MORI

LEAVES FROM THE JOURNAL

OF

A LIFE IN THE HIGHLANDS

FROM 1862 TO 1882

—————•◆•—————

NEW YORK:
R. WORTHINGTON, 770 BROADWAY.
1884.

Victoria R

1866.

PREFACE.

THE little volume " Our Life in the Highlands," published fifteen years ago, with its simple records of the never-to-be-forgotten days spent with him " who made the writer's life bright and happy," was received with a warmth of sympathy and interest which was very gratifying to her heart. The kind editor of that volume is no longer here to advise and help her, though friendly assistance has not been wanting on the present occasion. But remembering the feeling with which that little book was received, the writer thinks that the present volume may equally evoke sympathy, as, while describing a very altered life, it shows how her sad and suffering heart was soothed and cheered by the excursions and incidents it recounts, as well as by the simple mountaineers, from whom she learnt many a lesson of resignation and faith, in the pure air and quiet of the beautiful Highlands.

The writer wishes at the same time to express her gratitude to those who are mentioned throughout this volume for the devotion and kindness which contributed so much to her enjoyment of the varied scenes and objects of interest of which these pages contain the unpretending record.

OSBORNE:
December 22, 1883.

TO

MY LOYAL HIGHLANDERS

AND ESPECIALLY

TO THE MEMORY OF

MY DEVOTED PERSONAL ATTENDANT

AND FAITHFUL FRIEND

JOHN BROWN

THESE RECORDS OF MY WIDOWED LIFE

IN SCOTLAND

ARE

GRATEFULLY DEDICATED

VICTORIA R. I.

CONTENTS.

	DATE.	PAGE.
Building of the Prince's Cairn	21 Aug. 1862	7
Visit to the Old Cairn on the Prince's Birthday	26 Aug. 1862	8
First Visit to the Prince's Cairn after its Completion	19 May 1863	9
Visit to Blair	15 Sept. 1863	9
Carriage Accident	7 Oct. 1863 . .	11
Unveiling of the Prince's Statue at Aberdeen	13 Oct. 1863 . .	13
Expedition to Invermark	19 Sept. 1865 . ..	18
First Visit to Dunkeld	9 Oct. 1865 . ..	21
Second Visit to Dunkeld	1 Oct. 1866 . ..	28
Opening of the Aberdeen Waterworks	16 Oct. 1866	37
Halloween	31 Oct. 1866–67	38
Visit to Floors and the Scotch Border Country	20 Aug. 1867 . ..	39
Visit to Glenfiddich	24 Sept. 1867	46
Unveiling of the Prince's Statue at Balmoral	15 Oct. 1867	53
A House-warming at the Glassalt Shiel	1 Oct. 1868	53
"Juicing the Sheep"	21 Oct. 1868	55
A Highland "Kirstnin" (Christening)	24 Oct. 1868	56
A Second Christening	1 Nov. 1868	57
Widow Grant	22 Aug. 1869	57
Visit to Invertrossachs	1 Sept. 1869	58
Sheep Clipping	13 June 1870	73
Betrothal of Princess Louise to the Marquis of Lorne	3 Oct. 1870	73
Communion Sunday at Crathie	13 Nov. 1871	74
The "Spate"	11 June 1872	76
Visit to Holyrood and Edinburgh	13 Aug. 1872	79
Visit to Dunrobin	6 Sept. 1872	85
Dr. Norman Macleod	March 1873	100
Visit to Inverlochy	9 Sept. 1873 . .	113
Home-coming of their Royal Highnesses the Duke and Duchess of Edinburgh	29 Aug. 1874	133
Visit to Inveraray	21 Sept. 1875	134
Highland Funeral	21 Oct. 1875	149
Unveiling of the Statue of the Prince Consort at Edinburgh	17 Aug. 1876	151
Presentation of Colors to "The Royal Scots"	26 Sept. 1876	154
Expedition to Loch Maree	12 Sept. 1877	155
Visit to Broxmouth	23 Aug. 1878	167
Death of Sir Thomas Biddulph at Abergeldie Mains	28 Sept. 1878	174
Memorial Cross to the Princess Alice, Grand Duchess of Hesse	22 May 1879	175

	DATE.	PAGE.
Death of the Prince Imperial	19 June 1879	176
Home-coming of their Royal Highnesses the Duke and Duchess of Connaught	5 Sept. 1879	180
His Royal Highness the Duke of Connaught's Cairn	8 Sept. 1879	181
Visit to the Glen Gelder Shiel	6 Oct. 1879	181
Victory of Tel-el-Kebir and Home-coming of their Royal Highnesses the Duke and Duchess of Albany	11 Sept. 1882	182
Conclusion		185

MORE LEAVES FROM THE JOURNAL

OF

A LIFE IN THE HIGHLANDS.

CALEDONIA ! thou land of the mountain and rock,
  Of the ocean, the mist, and the wind—
Thou land of the torrent, the pine, and the oak,
  Of the roebuck, the hart, and the hind !

  *   *   *   *   *   *   *

Thou land of the valley, the moor, and the hill,
  Of the storm and the proud-rolling wave—
Yes, thou art the land of fair liberty still,
  And the land of my forefathers' grave !
                    THE ETTRICK SHEPHERD.

A nation famed for song and beauty's charms—
Zealous yet modest, innocent though free ;
Patient of toil, serene amidst alarms,
Inflexible in faith, invincible in arms.
                    BEATTIE'S *Minstrel.*

BUILDING OF THE PRINCE'S CAIRN.

BALMORAL, *Thursday, August 21, 1865.*

AT eleven o'clock started off in the little pony-chair (drawn by the *Corriemulzie* pony, and led by Brown), Bertie, who had come over from *Birkhall,* on foot, the two girls on ponies, and the two little boys, who joined us later, for *Craig Low-rigan ;* and I actually drove in the little carriage to the very top, turning off from the path and following the track where the carts had gone. Grant and Duncan pushed the carriage behind. Sweet Baby (Beatrice) we found at the top. The view was so fine, the day so bright, and the heather so beau-tifully pink—but no pleasure, no joy! all dead !

And here at the top is the foundation of the cairn—forty feet wide—to be erected to my precious Albert, which will be seen all down the valley. I and my poor six orphans all placed stones on it; and our initials, as well as those of the three absent ones, are to be carved on stones all round it. I felt very shaky and nervous.

It is to be thirty-five feet high, and the following inscription to be placed on it:—

TO THE BELOVED MEMORY

OF

ALBERT, THE GREAT AND GOOD PRINCE CONSORT,

RAISED BY HIS BROKEN-HEARTED WIDOW,

VICTORIA R,

AUGUST 21, 1862.

"He being made perfect in a short time fulfilled a long time;
For his soul pleased the Lord,
Therefore hastened He to take him
Away from among the wicked."
Wisdom of Solomon, iv. 13, 14.

Walked down to where the rough road is, and this first short attempt at walking in the heather shook me and tired me much.

VISIT TO THE OLD CAIRN ON THE PRINCE'S BIRTHDAY.

BALMORAL, *August 26,* 1862.

I WENT out at twelve with the two girls on ponies (I in the little carriage), Bertie on foot. We went to see the obelisk building to His dear memory: Bertie left us there, and we went on round by the village, up *Craig-Gowan,* in the little carriage, over the heather till we reached near to the old cairn of 1852. Grant said: "I thought you would like to be here to-day, on His birthday!"—so entirely was he of opinion that this beloved day, and even the 14th of December, must not be looked upon as a day of mourning. "That's not the light to look at it." There is so much true and strong faith in these good, simple people.

Walked down by the *Fog* * *House,* all pink with heather; the day beautifully fine and bright.

* Scotch for "Moss."

John Grant

FIRST VISIT TO THE PRINCE'S CAIRN AFTER ITS COMPLETION.

BALMORAL, *Tuesday, May* 19, 1863.

I WENT out in the little carriage (Donald Stewart leading the pony, as John Brown was unwell) with Lenchen and Dr. Robertson (Grant following), and drove up to the cairn on the top of *Craig Lowrigan*, which is a fine sharp pyramid admirably constructed out of granite without any mortar. The inscription is very well engraved and placed. There is a good path made up to the top of the hill.

VISIT TO BLAIR, 1863.

BALMORAL, *Tuesday, September* 15, 1863.

AT twenty minutes to eight we reached *Perth*, where we breakfasted and dressed, and at twenty minutes past nine I left with Lenchen, Augusta Bruce, and General Grey, for *Blair*, going past *Dunkeld*, where we had not been since 1844, and which is so beautifully situated, and *Pitlochry*, through the splendid *Pass of Killiecrankie* (which we so often drove through in 1844), past Mr. Butter's place *Faskally*, on to *Blair*, having a distant peep at the entrance to *Glen Tilt*, and *Schiehallion*, which it made and makes me sick to think of. At the small station were a few people—the poor Duke's Highlanders (keepers), the dear Duchess, Lord Tullibardine, and Captain Drummond of *Megginch*.

The Duchess was much affected, still more so when she got into the carriage with me. Lenchen and the others went in the boat carriage, the one *we* had gone in not two years ago!

We drove at once to the house which we had visited in such joyful and high spirits October 9, two years ago. The Duchess took me to the same room which I had been in on that day, and, after talking a little to me of this dreadful affliction,* she went to see if the Duke was ready. She soon returned, and I followed her down stairs along the passage, full of stags' horns, which we walked along, together with the poor Duke, in 1861. When I went in, I found him standing up very much altered; it was very sad. He kissed my hand, gave me the white rose which, according to tradition, is presented by the Lords of Athole on the occasion of the Sov-

---

* The Duke was suffering from an incurable illness.

ereign's visit, and we sat a little while with him. It is a
small room, full of his rifles and other implements and attri-
butes of sport—now forever useless to him! A sad, sad
contrast. He seemed very much pleased and gratified.

We went up stairs again and took some breakfast, in the
very same room where we breakfasted on that very happy,
never-to-be-forgotten day, full of joy and expectation. While
we were breakfasting the door opened, and in walked the
Duke in a thick MacDougal. Mrs. Drummond and Miss
Moncreiffe (the Duchess's pretty, amiable future daughter-in-
law) were there, and also Miss MacGregor, but we did not
see her. The poor Duke insisted on going with me to the
station, and he went in the carriage with the Duchess and
me. At the station he got out, walked about, and gave di-
rections. I embraced the dear Duchess and gave the Duke
my hand, saying, "Dear Duke, God bless you!" He had
asked permission that his men, the same who had gone with
us through the glen on that happy day two years ago, might
give me a cheer, and he led them on himself. Oh! it was so
dreadfully sad! To think of the contrast to the time two
years ago, when my darling was so well and I so happy with
him, and just beginning to recover from my great sorrow for
dearest Mama's death—looking forward to many more such
delightful expeditions; and the poor Duke then full of health
and strength, walking the whole way, and at the "March" *
stopping to drink our health and asking us to come again
whenever we liked, and giving a regular Highland cheer in
Highland fashion, returned by our men, the pipers playing,
and all, all so gay, so bright! And I so eager for next year's
expeditions, which I ought not to have been! Oh! how little
we know what is before us! How uncertain is life! I felt
very sad, but was so much occupied with the poor Duke,†
for whom I truly grieve, that I did not feel the trial of returning to *Blair* in such terribly altered circumstances, as I
should otherwise have done.

At *Stanley Junction* we joined the others, and proceeded as
usual to *Aboyne*, whence we drove in open carriages—Lenchen, Alfred, and Baby with me—and reached *Balmoral* at
twenty minutes past six. It was very cold. Bertie and Alix
were at the door, and stayed a little while afterwards. How
strange they should be at *Abergeldie!* A few years ago dear
Mama used to receive us.

* The boundary of the Duke's property. "March" is the word commonly used
in Scotland to express the outer limit or boundary of land.
† He died in the following year, January 16, 1864.

CARRIAGE ACCIDENT.

Wednesday, October 7, 1863.

A HAZY morning. I decided by Alice's advice, with a heavy heart, to make the attempt to go to *Clova*. At half-past twelve drove with Alice and Lenchen to *Altnagiuthasach*, where we lunched, having warmed some broth and boiled some potatoes, and then rode up and over the *Capel Month* in frequent slight snow-showers. All the high hills white with snow; and the view of the green *Clova* hills covered with snow at the tops, with gleams of sunshine between the showers, was very fine, but it took us a long time, and I was very tired towards the end, and felt very sad and lonely. *Loch Muich* looked beautiful in the setting sun as we came down, and reminded me of many former happy days I spent there. We stopped to take tea at *Altnagiuthasach*. Grant was not with us, having gone with Vicky.* We started at about twenty minutes to seven from *Altnagiuthasach*, Brown on the box next Smith,† who was driving, little Willem (Alice's black serving boy) behind. It was quite dark when we left, but all the lamps were lit as usual; from the first, however, Smith seemed to be quite confused (and indeed has been much altered of late), and got off the road several times, once in a very dangerous place, when Alice called out and Brown got off the box to show him the way. After that, however, though going very slowly, we seemed to be all right, but Alice was not at all reassured, and thought Brown's holding up the lantern all the time on the box indicated that Smith could not see where he was going, though the road was as broad and plain as possible. Suddenly, about two miles from *Altnagiuthasach*, and about twenty minutes after we had started, the carriage began to turn up on one side; we called out: "What's the matter?" There was an awful pause, during which Alice said: "We are upsetting." In another moment—during which I had time to reflect whether we should be killed or not, and thought there were still things I had not settled and wanted to do—the carriage turned over on its side, and we were all precipitated to the ground! I came down very hard, with my face upon the ground, near the carriage, the horses both on the ground,

* She and Fritz Wilhelm had come three days before to stay at Abergeldie with their children.
† Smith was pensioned in 1864 and died in 1866, having been thirty-one years in the Royal service.

and Brown calling out in despair, " The Lord Almighty have
mercy on us ! Who did ever see the like of this before ! I
thought you were all killed." Alice was soon helped up by
means of tearing all her clothes to disentangle her; but Lenchen, who had also got caught in her dress, called out very
piteously, which frightened me a good deal; but she was
also got out with Brown's assistance, and neither she nor
Alice was at all hurt. I reassured them that I was not hurt,
and urged that we should make the best of it, as it was an
inevitable misfortune. Smith, utterly confused and bewildered, at length came up to ask if I was hurt. Meantime
the horses were lying on the ground as if dead, and it was
absolutely necessary to get them up again. Alice, whose
calmness and coolness were admirable, held one of the lamps
while Brown cut the traces, to the horror of Smith, and the
horses were speedily released and got up unhurt. There was
now no means of getting home except by sending back Smith
with the two horses to get another carriage. All this took
some time, about half an hour, before we got off. By this
time I felt that my face was a good deal bruised and swollen,
and, above all, my right thumb was excessively painful and
much swollen ; indeed I thought at first it was broken, till
we began to move it. Alice advised then that we should sit
down in the carriage—that is, with the bottom of the carriage
as a back—which we did, covered with plaids, little Willem
sitting in front, with the hood of his " bournous " over his
head, holding a lantern, Brown holding another, and being
indefatigable in his attention and care. He had hurt his
knee a good deal in jumping off the carriage. A little claret
was all we could get either to drink or wash my face and
hand. Almost directly after the accident happened, I said
to Alice it was terrible not to be able to tell it to my dearest
Albert, to which she answered : " But he knows it all, and I
am sure he watched over us." I am thankful that it was by
no imprudence of mine, or the slightest deviation from what
my beloved one and I had always been in the habit of doing,
and what he sanctioned and approved.

The thought of having to sit here in the road ever so long
was, of course, not very agreeable, but it was not cold, and I
remembered from the first what my beloved one had always
said to me, namely, to make the best of what could not be altered. We had a faint hope, at one moment, that our ponies
might overtake us ; but then Brown recollected that they had
started before us. We did nothing but talk of the accident,

and how it could have happened, and how merciful the escape
was, and we all agreed that Smith was quite unfit to drive me
again in the dark. We had been sitting here about half an
hour when we heard the sound of voices and of horses' hoofs,
which came nearer and nearer. To our relief we found it
was our ponies. Kennedy (whom dear Albert liked, and who
always went out with him, and now generally goes with us)
had become fearful of an accident, as we were so long coming ; he heard Smith going back with the ponies, and then,
seeing lights moving about, he felt convinced something must
have happened, and therefore rode back to look for us, which
was very thoughtful of him, for else we might have sat there
till ten o'clock. We mounted our ponies at once and proceeded home, Brown leading Alice's and my pony, which he
would not let go for fear of another accident. Lenchen and
Willem followed, led by Alick Grant. Kennedy carried the
lantern in front. It was quite light enough to see the road
without a lantern. At the hill where the gate of the deer-
fence is, above the distillery, we met the other carriage, again
driven by Smith, and a number of stable-people come to raise
the first carriage, and a pair of horses to bring it home. We
preferred, however, riding home, which we reached at about
twenty minutes to ten o'clock. No one knew what had happened till we told them. Fritz and Louis were at the door.
People were foolishly alarmed when we got up stairs, and
made a great fuss. Took only a little soup and fish in my
room, and had my head bandaged.

I saw the others only for a moment, and got to bed rather
late.

UNVEILING OF THE PRINCE'S STATUE AT ABERDEEN.

Thursday, October 13, 1863.

I was terribly nervous. Longed not to have to go through
this fearful ordeal. Prayed for help, and got up earlier.

A bad morning. The three younger children (except
Baby), William of Hesse,* and the ladies and gentlemen all
gone on. I started sad and lonely, and so strange without
my darling, with dear Alice, Lenchen, and Louis. We could
not have the carriage open. At *Aboyne* we met Vicky and
Fritz, and both the couples went with me in the railway ; the

* Youngest brother of Prince Louis of Hesse.

Princes in Highland dress. I felt bewildered. It poured
with rain, unfortunately. To describe the day's proceedings
would be too painful and difficult; but I annex the account.
Vicky and Alice were with me, and the long, sad, and terrible procession through the crowded streets of *Aberdeen*, where
all were kindly, but all were silent, was mournful, and as unlike former blessed times as could be conceived. Unfortunately it continued pouring. The spot where the Statue is
placed is rather small, and on one side close to the bridge,
but Marochetti chose it himself.

I got out trembling; and when I had arrived, there was no
one to direct me and to say, as formerly, what was to be done.
Oh! it was and is too painful, too dreadful!

I received (only handed) the Provost's address, and
knighted him (the first since all ended) with General Grey's
sword. Then we all stepped on to the uncovered and wet
platform directly opposite the Statue, which certainly is low,
and rather small for out of doors, but fine and like. Principal Campbell's prayer was very long—which was trying in the
rain—but part of it (since I have read it) is really very good.

I felt very nervous when the Statue was uncovered, but
much regretted that when they presented arms there was no
salute with the drums, bugles, or the pipes, for the bands below were forbidden to play. I retired almost immediately.

Just below and in front of where we stood were Löhlein,
Mayet, Grant, Brown, Cowley, P. Farquharson, D. Stewart,
Nestor, Ross, and Paterson, whom we had brought with us
—and why was my darling not near me? It was dreadfully
sad.

Took a little luncheon in a room up stairs with our girls,
our footmen serving us. After this we left as we came.
Affie met us there, and then took leave at the station, William of Hesse joining him. It was quite fair, provokingly
so, when we got to *Aboyne.* Here we parted, took leave of
Vicky and Fritz, and drove back in an open carriage, reaching *Balmoral* at half-past six. Very tired; thankful it was
over, but the recollection of the whole scene, of the whole
journey, without my dear Albert, was dreadful! Formerly
how we should have dwelt on all!

[The following account of the ceremonial is taken from
the "Scotsman" newspaper of October 14, 1863.

The preparations made at the North-Eastern Station at
Aberdeen for the reception of Her Majesty and the Princes

and Princesses, were very simple and undemonstrative. Two huge flags were suspended across the inside entrance, and the floor of the passage leading into the portico at Guild Street was laid with crimson cloth. The following gentlemen were in waiting at the station, and received the royal party on the platform: The Duke of Richmond ; the Lord Provost and Magistrates ; the Earl of Aberdeen ; Lord Saltoun ; Sir J. D. H. Elphinstone ; Sir Alexander Bannerman, Bart. ; Lord Barcaple ; Mr. Thomson of Banchory ; Colonel Fraser of Castle Fraser ; Colonel Fraser, younger, of Castle Fraser ; Mr. Leslie of Warthill, M. P. ; Mr. Irvine of Drum, convener of the county ; Colonel Farquharson of Invercauld ; Sheriff Davidson ; John Webster, Esq., and several of the railway directors and officials.

On leaving the station, the procession was formed into the following order, and proceeded by way of Guild Street, Regent Quay, Marischal Street, Castle Street, and Union Street to the site of the Memorial :—

Body of Police.
Detachment of Cavalry.
The Convener and Master of Hospital of the
Incorporated Trades
The Principal and Professors of the University of Aberdeen.
The City Architect.
His Grace the Duke of Richmond, the Convener and Sheriff of the
County, and the Committee of Subscribers to the
Memorial.
The Lord Provost,
and Magistrates, and Town Council.
The Suite in Attendance on Her Majesty and Royal Family.
Lady Augusta Bruce (in attendance on the Queen).
Countess Hohenthal (in attendance on Crown-Princess).
Baroness Schenck (in attendance on Princess Louis of Hesse).
Sir George Grey.
The Princes Alfred, Arthur, and Leopold.
Lady Churchill (Lady-in-Waiting).
The Princess Helena.
The Princess Louise.
The Crown-Prince of Prussia.
The Prince Louis of Hesse.
The Crown-Princess of Prussia.
THE QUEEN.
Cavalry Escort.

The procession wound its way along the densely packed streets amid the deepest silence of the assemblage, everybody seeming to be animated by a desire to abstain from any popular demonstrations that might be distasteful to Her Majesty. On reaching the Northern Club buildings, Her Majesty, accompanied by the Prince and Princesses, Sir Charles Phipps,* Lord Charles Fitzroy, Major-General Hood, Dr. Jenner, General Grey, and the ladies and gentlemen of the suite, passed from their carriages into the lobby, and thence into the billiard room—a handsome lofty room, which forms a half oval at the end towards Union Terrace. The Lord Provost then presented the following address to Her Majesty :—

TO THE QUEEN'S MOST EXCELLENT MAJESTY.

The humble Address of Her Majesty's loyal and dutiful subjects, the contributors to the erection in Aberdeen of a Memorial Statue of His Royal Highness the Prince-Consort.

May it please your Majesty,

We your Majesty's most loyal and dutiful subjects, the contributors to the erection in Aberdeen of a Memorial Statue of His Royal Highness the Prince-Consort, humbly beg leave to approach your Majesty with the expression of our devoted attachment to your Majesty's person and government.

We are enabled this day to bring to completion the work which we undertook in sorrowing and grateful remembrance of that illustrious Prince, whose removal by the inscrutable will of Providence we, in common with all your Majesty's subjects, can never cease to deplore.

No memorial is necessary to preserve the name of one who adorned the highest station of the land by the brightest display of intellectual and moral greatness, as well as the purest and most enlightened zeal for the public good; whose memory is revered throughout the world, as that of few Princes has ever been; and whose example will ever be cherished as a most precious inheritance by this great nation. Yet, in this part of the United Kingdom, which was honored by the annual presence of the illustrious Prince, and in this city, which a few years ago was signally favored by the exertion of his great talents as President of the British Association for the Advancement of Science, an earnest desire pervaded all ranks to give permanent expression to the profound reverence and affection he had inspired.

How inadequate for such a purpose the memorial we have erected must be, we ourselves most deeply feel. But that your Majesty should have on this occasion graciously come forth again to receive the public homage of your loyal and devoted people, we regard as a ground of heartfelt thankfulness ; and viewing it as a proof that your Majesty approves the humble but sincere tribute of our sorrow, we shall ever be grateful for the exertion which your Majesty has made to afford us this proof.

* Keeper of the Privy Purse, who died February 24, 1866, to my great regret, for he was truly devoted and attached to the dear Prince and me, with whom he had been for twenty years.

That Almighty God, the source of all strength, may comfort your Majesty's heart, prospering all your Majesty's designs and efforts for your people's good; that He may bestow His choicest favors on your royal offspring, and continue to your devoted subjects for many years the blessings of your Majesty's reign, is our earnest and constant prayer.

In the name of the Contributors,

ALEX. ANDERSON,

Lord Provost of Aberdeen,

Chairman of the Committee of Contributors.

Aberdeen, October 13, 1863.

On receiving the address, Her Majesty handed the following reply to the Lord Provost :—

Your loyal and affectionate address has deeply touched me, and I thank you for it from my heart.

It was with feelings which I fail in seeking words to express that I determined to attend here to-day to witness the inaugurating of the statue which will record to future times the love and respect of the people of this county and city for my great and beloved husband. But I could not reconcile it to myself to remain at Balmoral while such a tribute was being paid to his memory without making an exertion to assure you personally of the deep and heartfelt sense I entertain of your kindness and affection ; and at the same time proclaim in public the unbounded reverence and admiration and the devoted love that fill my heart for him whose loss must throw a lasting gloom over all my future life.

Never can I forget the circumstances to which you so feelingly alluded —that it was in this city he delivered his remarkable address to the British Association a very few years ago; and that in this county we had for so many years been in the habit of spending some of the happiest days of our lives.

After the Queen's reply had been handed to the Lord Provost, Sir George Grey commanded his Lordship to kneel, when Her Majesty, taking a sword from Sir George, touched the Provost on each shoulder and said—" Rise, Sir Alexander Anderson." This ceremony concluded, the Queen and the whole of the royal party then proceeded to the platform. Her Majesty's appearance on which was the signal for the multitude gathered outside to uncover their heads. Her Majesty, who appeared to be deeply melancholy and much depressed, though calm and collected, advanced to the front of the platform, while the Princes, who were all dressed in Royal Stewart tartan, and the Princesses, who wore blue silk dresses, white bonnets, and dark gray cloaks, took up a position immediately behind her. The proceedings were opened with a prayer by Principal Campbell, who spoke for about

2

ten minutes, the assemblage standing uncovered in the rain, which was falling heavily at the time. During the time the learned Principal was engaged in prayer, Her Majesty more than once betrayed manifest and well-justified signs of impatience at the length of the oration. At the conclusion of the prayer, a signal was given, the bunting which had concealed the statue was hoisted to the top of a flagstaff, and the ceremony was complete.

Her Majesty, having scanned the statue narrowly, bowed to the assemblage and retired from the platform, followed by the royal party. After the illustrious company had lunched in the club, the procession was reformed and proceeded the same way as it came to the Scottish North-Eastern Station in Guild Street. Her Majesty left Aberdeen about three o'clock.]

EXPEDITION TO INVERMARK.

Tuesday, September 19, 1865.

ON waking I felt very low and nervous at the thought of the expedition. All so sadly changed. Started at eleven o'clock with Lenchen and Jane Churchill, Grant and Brown on the box—like in former happy times. General Grey had preceded us, and we found him at the *Bridge of Munich*, where our ponies were waiting. We had four gillies, three of whom were with us in 1861 (Smith, Morgan, and Kennedy). The heat was intense going up the *Polach*. I got well enough through the bog, but Jane Churchill's pony floundered considerably. We lunched when we had crossed the *Tanar* and gone a little way up *Mount Keen*, and General Grey then went on to meet Lord Dalhousie. Two of his foresters had come to show us the way. We remounted after sitting and resting a little while, and ascended the shoulder of *Mount Keen*, and then rode on. The distance was very hazy. We got off and walked, after which I rode down that fine wild pass called the *Ladder Burn;* but it seemed to strike me much less than when I first saw it, as all is flat now. At the foot of the pass Lord Dalhousie met us with General Grey, and welcomed us kindly; and at the Shiel, a little further on, where we had lunched in 1861, Lady Christian Maule, Lord Dalhousie's sister, met us. She was riding. We then went on a few yards further till we came to the *Well*, where we got

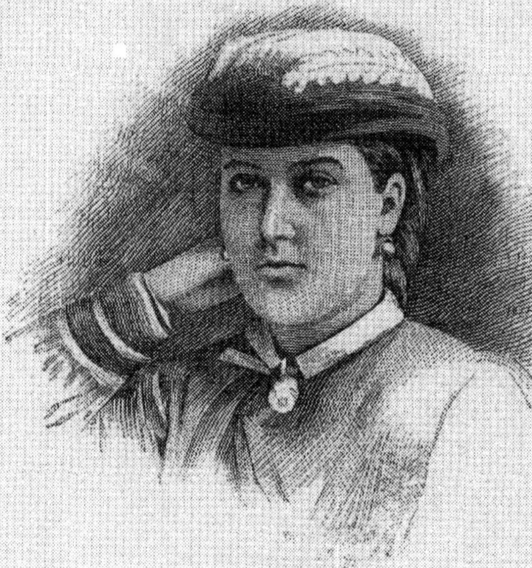
Helena

off. It is really beautiful, built of white stones in the shape of the ancient crown of *Scotland ;* and in one of the pillars a plate is inserted with this inscription : " Queen Victoria with the Prince Consort visited this well and drank of its refresh-ing waters on the 20th September, 1861, the year of Her Majesty's great sorrow ; " and round the spring, which bubbles up beautifully, and quite on a level with the ground, is inscribed in old English characters the following legend :—

> Rest, traveller, on this lonely green,
> And drink and pray for Scotland's Queen.

We drank with sorrowing hearts from this very well, where just four years ago I had drunk with my beloved Albert ; and Grant handed me his flask (one I had given him) out of which we had drunk on that day ! Lord Dalhousie has kindly built this well in remembrance of that occasion. It was quite a pilgrimage.

We afterwards had some tea, close by ; and this fine wide glen was seen at its best, lit up as it was by the evening sun, warm as on a summer's day, without a breath of air, the sky becoming pinker and pinker, the hills themselves, as you looked down the glen, assuming that beautifully glowing tinge which they do of an evening. The Highlanders and ponies grouped around the well had a most picturesque effect. And yet to me all seemed strange, unnatural, and sad.

We mounted again, and went on pursuing the same way as we had done four years ago, going past the old *Castle of Invermark.* As there was time, however, we rode on to *Loch Lee,* just beyond it, which we had only seen from a dis-tance on the last occasion. It is quite small, but extremely pretty, and was beautifully lit up, reminding me of the farth-est end of *Loch Muich.* After this we rode up to the house, the little drawing-room of which I well remembered ; it brought all back to me. Lady Christian took us up stairs. I had two nice small rooms. The two maids, Lenchen and Lady Churchill, and Brown were all in our passage, away from the rest of the house. I felt tired, sad, and bewildered. For the first time in my life I was alone in a strange house, without either mother or husband, and the thought over-whelmed and distressed me deeply. I had a dear child with me, but those loving ones above me were both gone, —their support taken away ! It seemed so dreadful ! How many visits we paid together, my darling and I, and how we ever enjoyed them ! Even when they were trying and formal, the happiness of being together, and a world in ourselves, was so great.

Dinner was below, in a pretty room which I also remembered. Only Lord Dalhousie, Lady Christian, the General, Lady Churchill, Lenchen, and I. I stayed but a short while below after dinner, and then went up with Lenchen and Jane Churchill, and afterwards walked out a little with Jane. It was very warm.

Wednesday, September 20.

A beautiful morning. Breakfasted alone with Lenchen in my own little sitting-room—waited on by Brown, who is always ready to try to do anything required. At eleven we went out, and I planted two trees, and Lenchen one (instead of her blessed Father, alas !). We then mounted our ponies as yesterday, and proceeded (accompanied by Lord Dalhousie, Lady Christian, and several of his foresters) by a shorter road past the well, where we did not get off, up the *Ladder Burn*, on our homeward journey. We went the same way, stopping at the " March," where, in a high wind, we got off and lunched under some stones. Good Lord Dalhousie * was most hospitable and kind. The luncheon over, they took leave and went back, and General Grey went on in advance. As it was only one o'clock when we sat down to luncheon, we remained sitting some little time before we commenced our downward course. It was to-day—strange to say—the anniversary of our first visit to *Invermark*. Then we proceeded down the same way we had come up, across the *Tanar*, and when we had gone up some little way we stopped again, as we were anxious not to hurry home, and moreover the carriage would not have been ready to meet us. We had some tea, sketched a little, and rode on again ; the sky had become dark and cloudy, and suddenly down came a most violent shower of rain which beat fiercely with the wind. We were just then going over the boggy part, which, however, we got across very well. As we came over the *Polach* the rain ceased. The view of the *Valley of the Gairn* and *Muich* as you descend is beautiful, and reminded me forcibly of our last happy expedition in 1861, when Albert stopped to talk to Grant about the two forests, and said he and Grant might possibly be dead before they were

---

* He died in 1874.

completed! There lay the landscape stretched out—the same as before : and all else was changed!

We got home at ten minutes past seven o'clock, when it was still raining a little.

FIRST VISIT TO DUNKELD.

Monday, October 9, 1865.

A THICK, misty, very threatening morning! There was no help for it, but it was sadly provoking. It was the same once or twice in former happy days, and my dear Albert always said we could not alter it, but must leave it as it was, and make the best of it. Our three little ones breakfasted with me. I was grieved to leave my precious Baby and poor Leopold behind. At ten started with Lenchen and Janie Ely (the same attendants on the box). General Grey had gone on an hour and a half before. We took post-horses at *Castleton.* It rained more or less the whole time. Then came the long well-known stage to the *Spital of Glenshee,* which seemed to me longer than ever. The mist hung very thick over the hills, We changed horses there, and about a quarter of an hour after we had left it, we stopped to lunch in the carriage. After some delay we went on and turned into *Strathardle* and then, leaving the *Blairgowrie* road, down to the farm of *Pitcarmich,* shortly before coming to which Mr. Small Keir * of *Kindrogan* met us and rode before us to this farm. Here we found General Grey and our ponies, and here the dear Duchess of Athole and Miss Mac-Gregor met us, and we got out and went for a short while into the farmhouse, where we took some wine and biscuit. Then we mounted our ponies (I on dear Fyvie, Lenchen on Brechin), and started on our course across the hill. There was much mist. This obscured all the view which otherwise would have been very fine. At first there was a rough road, but soon there was nothing but a sheep-track, and hardly that, through heather and stones up a pretty steep hill. Mr. Keir could not keep up with the immense pace of Brown and Fyvie, which distanced every one; so he had to drop behind, and his keeper acted as guide. There was by this time heavy driving rain, with a thick mist. About a little more than an hour took us to the "March," where two of

* His father was presented to me at Dunkeld in 1842.

the *Dunkeld* men met us, John McGregor, the Duke's head wood-forester, and Gregor McGregor, the Duchess's game-keeper; and the former acted as a guide. The Duchess and Miss MacGregor were riding with us. We went from here through larch woods, the rain pouring at times violently. We passed (after crossing the *Dunkeld March*) *Little Loch Oishne* and *Loch Oishne*, before coming to *Loch Ordie*. Here dripping wet we arrived at about a quarter-past six, hav-ing left *Pitcarmich* at twenty minutes to four. It was dark already from the very bad weather. We went into a lodge here, and had tea and whiskey, and Lenchen had to get her-self dried, as she was so wet. About seven we drove off from *Loch Ordie*. There was no outrider, so we sent on first the other carriage with Lenchen, Lady Ely, and Miss MacGregor, and General Grey on the box, and I went with the Duchess in a phaeton which had a hood—Brown and Grant going behind. It was pitch-dark, and we had to go through a wood, and I must own I was somewhat nervous.

We had not gone very far when we perceived that we were on a very rough road, and I became much alarmed, though I would say nothing. A branch took off Grant's cap, and we had to stop for Brown to go back and look for it with one of the carriage-lamps. This stoppage was most fortunate, for he then discovered we were on a completely wrong road. Grant and Brown had both been saying, "This is no car-riage-road; it is full of holes and stones." Miss MacGregor came to us in great distress, saying she did not know what to do, for that the coachman, blinded by the driving rain, had mistaken the road, and that we were in a track for carting wood. What was to be done, no one at this moment seemed to know—whether to try and turn the carriage (which proved impossible) or to take a horse out and send the postilion back to *Loch Ordie* to get assistance. At length we heard from General Grey that we could go on, though where we should get out, no one could exactly tell. Grant took a lamp out of the carriage and walked before the horses while Brown led them; and this reassured me. But the road was very rough, and we had to go through some deep holes full of water. At length, in about twenty minutes, we saw a light and passed a lodge, where we stopped and inquired where we were, for we had already come upon a good road. Our relief was great when we were told we were all right. Grant and Brown got up behind, and we trotted along the high road fast enough. Just before we came to the lodge, General Grey called out to ask which way the Duchess thought we should go, and Brown answered in her name, " The Duchess don't know at all where we are," as it was so dark she could not recognize familiar places.   At length at a quarter to nine we arrived quite safely at *Dunkeld* at the Duchess's nice, snug little cottage, which is just outside the town, surrounded by fine large grounds.   Two servants in kilts, and the steward, received us at the door.   You come at once on the middle landing of the staircase, the cottage being built on sloping ground.   The Duchess took me to my room, a nice little room, next to which was one for my wardrobe maid, Mary Andrews.*   Lenchen was up stairs near Miss MacGregor on one side of the drawing-room, which was given up to me as my sitting-room, and the Duchess's room on the other. Brown, the only other servant in the house, below, Grant in the adjoining buildings to the house.   The General and Lady Ely were at the hotel.   We dined at half-past nine in a small dining-room below, only Lenchen, the Duchess, Miss MacGregor, and I.   Everything so nice and quiet.   The Duchess and Miss MacGregor carving, her three servants waiting.   They were so kind, and we talked over the day's adventures.   Lenchen and every one, except the Duchess and myself, had been drenched.   The Duchess and her cousin stayed a short while, and then left us, and I wrote a little.   Strange to say, it was four years to-day that we paid our visit to *Blair* and rode up to *Glen Tilt.*   How different!

Tuesday, October 10.

A hopelessly wet morning.   I had slept well, but felt sad on awaking.   Breakfasted alone with Lenchen down stairs. each day waited on by Brown.   A dreadful morning, pouring rain.   Sat up stairs in the drawing-room, and wrote a good deal, being perfectly quiet and undisturbed.

Lenchen and I lunched with the Duchess and Miss Mac-Gregor, and at four we drove up to the Duchess's very fine model farm of *St. Colme's.* about four miles from *Dunkeld;* the Duchess and I in the phaeton, Lenchen, Janie Ely, and Miss MacGregor going in the other carriage.   We went all over the farm in detail, which is very like ours at *Osborne* and *Windsor,* much having been adopted from our farms there; and my dearest Husband had given the Duchess so much advice about it, that we both felt so sad *he* should not see it.

* She left my service in 1866.

We took tea in the farmhouse, where the Duchess has kept one side quite for herself, and where she intends to live sometimes with Miss MacGregor, and almost by themselves. From here we drove back and stopped at the "*Byres*," close by the stables, which were lit up with gas, and where we saw all the cows being milked. Very fine Ayrshire cows, and nice dairymaids. It is all kept up just as the late Duke wished it. We came home at half-past seven. It never ceased raining. The Cathedral bell began quite unexpectedly to ring, or almost toll, at eight o'clock, which the Duchess told us was a very old custom—in fact, the curfew-bell. It sounds very melancholy.

Dinner just as yesterday.

Wednesday, October 11.

Another wretchedly wet morning. Was much distressed at breakfast to find that poor Brown's legs had been dreadfully cut by the edge of his wet kilt on Monday, just at the back of the knee, and he said nothing about it, but to-day one became so inflamed, and swelled so much, that he could hardly move. The doctor said he must keep it up as much as possible, and walk very little, but did not forbid his going out with the carriage, which he wished to do. I did not go out in the morning, and decided to remain till Friday, to give the weather a chance. It cleared just before luncheon, and we agreed to take a drive, which we were able to do almost without any rain. At half-past three we drove out just as yesterday. There was no mist, so that, though there was no sunshine, we could see and admire the country, the scenery of which is beautiful. We drove a mile along the *Blair Road* to *Polney Loch*, where we entered the woods, and, skirting the loch, drove at the foot of *Craig y Barns* on grass drives—which were very deep and rough, owing to the wet weather, but extremely pretty—on to the *Loch Ordie* road. After ascending this for a little way we left it, driving all round *Cally Loch* (there are innumerable lochs) through *Cally Gardens* along another fine but equally rough wood drive, which comes out on the *Blairgowrie* high road. After this we drove round the three *Lochs* of the *Lowes*—viz. *Craig Lush, Butterstone,* and the *Loch of the Lowes* itself (which is the largest). They are surrounded by trees and woods, of which there is no end, and are very pretty. We came back by the *Blairgowrie* road and drove through *Dunkeld* (the people had been so discreet and quiet, I said I

would do this), crossing over the bridge (where twenty-two years ago we were met by twenty of the Athole Highlanders, who conducted us to the entrance of the grounds), and proceeded by the upper road to the *Rumbling Bridge*, which is Sir William Stewart of *Grand-tully's* property. We got out here and walked to the bridge, under which the *Braan* flowed over the rocks most splendidly; and, swollen by the rain, it came down in an immense volume of water with a deafening noise. Returning thence we drove through the village of *Inver* to the *Hermitage* on the banks of the *Braan*, which is *Dunkeld* property. This is a little house full of looking-glasses, with painted walls, looking on another fall of the *Braan*, where we took tea almost in the dark. It was built by James, the second Duke of Athole, in the last century. We drove back through *Dunkeld* again, the people cheering. Quite fair. We came home at half-past six o'clock. Lady Ely and General Grey dined with us. After dinner only the Duchess came to the drawing-room, and read to us again. Then I wrote, and Grant waited instead of Brown, who was to keep quiet on account of his leg.

Thursday, October 12.

A fair day, with no rain, but, alas! no sunshine. Brown's leg was much better, and the doctor thought he could walk over the hill to-morrow.

Excellent breakfasts, such splendid cream and butter! The Duchess has a very good cook, a Scotchwoman, and I thought how dear Albert would have liked it all. He always said things tasted better in smaller houses. There were several Scotch dishes, two soups, and the celebrated "haggis," which I tried last night, and really liked very much. The Duchess was delighted at my taking it.

At a quarter past twelve Lenchen and I walked with the Duchess in the grounds and saw the Cathedral, part of which is converted into a parish church, and the other part is a most picturesque ruin. We saw the tomb of the Wolf of Badenoch, son of King Robert the Second. There are also other monuments, but in a very dilapidated state. The burying-ground is inside and south of the Cathedral. We walked along the side of the river *Tay*, into which the river *Braan* flows, under very fine trees, as far as the American garden, and then round by the terrace overlooking the park, on which the tents were pitched at the time of the great déjeuner that the Duke, then Lord Glenlyon, gave us in 1842, which was our first acquaintance with the *Highlands* and Highland customs ; and it was such a fine sight ! Oh ! and here we were together—both widows !

We came back through the kitchen-garden by half-past one o'clock. After the usual luncheon, drove with Lenchen, the Duchess, and Miss MacGregor, at twenty minutes to four, in her sociable to *Loch Ordie*, by the lakes of *Rotmell* and *Dowally* through the wood, being the road by which we ought to have come the first night when we lost our way. It was cold, but the sky was quite bright, and it was a fine evening ; and the lake, wooded to the water's edge and skirted by distant hills, looked extremely pretty. We took a short row on it in a " coble " rowed by the head keeper, George M'Gregor. We took tea under the trees. The evening was very cold, and it was getting rapidly dark. We came back safely by the road the Duchess had wished to come the other night, but which her coachman did not think safe on account of the precipices ! We got home at nine. Only the Duchess and Miss MacGregor dined with us. The Duke's former excellent valet, Christie (a Highlander, and now the Duchess's house-steward), and George McPherson, piper, and Charles McLaren, footman, two nice, good-looking Highlanders in the Athole tartan, waited on us. The Duchess read again a little to us after dinner.

Friday, October 13.

Quite a fine morning, with bright gleams of sunshine lighting up everything. The piper played each morning in the garden during breakfast. Just before we left at ten, I planted a tree, and spoke to an old acquaintance, Willie Duff, the Duchess's fisherman, who had formerly a very long black beard and hair, which are now quite gray. Mr. Carrington, who has been Secretary in the Athole family for four generations, was presented. General Grey, Lady Ely, and Miss MacGregor had gone on a little while before us. Lenchen and I, with the Duchess, went in the sociable with four horses (Brown and Grant on the box). The weather was splendid, and the view, as we drove along the *Inverness Road*—which is the road to *Blair*—with all the mountains rising in the distance, was beautiful.

We passed through the village of *Ballinluig*, where there is a railway station, and a quarter of a mile below which the *Tay* and the *Tummel* unite, at a place called *Logierait*. All these names were familiar to me from our stay in 1844. We

saw the place where the monument to the Duke is to be raised,
on an eminence above *Logierait.* About eleven miles from
Dunkeld, just below *Croftinloan* (Captain Jack Murray's),
we took post-horses. You could see *Pitlochry* in the distance
to the left. We then left the *Inverness Road,* and turned
to the right, up a very steep hill past *Dunavourd* (Mr. Na-
pier's, son of the historian), past *Edradour* (the Duke's property), over a wild moor, reminding one very much of *Aberarder* (near *Balmoral*), whence, looking back, you have a
beautiful view of the hills *Schiehallion, Ben Lomond,* and *Ben
Lawers.* This glen is called *Glen Brearichan,* the little river
of that name uniting with the *Fernate,* and receiving afterwards the name of the *Ardle.* On the left hand a shoulder
of *Ben-y-Gloe* is seen.

We lunched in the carriage at ten minutes past twelve,
only a quarter of a mile from the West Lodge of *Kindrogan*
(Mr. Keir's). Here were our ponies, and General Grey,
Lady Ely, and Miss MacGregor. We halted a short while to
let General Grey get ahead, and then started on our ponies,
Mr. Keir walking with us. We passed Mr. Keir's house of
Kindrogan, out at the East Lodge, by the little village of
Enoch Dhu, up the rather steep ascent and approach of
Dirnanean, Mr. Small's place; passing his house as we went.
Mr. Small was absent, but two of his people, fine, tall-look-
ing men, led the way; two of Mr. Keir's were also with us.
We turned over the hill from here, through a wild, heathery
glen, and then up a grassy hill called the *Larich,* just above
the *Spital.* Looking back the view was splendid, one range
of hills behind the other, of different shades of blue. After
we had passed the summit, we stopped for our tea, about
twenty minutes to four, and seated ourselves on the grass,
but had to wait for some time till a kettle arrived which had
been forgotten, and had to be sent for from the *Spital.* This
caused some delay. At length, when tea was over, we walked
down a little way, and then rode. It was really most distressing to me to see what pain poor Brown suffered, especially in going up and down the hill. He could not go fast,
and walked lame, but would not give in. His endurance on
this occasion showed a brave heart indeed, for he resisted all
attempts at being relieved, and would not relinquish his
charge.

We took leave of the dear kind Duchess and Miss Mac-
Gregor, who were going back to *Kindrogan,* and got into the
carriage. We were able to ascend the *Devil's Elbow* before

it was really dark, and got to *Castleton* at half-past seven, where we found our own horses, and reached *Balmoral* at half-past eight.

————

SECOND VISIT TO DUNKELD.

Monday, October 1, 1866.

A VERY fine morning. Got up earlier, and breakfasted earlier, and left at a quarter to ten with Louise and Janie Ely (attended by Brown and Grant as formerly); Arthur having gone on with General Grey. We met many droves of cattle on the road, as it was the day for the tryst at *Castleton.* It was very hot, the sun very bright, and the *Cairn Wall* looked wild and grand. But as we went on the sky became dull and over-cast, and we almost feared there might be rain. We walked down the *Devil's Elbow*, and when within a mile and a half of the *Spital* we stopped and lunched in the carriage, and even sketched a little. A little way on the north side of the *Spital* were the ponies, Gordon for me, Brechin for Louise, and Cromar for Janie Ely. There was a pony for Arthur, which he did not ride, and for Grant or any one who was tired. The dear Duchess of Athole and Miss MacGregor came to meet us here, and when we had reached the spot where the road turns up the hill, we found Mr. Keir and his son, and Mr. Small of *Dirnanean*—a strong, good-looking, and pleasing person about thirty-two—and his men, the same two fine tall men, preceding us as last year. It was a steep climb up the hill which we had then come down, and exces- sively hot. The view both ways beautiful, though not clear. The air was very heavy and oppressive. We went the same way as before, but the ground was very wet from the great amount of rain. We stopped a moment in passing, at *Dirnanean*, to speak to Miss Small, Mr. Small's sister, a tall, stout young lady,* and then went on to *Kindrogan*, Mr. Keir's. All about here the people speak Gaelic, and there are a few who do not speak a word of English. Soon after entering Mr. Keir's grounds we got off our ponies, and went along a few yards by the side of the river *Ardle* to where Mr. Keir had got a fire kindled and a kettle boiling, plaids spread and tea prepared. Mrs. Keir and her two daughters were there. She is a nice quiet person, and was a Miss Menzies,

———
* Their father, a man of immense size, was presented to me at Dunkeld in 1842.

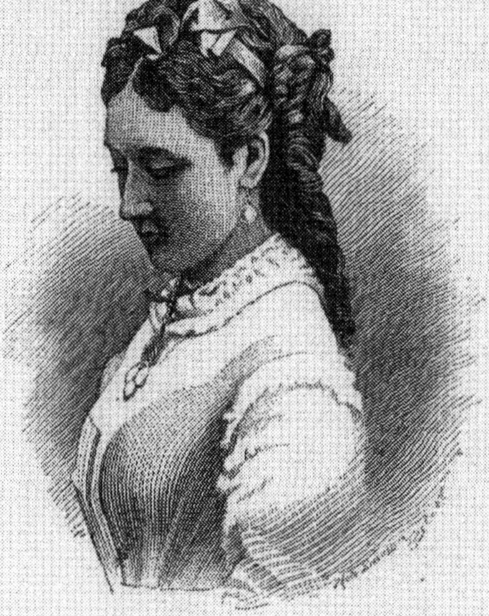

Louise

daughter of Sir Niel Menzies, whom I saw at *Taymouth* in 1842. Only we ladies remained. The tea over, we walked up to the house, which is a nice comfortable one. We waited here a little while, and I saw at the door Major Balfour of *Fernie*, the intended bridegroom of Mr. Keir's youngest daughter. At a little over a quarter-past five started in my sociable, with Louise and the Duchess. We came very fast and well with the Duchess's horses by exactly the same road we drove from *Dunkeld* last year. The horses were watered at the small halfway house of *Ballinluig*, and we reached *Dunkeld* in perfect safety at ten minutes past seven, I am where I was before, Louise in Lenchen's room, and Arthur in a room next to where Brown was before, and is now. All the rest the same, and snug, peaceful, and comfortable.

DUNKELD. Tuesday. October 2.

MILD and muggy, the mist hanging on the hills. Breakfasted with the children. Andrew Thomson attends to Arthur. Emilie * and Annie Macdonald † are with me here ; they help Louise, who, however, is very handy and can do almost everything for herself.

At half-past eleven I drove out alone with the Duchess through the woods to *Polney*, and then along the road, and turned in at *Willie Duff's Lodge*, and down the whole way along the river under splendid trees which remind me of *Windsor Park*. How dearest Albert would have admired them ! We ended by a little walk, and looked into the old ruin. At twenty minutes to four we drove, the Duchess, Louise, and I—Janie Ely and Miss MacGregor following— to *Crieff*-gate on the road of the *Loch of the Lowes*, where we got on ponies and rode for about an hour and a half through beautiful woods (saw a capercailzie, of which there are many here), but in a very thick mist (with very fine rain) which entirely destroyed all idea of view and prevented one's seeing anything but what was near. We came down to *St. Colme's*, where we got off, but where again, like last year, we saw nothing of the beautiful view. Here we took tea out of the tea set I had given the Duchess. She has furnished all her rooms here so prettily. How Albert would have liked all this ! Dinner as yesterday. Brown waited at dinner.

---

* Emilie Dittweiler, my first dresser, a native of Carlsruhe, in the Grand Duchy of Baden, who has been twenty-four years in my service.

† My first wardrobe woman, who has been twenty-seven years in my service, daughter of Mitchel, the late blacksmith at Clachanturn, near Abergeldie, and widow of my footman, John Macdonald, who died in 1865 (*vide* " Our Life in the Highlands ").

Just returned from a beautiful and successful journey of
seventy miles (in ten hours and a half). I will try and begin
an account of it. At nine the Duchess sent up to say she
thought the mist would clear off (it was much the same as
yesterday), and to suggest whether we had not better try and
go as far as her horses would take us, and return if it was
bad. I agreed readily to this. Arthur left before our breakfast to go to the *Pass of Killiecrankie* with Lady Ely and General Grey. At a quarter past ten, well provided, we started,
Louise, the Duchess, Miss MacGregor, and I (in our riding
habits, as they take less room). The mist was very thick at
first, and even accompanied by a little drizzling rain, so that
we could see none of the distant hills and scenery. We
crossed the *Tay Bridge*, drove through *Little Dunkeld* and
along the *Braan* through *Inver* (where Niel Gow, the fiddler,
lived), afterwards along the *Tay* opposite to *St. Colme's.*
Four miles from *Dunkeld*, at *Inchmagranachan Farm*, the
Highlands are supposed to begin, and this is one of the
boundaries of *Athole*. We, drove through some beautiful
woods—oak and beech with brushwood, reminding one of
Windsor Park—overtopped by rocks. A mile further *Dalguise* begins (the property of Mr. Stewart, now at the *Cape of
Good Hope*), which is remarkable for two large orchards at
either end, the trees laden with fruit in a way that reminded
me of *Germany*. *Kinnaird* is next, the jointure house of the
late Lady Glenlyon (mother to the late Duke). Just beyond
this the *Tummel* and the *Tay* join at the point of *Logierait.*

We now entered *Strath Tay*, still the Duke of Athole's
property, on the side along which we drove. The *Tay* is a
fine large river; there are many small properties on the opposite side in the woods. The mist was now less thick and
there was no rain, so that all the near country could be well
seen. Post-horses from Fisher of *Castleton's* brother, the innkeeper at *Dunkeld*, were waiting for us at *Skituan*, a little beyond *Balnaguard* (where we changed horses in 1842, and
this was the very same road we took then). Now an un-
sightly and noisy railroad runs along this beautiful glen, from
Dunkeld as far as *Aberfeldy*. We passed, close to the road,
Grandtully Castle, belonging to Sir William Stewart, and
rented by the Maharajah Duleep Singh. It is a curious old
castle, much in the style of *Abergeldie*, with an avenue of trees
leading up to it.

At *Aberfeldy*, a pretty village opposite to *Castle Menzies*, one or two people seemed to know us. We now came in among fine high-wooded hills, and here it was much clearer. We were in the *Breadalbane* property and approaching *Taymouth*. We passed, to the left, *Bolfrax*, where Lord Breadalbane's factor still lives, and to the right the principal lodge of *Taymouth*, which I so well remember going in by; but as we could not have driven through the grounds without asking permission and becoming known, which for various reasons we did not wish, we decided on not attempting it, and contented ourselves with getting out at a gate, close to a small fort, into which we were admitted by a woman from the gardener's house, close to which we stopped, and who had no idea who we were. *We got out and looked down from this height upon the house below, the mist having cleared away sufficiently to show us everything ; and here unknown, quite in private, I gazed, not without deep inward emotion, on the scene of our reception, twenty-four years ago, by dear Lord Breadalbane in a princely style, not to be equalled for grandeur and poetic effect ! Albert and I were only twenty-three, young and happy. How many are gone who were with us then ! I was very thankful to have seen it again. It seemed unaltered.* Everything was dripping from the mist. *Taymouth* is twenty-two miles from *Dunkeld*.

We got into the carriage again; the Duchess this time sitting near to me to prevent our appearance creating suspicion as to my being there. We drove on a short way through splendid woods with little waterfalls, and then turned into the little village of *Kenmore*, where a tryst was being held, through the midst of which we had to drive ; but the people only recognized the Duchess. There was music going on, things being sold at booths, and on the small sloping green near the church cattle and ponies were collected—a most picturesque scene. Immediately after this we came upon the bridge, and *Loch Tay*, with its wooded banks, clear and yet misty, burst into view. This again reminded me of the past—of the row up the loch, which is sixteen miles long, in 1842, in several boats, with pibrochs playing, and the boatmen singing wild Gaelic songs. The McDougall steered us then, and showed us the real Brooch of Lorne taken from Robert Bruce.

To the right we could see the grounds and fine park, look-

---

* The passage between the asterisks was quoted in a note in "Our Life in the Highlands," page 22.

ing rather like an English one. We stopped at *Murray's Lodge*, but, instead of changing horses here, drove five miles up the loch, which was quite clear, and the stillness so great that the reflection on the lake's bosom was as strong as though it were a real landscape. Here we stopped, and got out and sat down on the shore of the loch, which is covered with fine quartz, of which we picked up some; took our luncheon about half-past one, and then sketched. By this time the mist had given way to the sun, and the lake, with its richly wooded banks and changing foliage, looked beautiful.

At half-past two we re-entered our carriage, the horses having been changed, and drove back up a steep hill, crossing the river *Lyon* and going into *Glenlyon*, a beautiful wild glen with high green hills and rocks and trees, which I remember quite well driving through in 1842—then also on a misty day: the mist hung over, and even in some places below the tops of the hills. We passed several small places— *Glenlyon House*, the property of F. G. Campbell of *Troup*. To the left also *Fortingal* village—Sir Robert Menzies'—and a new place called *Dunaven House*. Small, picturesque, and very fair cottages were dotted about, and there were others in small clusters; beautiful sycamores and other trees were to be seen near the riverside. We then passed the village of *Coshieville* and turned by the hill-road—up a very steep hill with a burn flowing at the bottom, much wooded, reminding me of *M'Inroy's Burn*—passed the ruins of the old castle of the Stewarts of *Garth*, and then came on a dreary wild moor —passing below *Schiehallion*, one of the high hills—and at the summit of the road came to a small loch, called *Ceannairdiche.*

Soon after this we turned down the hill again into woods, and came to *Tummel Bridge*, where we changed horses. Here were a few, but very few people, who I think, from what Brown and Grant—who, as usual, were in attendance—said, recognized us, but behaved extremely well, and did not come near. This was at twenty minutes to four. We then turned as it were homewards, but had to make a good long circuit, and drove along the side of *Loch Tummel*, high above the loch, through birch wood, which grows along the hills much the same as about *Birkhall*. It is only three miles long. Here it was again very clear and bright. At the end of the loch, on a highish point called after me " *The Queen's View* " —though I had not been there in 1844—we got out and took tea. But this was a long and unsuccessful business; the fire would not burn, and the kettle would not boil. At length

Brown ran off to a cottage and returned after some little while with a can full of hot water, but it was no longer boiling when it arrived, and the tea was not good. Then all had to be packed, and it made us very late.

It was fast growing dark. We passed *Alleine*, Sir Robert Colquhoun's place, almost immediately after this, and then, at about half-past six, changed horses at the *Bridge of Garry*, near, or rather in the midst of, the *Pass of Killiecrankie:* but from the lateness of the hour and the dulness of the evening—for it was raining—we could see hardly anything.

We went through *Pitlochry*, where we were recognized, but got quite quietly through, and reached *Ballinluig*, where the Duchess's horses were put on, at a little before half-past seven. Here the lamps were lit, and the good people had put two lighted candles in each window! They offered to bring "Athole brose," which we, however, declined. The people pressed round the carriage, and one man brought out a bull's-eye lantern which he turned upon me. But Brown, who kept quite close, put himself between me and the glare. We ought to have been home in less than an hour from this time, but we had divers impediments—twice the plaid fell out and had to be picked up; and then the lamp which I had given to the Duchess, like the one our outrider carries, was lit, and the coachman who rode outrider, and who was not accustomed to use it, did not hold it rightly, so that it went out twice, and had to be relit each time. So we only got home at a quarter to nine, and dined at twenty minutes past nine. But it was a very interesting day. We must have gone seventy-four miles.

Thursday, October 4.

Again heavy mist on the hills—most provoking—but without rain. The Duchess came to ask if I had any objection to the servants and gillies having a dance for two hours in the evening, to which I said, certainly not, and that I would go to it myself. At a quarter to twelve I rode in the grounds with the Duchess, going round *Bishop's Hill* and up to the *King's Seat*, a good height, among the most splendid trees—beeches, oaks Scotch firs, spruce—really quite like *Windsor*, and reminding me of those fine trees at the *Belvidere*, and a good deal of *Reinhardtsbrunn* (in the forest of *Thuringia*). But though less heavy than the two preceding mornings and quite dry, it was too hazy to see any distant hills, and *Craigy Barns*, that splendid rocky, richly wooded hill overtopping

3

the whole, only peeped through the mist occasionally.   From
the *King's Seat* we came down by the fort and upon the old
" *Otter Hound Kennels*," where we saw Mrs. Fisher, the
mother of Agnes Brierly, who was formerly schoolmistress to
the *Lochnagar* girls' school near *Balmoral*.   We came in at a
little after one, expecting it would clear and become much
finer, instead of which it got darker and thicker.

At twenty minutes to four drove with the Duchess, Miss
MacGregor and Janie Ely following, to *Loch Clunie* by the
Loch of the Lowes, and passed *Laighwood Farm*.   We drove
round the loch ; saw and stopped to sketch the old castle of
Clunie, on a little island in the loch, the property of Lord
Airlie.   The scenery is tame, but very pretty with much wood,
which is now in great beauty from the change of the leaf.
The distance was enveloped in mist, and, as we drove back
towards *Dunkeld* by the *Cupar Angus Road*, it was quite like
a thick *Windsor* fog, but perfectly dry.

We stopped to take tea at *Newtyle*, a farm of the Duchess,
about two miles from *Dunkeld*, where she has a small room,
and which supplies turnips, etc., for the fine dairy cows.   We
got home by five minutes to seven.   We passed through the
town, where the people appeared at their doors cheering, and
the children made a great noise.   Dinner as before.   At half-
past ten we went down (through the lower passages) to the
servants' hall, in which the little dance took place.   All the
Duchess's servants, the wives of the men-servants. the keepers,
the wood-forester (J. M'Gregor, who has an extensive charge
over all the woods on the *Athole* property), the gardener, and
some five or six others who belong to my guard (eight people,
belonging to the Duchess or to town, who take their turn of
watching two by two at night), besides all our servants, were
there ; only Grant and two of the gillies did not appear, which
vexed us ; but the gillies had not any proper shoes, they said,
and therefore did not come.   Janie Ely came ; also Mr. Keir,
and both were very active ; General Grey only looked in for
a moment as he was suffering severely from cold.   The fid-
dlers played in very good time, and the dancing was very
animated, and went on without ceasing.   Louise and Arthur
both danced a good deal.   Nothing but reels were danced.
Even the Duchess's old French maid, Clarice, danced !   She
no longer acts as the Duchess's maid, but still lives near, in
the adjacent so-called " brick buildings."

A brighter morning, though still hazy. The sun came out and the mist seemed dispersing. At twenty minutes to one started with the Duchess and Louise, the two ladies following, for *Loch Ordie.* Several times during the drive the mist regained its mastery, but then again the sun struggled through, blue sky appeared, and the mist seemed to roll away and the hills and woods to break through. We drove by *Craig Lush* and *Butterstone Lochs,* and then turned by the *Riechip Burn* —up a very steep hill, finely wooded, passing by *Riechip* and *Raemore,* two of the Duke of Athole's shooting lodges, both let. After the last the road opens upon a wild moor (or "muir") for a short while, before entering the plantations and woods of *Loch Ordie.* Here, quite close to the lodge, on the grass, we took luncheon. The Duchess had had a hot venison pie brought, which was very acceptable. The sun had come out, and it was delightfully warm, with a blue sky and bright lights, and we sat sketching for some time. The good people have made a cairn amongst the trees where we had tea last year.

At four we drove away, and went by the road which leads towards *Tullymet,* and out of the woods by *Hardy's Lodge,* near a bridge. We stopped at a very picturesque place, surrounded by woods and hills and little shields, reminding me of the *Laucha Grund* at *Reinhardtsbrunn.* Opposite to this, on a place called *Ruidh Reinnich,* or the "ferny shieling," a fire was kindled, and we took our tea. We then drove back by the upper *St. Colme's Road,* after which we drove through the town, up *Bridge Street,* and to the *Market Cross,* where a fountain is being erected in memory of the Duke. We went to see the dairy, and then came home on foot at a quarter to seven. Rested on the sofa, as my head was bad; it got better, however, after dinner.

A beautiful, bright, clear morning, most provokingly so. After breakfast at half-past nine, we left, with real regret, the kind Duchess's hospitable house, where all breathes peace and harmony, and where it was so quiet and snug. It was a real holiday for me in my present sad life. Louise and the Duchess went with me; the others had gone on. Some of the principal people connected with the Duchess stood along the approach as we drove out. We went the

usual way to *Loch Ordie*, and past the lodge, on to the east
end of the loch, the latter part of the road being very rough
and deep.   Here we all mounted our ponies at half-past
eleven, and proceeded on our journey.   A cloudless sky, not
a breath of wind, and the heat intense and sickening.   We
went along a sort of cart-road or track.   The burn of *Riechip*
runs out of this glen, through which we rode, and which
really is very beautiful, under the shoulder of *Benachallie.*
The shooting tenant of *Raemore*, a Mr. Gordon, was out on
the opposite side of the glen on a distant hill.   We rode on
through the woods ; the day was very hazy.   After a few
miles the eastern shore of *Loch Oishne* was reached, and we
also skirted *Little Loch Oishne* for a few hundred yards.   We
followed from here the same road which we had come on
that pouring afternoon in going to *Dunkeld* last year, till at a
quarter to one we reached the *Kindrogan March.*   Here Mr.
Keir, his son, and his keeper met us.   Thence we rode by
Glen Derby, a wild open glen with moors.   Descending into
it, the road was soft but quite safe, having been purposely
cut and put in order by Mr. Keir.   We then ascended a
steepish hill, after passing a shepherd's hut.   Here Arthur
and General Grey rode off to *Kindrogan*, young Mr. Keir
with them, whence they were to drive on in advance.   As we
descended, we came upon a splendid view of all the hills,
and also of *Glen Fernate*, which is the way to *Fealar.*

At half-past two we five ladies lunched on a heathery knoll,
just above Mr. Keir's wood, and were indeed glad to do so,
as we were tired by the great heat.   As soon as luncheon
was over, we walked down through the wood a few hundred
yards to where the carriage was.   Here we took leave, with
much regret, of the dear kind Duchess and amiable Miss
MacGregor, and got into the carriage at half-past three, stopping for a moment near *Kindrogan* to wish Mrs. Keir and
her family good-by.   We drove on by *Kirkmichael*, and then
some little way until we got into the road from *Blairgowrie.*
The evening was quite splendid, the sky yellow and pink,
and the distant hills coming out soft and blue, both behind
and in front of us.   We changed horses at the *Spital*, and
about two miles beyond it—at a place called *Loch-na-Braig*
—we stopped, and while Grant ran back to get from a small
house some hot water in the kettle, we three, with Brown's
help, scrambled over a low stone wall by the roadside, and
lit a fire and prepared our tea.   The kettle soon returned,
and the hot tea was very welcome and refreshing.

Grey

We then drove off again. The scenery was splendid till daylight gradually faded away, and then the hills looked grim and severe in the dusk. We cleared the *Devil's Elbow* well, however, before it was really dark, and then many stars came out, and we reached *Balmoral* in safety at half-past eight o'clock.

OPENING OF THE ABERDEEN WATERWORKS.

Tuesday, October 16, 1866.

AT a quarter-past ten left for *Ballater* with Lenchen and Louise; Christian, Arthur, the Duchess of Roxburghe, and Emily Cathcart in the second; the gentlemen (General Grey,* etc.) having gone on in front. We went by the railway, which was useful on this occasion. We went about three-quarters of an hour by railway, and then stopped close to *Inchmarlo*, Mr. Davidson's place, not far from *Kincardine O'Neil*. Here we got into carriages—Lenchen and Louise with me,—Christian, Arthur and the two equerries, etc., in the next. About twenty minutes' drive took us to *Invercannie*, where the ceremony took place. I got out and stood outside the tent while the Lord Provost (whom I knighted at *Aberdeen* in 1863) read the address. Then I had to read my answer, which made me very nervous; but I got through it well, though it was the first time I had read anything since my darling Husband was taken from me. Then came the turning of the cock, and it was very pretty to see the water rushing up.

These waterworks are on a most extensive scale, and are estimated to convey to the city 6,000,000 gallons of water daily. The water is from the river *Dee*, from which it is diverted at *Cairnton*, about four miles above *Banchory*. The principal features of the works are a tunnel 760 yards in length, which is cut through the hill of *Cairnton*, composed of solid rock of a very hard nature. At the end of the tunnel is the *Invercannie* Reservoir, where the ceremony took place. This reservoir is estimated to contain 15,000,000 gallons of water. It is just two years and a half since the first turf of the undertaking was cut, and the cost of the works is 130,000*l*.

* He died on March 31, 1870. He had been with me as equerry from the time I came to the Throne. In 1846 he became Private Secretary to the Prince, and from December, 1861, held the same position with me till his death. He was highly esteemed and valued by us both, and his loss grieved me deeply.

The ceremony was over in less than a quarter of an hour, and we returned as we came, stopping a moment at the door of Mr. Davidson's house, where his daughter presented me with a nosegay. The day was fine and mild. The people were very kind, and cheered a good deal.

We got back at twenty minutes past two.

HALLOWEEN.

October 31, 1866–1867.

WHILE we were at Mrs. Grant's we saw the commencement of the keeping of Halloween. All the children came out with burning torches, shouting and jumping. The Protestants generally keep Halloween on the old day, November 12, and the Catholics on this day; but hearing I had wished to see it two years ago, they all decided to keep it to-day. When we drove home we saw all the gillies coming along with burning torches, and torches and bonfires appeared also on the opposite side of the water. We went up stairs to look at it from the windows, from whence it had a very pretty effect.

On the same day in the following year, viz., Thursday, October 31, 1867, we had an opportunity of again seeing the celebration of Halloween, and even of taking part in it. We had been out driving, but we hurried back to be in time for the celebration. Close to Donald Stewart's house we were met by two gillies bearing torches. Louise got out and took one, walking by the side of the carriage, and looking like one of the witches in " Macbeth." As we approached *Balmoral*, the keepers and their wives and children, the gillies and other people met us, all with torches; Brown also carrying one. We got out at the house, where Leopold joined us, and a torch was given to him. We walked round the whole house, preceded by Ross playing the pipes, going down the steps of the terrace. Louise and Leopold went first, then came Janie Ely and I, followed by every one carrying torches, which had a very pretty effect. After this a bonfire was made of all the torches, close to the house, and they danced reels whilst Ross played the pipes.

VISIT TO FLOORS AND THE SCOTCH BORDER COUNTRY,
AUGUST 20, 1867.

Tuesday, August 20, 1867.

AT ten o'clock I left *Windsor* (those night departures are
always sad) with Louise, Leopold, and Baby (Beatrice);
Lenchen, Christian, and their little baby boy meeting us at
the station.   Jane Churchill, Harriet Phipps, the two gov-
ernesses, Sir. Thomas Biddulph, Lord Charles Fitz-Roy,
Colonel G. Gordon, Mr. Duckworth, and Dr. Jenner were in
attendance.   I had been much annoyed to hear just before
dinner that our saloon carriage could not go under some
tunnel or arch beyond *Carlisle*, and that I must get out and
change carriages there.

Wednesday, August 21.

The railway carriage swung a good deal. and it was very
hot, so that I did not get much sleep.   At half-past seven I
was woke up to dress and hurry out at *Carlisle*, which we did
at a quarter to eight.   Here in the station we had some
breakfast, and waited an hour till our carriage was taken off
and another put on (which they have since found out was
quite unnecessary!).   The morning, which had been gloomy,
cleared and became very fine, and we went on along such a
pretty line through a very pretty country, through *Eskdale*
and past *Netherby*, as far as *Riddings*, and then leaving the
Esk entered *Liddesdale*, the railway running along the *Liddel
Water* to *Riccarton* station, where we stopped for a moment.
We next came along the *Slitrig Water* to *Hawick*, where we
went slowly, which the people had begged us to do, and
where were great crowds.   Here we entered *Teviotdale* and
descended it, entering the valley of the *Tweed* at *St. Boswell's*.   Between *St. Boswell's* and *Kelso* at *Roxburgh* station,
we crossed the *Teviot* again.   We passed close under the
Eildon Hills, three high points rising from the background.
The country is extremely picturesque, valleys with fine trees
and streams, intermingled with great cultivation.   Only after
half-past eleven did we reach *Kelso* station, which was very
prettily decorated, and where were standing the Duke and
Duchess of Roxburghe, Lord Bowmont, the Duke of Buccleuch, and Lord C. Ker, as well as General Hamilton, commanding the forces in *Scotland*.   We got out at once.   I embraced the dear Duchess, and shook hands with the two

Dukes, and then at once entered the carriage (mine) with Lenchen, Louise, and the Duchess ; Beatrice, Leopold, and Christian going in the second, and the others following in other carriages.

The morning beautiful and very mild.   We drove through the small suburb of *Maxwell Heugh*, down into the town of *Kelso*, and over the bridge which commands a beautiful view of the broad stream of the *Tweed* and of the *Park of Floors*, with the fine house itself.   Everywhere decorations, and great and most enthusiastic crowds.   The little town of *Kelso* is very picturesque, and there were triumphal arches, and no end of pretty mottoes, and every house was decorated with flowers and flags.   Fifty ladies dressed in white strewed flowers as we passed.   Volunteers were out and bands playing. At the Market Place the carriage stopped ; an address was presented, not read ; and a little girl was held up to give me an enormous bouquet.   Immense and most enthusiastic cheering.   We then drove on, amidst continued crowds and hearty cheers, up to the very park gates, where the old Sheriff, eighty-five years old, was presented.   The park is remarkably fine, with the approach under splendid beech, sycamore, and oak trees.   The house very handsome, built originally by Sir John Vanbrugh in 1718, but much improved by the present Duke.   You drive under a large porch, and then go up a flight of steps to the hall.   The Duke's band was stationed outside.   Mr. and Lady Charlotte Russell, Mr. Suttie, and Lady Charles Ker were in the hall.   The Duchess took us into the library, where the Duke of Buccleuch joined us, and, after waiting a little while, we had breakfast (ourselves alone) in the really splendid dining-room adjoining, at ten minutes past twelve.   This over, the Duchess showed us to our rooms up stairs.   I had three that were very comfortable, opening one into the other ; a sitting-room, dressing-room, and the largest of the three, the bedroom, simple, with pretty chintz, but very elegant, nice and comfortable.   The children were close at hand.   But the feeling of loneliness when I saw no room for my darling, and felt I was indeed alone and a widow, overcame me very sadly !   It was the first time I had gone in this way on a visit (like as in former times), and I thought so much of all dearest Albert would have done and said, and how he would have wandered about everywhere, admired everything, looked at everything—and now!   Oh! must it ever, ever be so ?

At half-past two lunched (as at home) in the fine dining-room. A lovely day. The view from the windows beautiful. The distant *Cheviot* range with a great deal of wood, *Kelso* embosomed in rich woods, with the bridge, and the *Tweed* flowing beneath natural grass terraces which go down to it. Very fine. It reminded me a little of the view from the *Phœnix Park* near *Dublin*.

At half-past five walked out with Lenchen and the kind Duchess to a spot where I planted a tree,* and then we walked on to the flower-garden, where there are a number of very fine hot-houses, and took tea in a pretty little room adjoining them, which is entirely tiled. After this we took a pleasant drive in the fine park which is full of splendid timber, along the *Tweed*, and below the ruins of the celebrated old *Castle of Roxburgh*, of which there is very little remaining. It is on a high eminence ; the *Tweed* and *Teviot* are on either side of it, so that the position is remarkably strong. It stood many a siege, and was frequently taken by the English and retaken by the Scotch. Scotch and even English kings, amongst them Edward II., held their Court there.

We came home at eight. The Duke and Duchess dined with us, and after dinner we watched the illuminations and many bonfires from the library, and afterwards went for a moment into the drawing-room to see the ladies and gentlemen, after which I went up to my room, where I sat and rested, feeling tired and only able to read the newspapers.

Thursday, August 22.

A fine morning, though rather hazy. The night and moonlight had been beautiful. Breakfasted with our family in the breakfast-room. At twenty minutes to eleven went and sat out under some trees on the lawn near the house writing, where I was quite quiet and undisturbed, and remained till half-past twelve, resting, reading, etc. Immediately after luncheon started in two carriages. the Duchess and our two daughters with me; Christian, the Duke, Lady Charlotte Russell, and Lord Charles Fitz-Roy in the second carriage (with post-horses). We had the Duke's horses as far as *Ravenswood*. We drove through *Kelso*, which was full of people, crossed the *Tweed* and *Teviot* (where the waters join), and passed below the old *Castle of Roxburgh*. The country is very pretty, hilly, wooded, and cultivated. Not long after we started, the second carriage disappeared, and we waited for it. It

* The gardener, Hector Rose, became head gardener at Windsor in the spring of 1868, and died, alas! June 5, 1872, after having filled his situation admirably.

seems that, at the first hill they came to, the wheelers would not hold up. So we stopped (and this delayed us some time), the leaders replaced the wheelers, and they came on with a pair. Then we drove up to *St. Boswell's Green*, with the three fine *Eildon* hills before us—which are said to have been divided by Michael Scott, the wizard—seeing *Mertoun*, my excellent Lord Polwarth's place, on the other side of the road. Alas! he died only last Friday from a second stroke, the first of which seized him in February; and now, when he had intended to be at the head of the volunteers who received me at *Kelso*, he is lying dead at his house which we passed so near! It lies low, and quite in among the trees. I lament him deeply and sincerely, having liked him very much, as did my dearest Albert also, ever since we knew him in 1858.

We changed horses at *Ravenswood*, or old *Melrose* (where I had my own), having caught a glimpse of where *Dryburgh Abbey* is, though the railway almost hides it. The Duke of Buccleuch met us there, and rode the whole way. Everywhere, wherever there were dwellings, there was the kindest welcome, and triumphal arches were erected. We went by the side of the *Eildon Hills*, past an immense railway viaduct, and nothing could be prettier than the road. The position of *Melrose* is most picturesque, surrounded by woods and hills. The little village, or rather town, of *Newstead*, which we passed through just before coming to *Melrose*, is very narrow and steep. We drove straight up to the *Abbey* through the grounds of the Duke of Buccleuch's agent, and got out and walked about the ruins, which are indeed very fine, and some of the architecture and carving in beautiful preservation. David I., who is described as a " sair Saint," originally built it, but the Abbey, the ruins of which are now standing, was built in the fifteenth century. We saw where, under the high altar, Robert Bruce's heart is supposed to be buried; also the tomb of Alexander II., and of the celebrated wizard, Michael Scott. Reference is made to the former in some lines of Sir Walter Scott's in the " Lay of the Last Minstrel," which describes this Border country :—

> They sat them down on a marble stone;
> A Scottish monarch slept below.

And then when Deloraine takes the book from the dead wizard's hand, it says—

> He thought, as he took it, the dead man frowned.

Most truly does Walter Scott say—

> If thou wouldst view fair Melrose aright,
> Go visit it by the pale moonlight.

It looks very ghostlike, and reminds me a little of *Holyrood Chapel*. We walked in the churchyard to look at the exterior of the Abbey, and then re-entered our carriages and drove through the densely crowded streets. Great enthusiasm and hearty affectionate loyalty. Many decorations. A number of people from *Galashiels*, and even from the North of *England*, had come into the town and swelled the crowd; many also had spread themselves along the outskirts. We took the other side of the valley returning, and saw *Galashiels*, very prettily situated, a flourishing town famous for its tweeds and shawls; the men are called the " braw lads of *Gala Water*."

Another twenty minutes or half-hour brought us to *Abbotsford*, the well-known residence of Sir Walter Scott. It lies low and looks rather gloomy. Mr. Hope Scott and Lady Victoria * (my god-daughter and sister to the present Duke of Norfolk) with their children, the young Duke of Norfolk, and some other relations, received us. Mr. Hope Scott married first Miss Lockhart, the last surviving grandchild of Sir Walter Scott, and she died leaving only one daughter, a pretty girl of eleven, to whom this place will go, and who is the only surviving descendant of Sir Walter. They showed us the part of the house in which Sir Walter lived, and all his rooms—his drawing-room with the same furniture and carpet, the library where we saw his MS. of " Ivanhoe," and several others of his novels and poems in a beautiful handwriting with hardly any erasures, and other relics which Sir Walter had himself collected. Then his study, a small dark room, with a little turret in which is a bust in bronze, done from a cast taken after death, of Sir Walter. In the study we saw his journal, in which Mr. Scott asked me to write my name (which I felt it to be a presumption in me to do), as also the others.

We went through some passages into two or three rooms where were collected fine specimens of old armor, etc., and where in a glass case are Sir Walter's last clothes. We ended by going into the dining-room, in which Sir Walter Scott died, where we took tea. . . .

We left at twenty minutes to seven—very late. It rained

* She died in 1870.

a little, but soon ceased. We recrossed the *Tweed*, and went by *Gattonside* to *Leaderfoot Bridge*. Here we were met by the *Berwickshire* Volunteers, commanded by Lord Binning (Lord Haddington's son), who as Deputy Lieutenant rode a long way with us. Here was a steep hill, and the road surrounded by trees. We passed soon after through *Gladswood*, the property of Mr. Meiklam, at whose house-door we stopped, and he and Mrs. Meiklam were presented, and their daughter gave me a nosegay. Just after this we entered *Berwickshire*. Changing horses and leaving this place, going over *Gateheugh*, we came upon a splendid view, overlooking a great extent of country, with a glen deep below the road, richly wooded, the river at the bottom, and hills in the distance; but unfortunately the "gloaming" * was already commencing—at least, the sun was gone down, and the evening was gray and dull, though very mild. We passed *Bemersyde*, which is eventually to belong to Alfred's Equerry, Mr. Haig,† and through the village of *Mertoun*, behind the park; and it was striking to see the good feeling shown by the people, who neither displayed any decorations nor cheered, though they were out and bowed, as their excellent master, Lord Polwarth, was lying dead in his house.

It was nearly dark by this time, but we got well and safely home by ten minutes to nine. The Duke of Buccleuch rode with us some way beyond *Gladswood*. We did not come through *Kelso* on our way back. In passing *Mertoun* we left the old tower of *Smailholm* to the left, the scene of the "Eve of St. John." We only sat down to dinner at half-past nine, and I own I was very tired. The Duke of Buccleuch was only able to come when dinner was half over. Besides him the Duke and Duchess of Roxburghe, Lord Bowmont, Lady Charles Ker, and Mr. Suttie made the party at dinner. Lady Susan was prevented by indisposition from being there. Nobody could be kinder, or more discreet, or more anxious that I should be undisturbed when at home, than the Duke and Duchess. I only stopped a few minutes down stairs after dinner, and then went up to my room, but it was then nearly eleven. The others went into the drawing-room to meet some of the neighbors.

Friday, August 23.

A dull morning, very close, with a little inclination to rain, though only for a short time. Breakfast as yesterday. At

* The Scotch word for "twilight."
† He succeeded to the property in 1878.

twenty minutes to eleven we started: I with our daughters
and the Duchess; Christian with dear Beatrice, the Duke of
Marlborough (the Minister in attendance), and Lady Susan
Melville, in the second carriage; and the Duke of Roxburghe,
Lord Charles Fitz-Roy, Sir Thomas Biddulph, in the third,
with Colonel Gordon and Dr. Jenner on the box.* We proceeded through *Kelso*, which was very full, and the people
most loyal; by the village of *Heiton*, prettily decorated with
an arch (two young girls dressed in white threw nosegays),
and up the rivers *Teviot* and *Jed*, which flow through charming valleys. The town of *Jedburgh* is very prettily situated,
and is about the same size as *Kelso*, only without its large
shops. It is, however, the capital of the county. It was very
crowded, and very prettily decorated. The town is full of
historical recollections. King Malcolm IV. died there;
William the Lion and Alexander II. resided there; Alexander III. married his second wife, Joletta, daughter of the
Comte de Dreux, there; and Queen Mary was the last
sovereign who came to administer severe justice. The
Duchess pointed out to me a house up a side street in the
town where Queen Mary had lived and been ill with fever.
In the square an address was presented, just as at *Kelso*, and
then we went on down a steep hill, having a very good view
of the old Abbey, as curious in its way as *Melrose*, and also
founded by David I. There is a very fine ruined abbey in
Kelso also.

There were four pretty triumphal arches; one with two
very well chosen inscriptions, viz., on one side " Freedom
makes all men to have lyking," and on the other side " The
love of all thy people comfort thee."

We went on through a beautiful wooded valley up the *Jed*,
in the bank of which, in the red stone, are caves in which
the Covenanters were hid. We passed Lord Cranstoun's
place, *Crailing*, and then turned, and close before the town
we turned into *Jed Forest*—up an interminable hill, which
was very trying to the horses and the postilions—and returned through the grounds of *Hartrigge*, the late Lord
Campbell's, now occupied by a Mr. Gordon.

We then returned by the same road we came, passing
Lord Minto's place, and *Kirkbank*, belonging to the Duke of
Buccleuch, where his late brother, Lord John Scott, used to
live. Here the horses were watered. We stopped for a few

* Brown and the sergeant footman, Collins, were (as usual) on the seat behind
my carriage.

minutes, and the Duke of Buccleuch, who had ridden with us the greater part of the way, into *Jedburgh* and back to this place, took leave. We only got home near three o'clock. We lunched at once, and then I rested. Only at half-past six did I go out with Lenchen and the good Duchess, and walked with them to the flower-garden, where, as it began to rain, we took tea in the small room there. Lenchen walked back with the Duchess, who returned to me, and I sat out a little while with her, and then walked back to the house. It was a very oppressive evening.

At half-past eight we dined. The Duke and Duchess, Mr. and Lady Charlotte Russell, and Lord Charles Ker dined. Went up stairs and wrote. At ten minutes to eleven we left *Floors*, where I had been most kindly received, and had been very comfortable and enjoyed all I saw, and felt much all the kindness of high and low. The carriages were open, and the night very warm and starlight. There were lamps all along the drive in the Park; the bridge was illuminated, and so was the whole town, through which we went at a foot's pace. It was densely crowded, the square especially, and the people very enthusiastic. The dear Duchess went with us to the station, whither the Duke and his sons had preceded us with the others. It was a very pretty sight. The *Free Kirk*, a pretty building, was lit up with red light, which almost gave it the appearance of being on fire. We took leave of the dear Duchess and the Duke, got into our railway carriage, and started at once.

Saturday, August 24.

We passed through *Edinburgh*. At eight A.M. we were at *Ballater*. Some coffee and tea were handed in to us before we left the train and got into our carriages.

A fine and very mild morning, the heather hardly out, but all very green; and at ten minutes to nine we were at our dear *Balmoral*.

VISIT TO GLENFIDDICH.

Tuesday, September 24, 1867.

A BRIGHT morning, but a fearful gale blowing. The maids, Emilie and Annie and Lady Churchill's maid, with Ross and the luggage, started at a little past seven.

Breakfasted at a quarter past nine; and at ten, taking

Jane Churchill
1875

leave of Lenchen, darling Beatrice, and the boys, and Christian, started with Louise and Jane Churchill—Brown, as usual, on the box. Sir Thomas Biddulph had gone on at eight. We drove up by *Alt Craichie* on to *Gairnshiel,* and anything like the wind I cannot describe. It blew through everything. Just beyond *Gairnshiel* we took another change of my own horses, which took us up that very steep hill called *Glaschoil.* Here we met the luggage with Blake,* which had stuck completely, but was going on with the help of four cart or farm horses, and then we went on by *Tornahoish* and *Cock Brigg,* where we crossed the *Don.* At the small inn at the foot of the hill, called *Bridge End,* we found the maids' carriage halting. They were waiting for the luggage, but we sent them on. Our postilions next took a wrong road, and we had to get out to enable them to turn. Then came a very steep hill, the beginning of very wild and really grand scenery. Louise and Jane Churchill walked up to the top of this hill, and then we went down another very steep one, seeing a fearfully long ascent before us. We changed horses, and took a pair of post-horses here. Steep green hills with a deep ravine on our left as we went up, and then down again, this fearful hill—surely three miles in length—called *Lecht.* At the bottom we entered a glen, or rather pass, very wild, and the road extremely bad, with rapid turnings. Near this there are iron mines belonging to the Duke of Richmond. Here we met a drove of very fine Highland cattle grazing. Turning out of this glen we came into much more cultivated land with farms and trees, skirted by hills in the distance—all very clear, as the views had been all along. By half-past one we came close by *Tomintoul,* which lies very prettily amongst the trees, hills, and fields; then leaving it to our left, we went on about a mile and a half beyond the town; and here by the roadside, on some grass below a heathery bank, at about a quarter-past two, we took our luncheon, and walked a little. The Duke of Richmond's keeper, Lindsay by name, joined us here and rode before us. We changed horses (again a pair) and drove on, entering *Glen Livet* through the small village of *Knockandhu* —*Blairfindy Castle* on the left, just behind the celebrated *Glenlivet Distillery.* We drove on six miles; pretty country all along, distant high hills and richly cultivated land, with houses and cottages dotted about. At *Tomnavoulin,* a farm, not far from a bridge, we met Sir Thomas Biddulph (who had

* A footman, now one of the Pages of the Presence.

driven on in a dogcart) and our ponies. Though the wind
had gone down a good deal, there was quite enough to make
it disagreeable and fatiguing, and so we decided to drive, and
Sir Thomas said he would ride across with the ponies and
meet the Duke, while his head keeper was to come on the
box with Brown and show us the way (Grant did not go with
us this time). We drove on for an hour and more, having
entered *Glen Rinnes* shortly after *Tomnavoulin*, with the hills
of *Ben Rinnes* on the left. There were fine large fields of
turnips, pretty hills and dales, with wood, and distant high
hills, but nothing grand. The day became duller, and the
mist hung over the hills ; and just as we sat down by the
roadside on a heathery bank, where there is a very pretty
view of *Glenlivet*, to take our tea, it began to rain, and continued doing so for the remainder of the evening. Lindsay,
the head keeper, fetched a kettle with boiling water from a
neighboring farmhouse. About two miles beyond this we
came through *Dufftown*—a small place with a long steep
street, very like *Grantown*—and then turned abruptly to the
right past *Auchindoun*, leaving a pretty glen to the left.
Three miles more brought us to a lodge and gate, which was
the entrance of *Glenfiddich*. Here you go quite into the hills.
The glen is very narrow, with the *Fiddich* flowing below,
green hills rising on either side with birch trees growing on
them, much like at *Inchrory*, only narrower. We saw deer
on the tops of the hills close by. The carriage-road—a very
good one—winds along for nearly three miles, when you
come suddenly upon the lodge, the position of which reminds
me very much of *Corn Davon*,* only that the glen is narrower
and the hills just round it steeper. It is a long shooting
lodge, covering a good deal of ground, but only one story
high. We reached it at half-past six, and it was nearly dark.
Sir Thomas received us, but he had missed the Duke! A
message had, however, at once been sent after him. On
entering the house there is one long, low passage, at the end
of which, with three windows, taking in the whole of each
side and looking three different ways, is the drawing-room
where tea was prepared. We went along the passage to our
rooms, which were all in a row. Another long passage, a
little beyond the hall door, went the other way at right angles
with the first, and along that were offices and servants' bedrooms. Next to the drawing-room came the dining-room,
then Sir Thomas Biddulph's room, then the Duke's, then

* Near Balmoral, not far from Loch Bulig.

Brown's and Ross's (in one) then Louise's, then mine, then Emilie's and Annie's (in one), then a little further back, Jane Churchill's and her maid's—all very comfortably and conveniently together. But though our maids had arrived, nor a bit of luggage. We waited and waited till dinner-time, but nothing came. So we ladies (for Sir Thomas had wisely brought some things with him) had to go to dinner in our riding-skirts, and just as we were. I, having no cap, had to put on a black lace veil of Emilie's, which she arranged as a coiffure. I had been writing and resting before dinner. The Duke (who remained at *Glenfiddich*) and Sir Thomas dined with us ladies.

None of the maids or servants had any change of clothing. Dinner over, I went with Louise and Jane to the drawing-room, which was given me as my sitting-room, and Jane read. While at dinner at half-past nine, Ross told us that Blake, the footman, had arrived with some of the smaller things, but none of the most necessary—no clothes, etc. The break with the luggage had finally broken down at *Tomintoul;* from thence Blake had gone with a cart to *Dufftown*, where he had got a small break, and brought the light things on, but the heavier luggage was coming in a cart, and they hoped would be here by twelve o'clock. At first it seemed as if no horses were to be had, and it was only with the greatest difficulty that some were at last obtained. Louise and Jane Churchill left me at near eleven o'clock.

I sat up writing and waiting for this luggage. A man was sent out on a pony with a lantern in search of it, and I remained writing till a quarter-past twelve, when, feeling very tired, I lay down on the sofa, and Brown (who was indefatigable) went out himself to look for it. At one, he came back, saying nothing was to be seen or heard of this luckless luggage, and urged my going to bed. My maids had unfortunately not thought of bringing anything with them, and I disliked the idea of going to bed without any of the necessary toilette. However, some arrangements were made which were very uncomfortable; and after two I got into bed, but had very little sleep at first; finally fatigue got the better of discomfort, and after three I fell asleep.

Wednesday, September 25.

Slept soundly till half-past seven, and heard that the luggage had only arrived at half-past four in the morning. Breakfasted with Louise. who made my coffee beautifully,

4

with Brown, who waited at breakfast, Ross coming in and out
with what had to be carried. It rained soon after I got up,
and continued raining till near eleven. I read and wrote,
etc. At half-past eleven, it having cleared, I rode up the
small narrow glen, down which flows a " burnie " (called the
Garden Burn), the banks covered with fern and juniper,
heather and birch, etc., past the kitchen-garden. Louise
walked with me. Went up nearly to the top and walked
down it again, then on to the stables, which are at a small
distance from the house, where I saw an old underkeeper, P.
Stewart by name, seventy-four years old, with a Peninsular
and Waterloo medal, who had been in the 92d Highlanders,
and was a great favorite of the late Duke's. Home by twenty
minutes to one. The day became very fine and warm.
Lunched in my own room with Louise at the same small
table at which we had breakfasted, Ross and the Duke's
piper playing outside the window.

After luncheon rode (on Sultan, as this morning) with Louise and Jane Churchill, the Duke walking (and Jane also part
of the way), down to the end of *Glenfiddich;* turning then to
the left for *Bridgehaugh* (a ford), and going on round the hill
of *Ben Main.* We first went along the road and then on the
heather " squinting " the hill—hard and good ground, but disagreeable from the heather being so deep that you did not see
where you were going—the Duke's forester leading the way,
and so fast that Brown led me on at his full speed, and we
distanced the others entirely. At five we got to the edge of
a small ravine, from whence we had a fine view of the old
ruined castle of *Achendown*, which formerly belonged to the
old Lords Huntly. Here we took our tea, and then rode
home by another and a shorter way—not a bad road, but on the
steeper side of the hill, and quite on the slant, which is not
agreeable. We came down at the ford, and rode back as we
went out, getting home at seven. A very fine evening. It was
very nearly dark when we reached home. I was very tired;
I am no longer equal to much fatigue.

Thursday, September 26.

Slept very well, and was much rested. At half-past twelve I
started with Louise on ponies (I on Sultan), and Jane
Churchill, the Duke of Richmond, and Sir Thomas walking,
rode past the stables on a good road, and then turned to the
right and went up *Glenfiddich* for about four miles. The
scenery is not grand, but pretty; an open valley with green

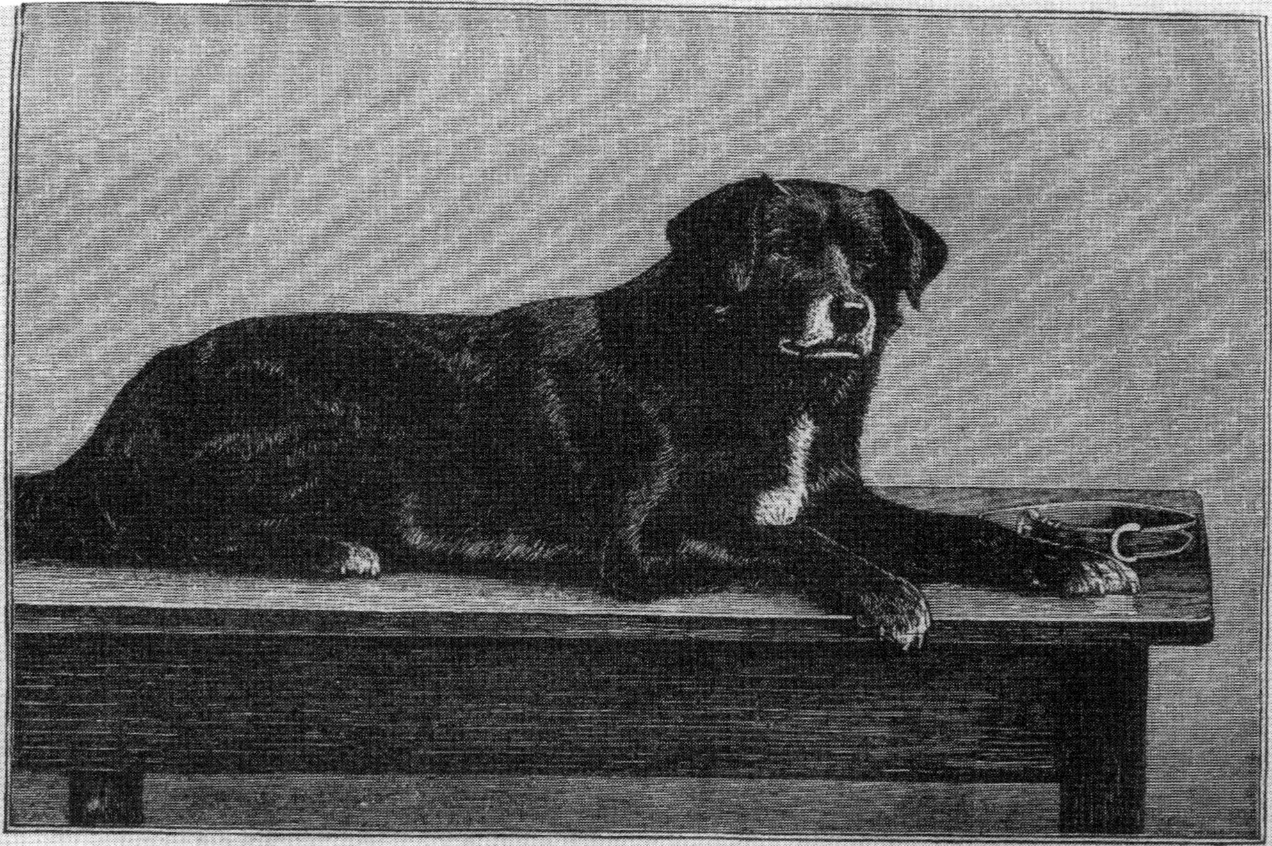

SHARP.

and not very high hills, some birches, and a great deal of fern and juniper. After about three miles the glen narrows and is extremely pretty ; a narrow steep path overhanging a burn leads to a cave, which the Duke said went a long way under the hill. It is called the *Elf House.* There is a small space of level ground, and a sort of seat arranged with stones on which Louise and I sat : and here we all lunched, and then tried to sketch. But I could make nothing of the cave, and therefore scrambled up part of the hill with great trouble, and tried again but equally unsuccessfully, and had to be helped down, as I had been helped up, by Brown. We were here nearly an hour, and then, after walking down the steep path, we got on our ponies and rode up to the left, another very steep and narrow path, for a short while on the brink of a steep high bank with the *Fiddich* below. We emerged from this ravine and came upon moors in the hills (the whole of this is "the forest"), and rode on a mile and a half till near the head of the *Livet* on the right of the *Sowie*, a high, bare, heathery, mossy hill ; *Cairn-ta-Bruar* to the left. Here we had a fine view of *Ben Aven* and *Ben-na-Bourd,* and this was the very way we should have ridden from *Tomnavoulin.* We had a slight sprinkling of rain, but very little at this time. We saw eight stags together at a distance. Oh! had dearest Albert been here with his rifle! We rode on and back till we came to a sheltered place near the burnside, about one mile and three-quarters from *Glenfiddich Lodge,* where one of the Duke's keepers had prepared a fire and got a kettle boiling, and here we took our tea. Afterwards I sketched, but we were surrounded by a perfect cloud of midges which bit me dreadfully. The gentlemen left us, after tea, and walked home. I walked a little while, and then rode back by a quarter to seven. A beautiful mild evening, the sky a lovely color. Dear good Sharp * was with us and out each day, and so affectionate.

A. Thomson, S. Forbes, Kennedy, and J. Stewart, the latter with the ponies, as well as the Duke's forester Lindsay, were out with us. Dinner as yesterday. Jane Churchill finished reading "Pride and Prejudice" to us after dinner. A very clear starlight night.

Friday, September 27.

A fair but dull morning. These quiet breakfasts with dear Louise, who was most amiable, attentive, and cheerful,

* A favorite collie of mine.

were very comfortable, just as they had been in 1865 with good Lenchen, and in 1866 with Louise at *Dunkeld*. Sketched hastily the stables from one window, and the approach from the other. The house in itself is really a good one, the rooms so well-sized and so conveniently placed. all close to each other. The cuisine, though very simple, was excellent, and the meat etc. the very best—only a female cook. The Duke was very kind.

At a quarter-past ten we left, taking leave of the Duke at the door. Sir Thomas sat with Brown on the box. The day was raw. We drove precisely the same way as we came. In *Dufftown* the people had turned out, the bell was rung and the band played, but they seemed hardly sure till we had passed who it was. We drove through at a great rate. The day being fair, we could see the country better. At one we got to the same place where we had lunched on Tuesday, and here changed horses, and Sir Thomas left us and got into his dogcart and drove after us. The sun had come out, and the day was fine and warm. As we passed *Tomnavoulin*, and in various other places, people were out. We drove on for about two or three miles, and then stopped at twenty minutes to two, just before we turned into the glen of the *Lecht Hills;* and here just below the road, under a bank on the grass, we sat down and took our luncheon, and sketched. Sir Thomas drove on, and we saw him again near the top of the hills, while we began the first very steep ascent, which seemed almost beyond the horses' power; but though only a pair, they got us up admirably. Brown walked by the carriage all the time, being very anxious about the road. Then down ever so long, having a splendid view of the hills—the road being dreadfully rough and bad besides— then up again, and when it came to that very steep winding hill going down to *Bridge End*, we got out and walked to the bottom and across the ford at *Tornahoish* over a foot-bridge. The view here was splendid, all the hills rising around, with the old *Castle of Corgarff*, and the river *Don* with the valley of the *Don-side* in the foreground.

Here we found our horses and drove on. It was raining at this time (about four), and it rained several times during the evening. We drove on, and after we passed *Tornahoish* two or three miles, and had got up the long hill, we found a sort of hole in the bank (such as are often met with where gravel and stones have been taken out), where we took our tea. The kettle took some time boiling, as we had only cold

water from the burn. When we go out only for the afternoon we take two bottles filled with hot water, which saves
much time. Poor Louise had been suffering from toothache
all the time. We got safely home at ten minutes past seven
o'clock.

UNVEILING OF THE PRINCE'S STATUE AT BALMORAL.

Tuesday, October 15, 1867.

OUR blessed Engagement Day! A dear and sacred day—
already twenty-eight years ago. How I ever bless it! A
wet morning—most annoying and provoking!

At a quarter-past eleven in this distressing rain, which
twice had given hopes of ceasing, I, with all the family and
Janie Ely, drove to the spot, just above *Middleton's Lodge,*
where were assembled all the servants and tenants, and the
detachment of the 93d Highlanders drawn up opposite, just
behind the Statue. I and the children stood just in front of
the Statue, which was covered. A verse of the 100th Psalm
was sung, and Mr. Taylor then stepped forward and offered
up a beautiful prayer (in pelting rain at that moment), after
which the order was given to uncover the Statue; but (as
happened at *Aberdeen*) the covering caught, and it was a little
while before it could be loosened from the shoulder.

The soldiers presented arms and the pipes played, as we
gazed on the dear noble figure of my beloved one, who used
to be with us here in the prime of beauty, goodness, and
strength.

Then Dr. Robertson stepped forward, and made a very
pretty little speech in the name of the servants and tenants,
thanking me for the gift of the statue. He spoke remarkably well. This was followed by the soldiers firing a *feu de
joie;* then all cheered, and the whole concluded by " God
save the Queen " being sung extremely well.

FIRST VISIT TO THE GLASSALT SHIEL.—A HOUSE-WARMING.

Thursday, October 1, 1868.

AT nearly four o'clock left with Louise and Jane Churchill
for the *Glassalt Shiel.* It was a beautiful evening, clear and

frosty. We drove by *Birkhall* and the *Linn of Muich*, where we stopped to take tea; we had just finished when Arthur arrived from *Ballater* with Grant, who had gone to meet him there. He had travelled straight from *Geneva*, and looked rather tired, having besides had a bad passage. After walking a little we drove on, Arthur getting into the carriage with us, and Grant going with Brown on the box. We arrived at half-past six at the *Glassalt Shiel*, which looked so cheerful and comfortable, all lit up, and the rooms so cozy and nice. There is a wonderful deal of room in the compact little house. A good staircase (the only one) leads to the upper floor, where are the rooms for Louise, Jane Churchill, her maid, and Arthur, in one passage; out of this there is another, where are three rooms for Brown, the cook, and another servant; in one of these Grant and Ross slept, and C. Thomson in the other. Below are my sitting-room, bedroom, and my maids' room; and on the other side of our little hall the dining-room; then a nice kitchen, small steward's room, store-closet, and another small room where two menservants slept. The small passage near my bedroom shuts off the rest, and makes it quite private and quiet. Good stables and the keeper's cottage, where our gillies sleep, just outside at the back.

We dined at about half-past eight in the small dining-room. This over, after waiting for a little while in my sitting-room, Brown came to say all the servants were ready for the house-warming, and at twenty minutes to ten we went into the little dining-room, which had been cleared, and where all the servants were assembled, viz., my second dresser,* C. Wilmore, Brown, Grant, Ross (who played), Hollis (the cook), Lady Churchill's maid, Maxted, C. and A. Thomson, Blake (the footman), the two housemaids, Kennedy, J. Stewart (the stableman), and the policeman (who only comes to do duty outside at night). We made nineteen altogether. Five animated reels were danced, in which all (but myself) joined. After the first reel "whiskey-toddy" was brought round for every one, and Brown begged I would drink to the "fire-kindling." Then Grant made a little speech, with an allusion to the wild place we were in, and concluding with a wish "that our Royal Mistress, our good Queen," should "live long." This was followed by cheers given out by Ross in regular Highland style, and all drank my health. The merry pretty little ball ended at a quarter-past eleven. The men, however, went on singing in the steward's room for some

---

* She was in my service for thirteen years, and left in 1881.

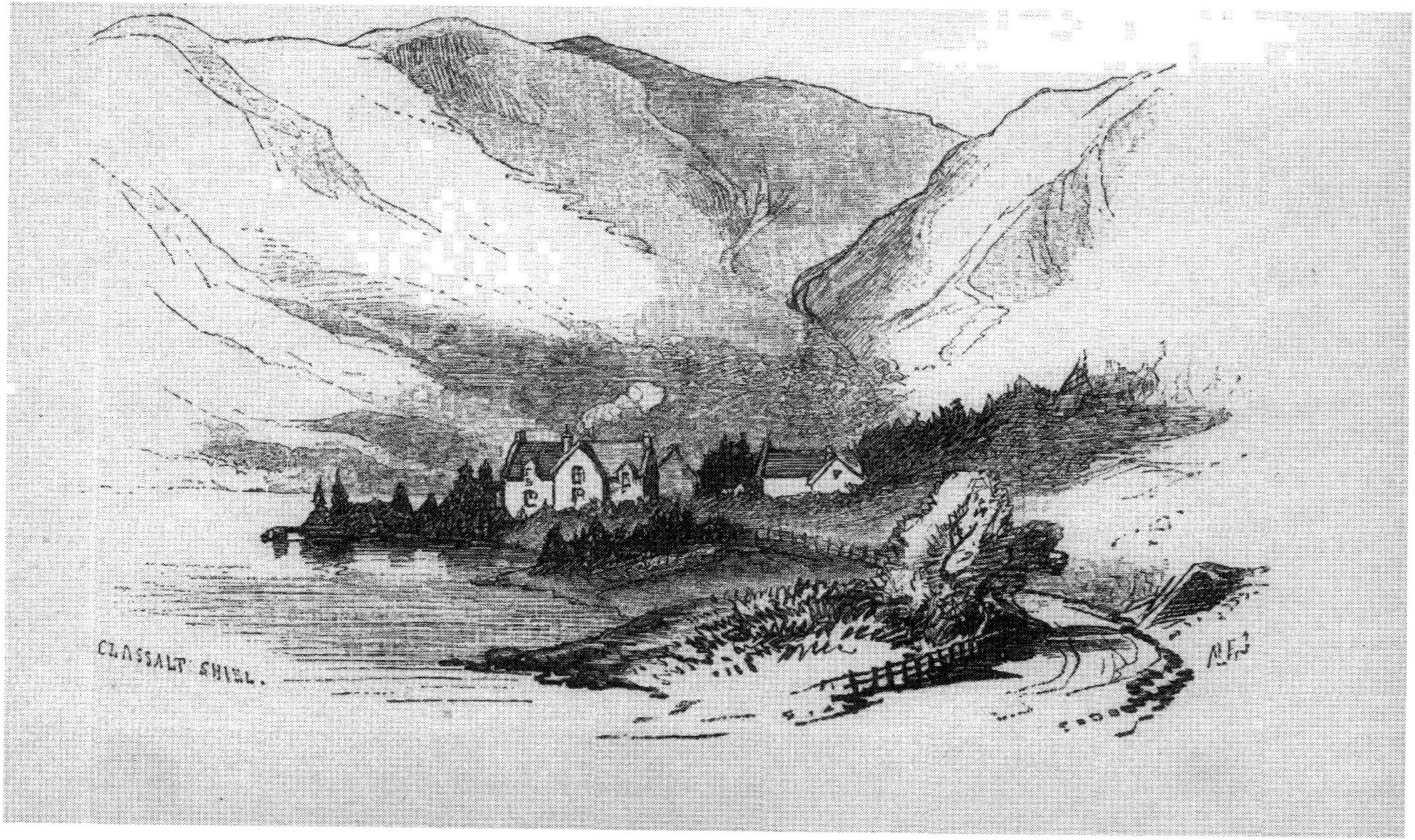
CLASSALT SHIEL.

time, and all were very happy, but I heard nothing, as the little passage near my bedroom shuts everything off.

Sad thoughts filled my heart both before dinner and when I was alone and retired to rest. I thought of the happy past and my darling husband whom I fancied I must see, and who always wished to build here, in this favorite wild spot, quite in amidst the hills. At *Altnagiuthasach* I could not have lived again now—alone. It is far better to have built a totally new house; but then the sad thought struck me that it was the first *Widow's house*, not built by him or hallowed by his memory. But I am sure his blessing does rest on it, and on those who live in it.

"JUICING THE SHEEP," 1868.

Thursday, October 21.

AT a quarter to twelve I drove off with Louise and Leopold in the wagonette up to near the "*Bush*" (the residence of William Brown,* the farmer) to see them "juice the sheep." This is a practice pursued all over the *Highlands* before the sheep are sent down to the low country for the winter. It is done to preserve the wool. Not far from the burnside, where there are a few hillocks, was a pen in which the sheep were placed, and then, just outside it, a large sort of trough filled with liquid tobacco and soap, and into this the sheep were dipped one after the other; one man (James Brown,† my shepherd, the elder brother, who came up on purpose to help) took the sheep one by one out of the pen and turned them on their backs; and then William and he, holding them by their legs, dipped them well in, after which they were let into another pen into which this trough opened, and here they had to remain to dry. To the left, a little lower down, was a cauldron boiling over a fire and containing the tobacco with water and soap; this was then emptied into a tub, from which it was transferred into the trough. A very rosy-faced lassie with a plaid over her head, was superintending this part of the work, and helped to fetch the water from the burn, while children and many collie dogs were grouped about, and several men and shepherds were helping. It was a very curious and picturesque sight.

---

* Brown's fourth brother.   † Brown's eldest brother

A HIGHLAND " KIRSTNIN " (CHRISTENING), 1868.

Sunday, October 24.

AT a quarter to four I drove, with Louise, Beatrice, and Lady Ely, to John Thomson the wood forester's house for the christening of their child, three weeks old. Here, in their little sitting-room, in front of the window, stood a table covered with a white cloth, on which was placed a basin with water, a bible, and a paper with the certificate of the child's birth.

We stood on one side, and John Thomson in his Highland dress next the minister, who was opposite me at the head of the table. Barbara, his wife, stood next to him, with the baby in her arms, and then the old Thomsons and their unmarried daughter, the Donald Stewarts, Grants and Victoria, Morgan and sister, and Brown.

Dr. Taylor (who wore his gown) then began with an address and prayer, giving thanks " for a living mother and a living child," after which followed another prayer; he then read a few passages from Scripture, after which came the usual questions which he addressed to the father, and to which he bowed assent. Then the minister told him— " Present your child for baptism." After this the father took the child and held it while the minister baptized it, sprinkling it with water, but not making the sign of the cross, saying first to those present : " The child's name is Victoria ; " and then to the child :

" Victoria, I baptize thee in the name of the Father, and of the Son, and of the Holy Ghost, One God blessed forever. —Amen."

The Lord bless thee and keep thee ! The Lord make His face to shine upon thee and be gracious unto thee ! The Lord lift up His countenance upon thee and give thee peace !

The service was concluded with another short prayer and the usual blessing. I thought it most appropriate, touching, and impressive. I gave my present (a silver mug) to the father, kissed the little baby, and then we all drank to its health and that of its mother in whisky, which was handed round with cakes. It was all so nicely done, so simply, and yet with such dignity.

A SECOND CHRISTENING, 1868.

ON Monday, November 1, I drove down at a quarter to four with Louise, Beatrice. Leopold (who was on the box with Brown), and Lady Ely, to the *Bush* (William Brown's) to witness the christening of his first child, just a week old, which was to be called Albert. The service was nearly the same, only two instead of three prayers, and the young mother with the child, who was only a week old, was seated by the fire, looking very nice, with the baby on her lap. The old mother, Mrs. Brown, in her white mutch, the three brothers, and a few neighbors stood round the room. I gave my present. It was a touching and impressive sight to see the young father holding his child with an expression of so much devotion and earnestness. On this occasion a dinner was given by the father after we left, in which Dr. Taylor took part.

WIDOW GRANT, 1869.

ON Sunday, August 22, 1869, I went to see old Mrs. Grant, whom l was grieved to see sitting in her chair supported by pillows, and her poor feet raised upon cushions, very much altered in her face, and I fear, dying of dropsy.

On August 26 I again saw her, and gave her a shawl and a pair of socks, and found the poor old soul in bed, looking very weak and very ill, but bowing her head and thanking me in her usual way. I took her hand and held it.

On the 27th she died.

On the 28th I stopped at her cottage and went in with Louise and Leopold. We found all so clean and tidy, but all so silent. Mrs. Gordon, her daughter, was there, having arrived just in time to spend the last evening and night with her; and then she lifted the sheet, and there the poor old woman, whom we had known and seen from the first here these twenty-one years, lay on a bier in her shroud, but with her usual cap on, peaceful and little altered, her dark skin taking away from the usual terrible pallor of death. She had on the socks I gave her the day before yesterday. She was in her eighty-ninth year.

VISIT TO INVERTROSSACHS, 1869.

Wednesday, September 1, 1869

WE got up at half-past seven, breakfasted at eight, and at half-past eight left *Balmoral* with Louise, Beatrice, and Jane Churchill (Brown as always, unless I mention to the contrary, on the box), for *Ballater*. A high and rather cold wind, but very bright sun, dreadfully dusty. Colonel Ponsonby met us at the railway station. Emilie Dittweiler and Annie Macdonald, Ocklee (for the two girls), Jane Churchill's maid, Charlie Thomson, and the footman Cannon, went with us; Blake, Spong with the luggage, A. Thomson, with Sharp (my faithful collie dog) and Annie Gordon (house-maid), Kennedy, Arthur Grant, and Hiley (the groom) with the ponies, all went yesterday, and three cooks came from *London*. We had a saloon carriage, but not my own. It grew hot in the railway train. We stopped at *Aberdeen* and the *Bridge of Dun*, where Jane Churchill got into our carriage, and had luncheon with us; but we could have no one to help to pack and unpack it, which is now so comfortably arranged in my own railway carriage, where there is a communication with the attendants.

Stopping a moment at *Cupar Angus*, we passed through *Perth*, and had another short halt at *Dunblane*, where the people crowded very much. Here we got a view of the old Cathedral, and turned off to *Callander*, which we reached at a quarter-past three. There was a very well-behaved crowd at the quiet station. Mr. and Lady Emily Macnaghten,[*] to whose house (which they had most kindly lent us) we were going, and Sir Malcolm and Lady Helen MacGregor (he is Miss MacGregor's nephew, she Lady Emily Macnaghten's niece), received us there. Their little girl gave me a nosegay. We at once got into our celebrated sociable, which has been to the top of the *Furca* in *Switzerland*, etc., and had been sent on before, Colonel Ponsonby and Brown going on the box. We drove off at once with post-horses through the small town of *Collander*, which consists of one long street with very few shops, and few good houses, but many poor ones. Poor Kanné[†] (who was to have managed everything, but had fallen ill) was still laid up there. We drove on, and,

---

[*] She died in 1874.
[†] My Director of Continental journeys, who had been sent to look at the house and to make arrangements for my reception.

after about three-quarters of a mile's drive, came to *Loch Vennachar*, a fine lake about four miles long, with *Ben Venue* and other high and beautiful mountains rising behind and around it. The road is thickly wooded with oak, birch, beech, mountain-ash, etc. The house stands extremely well on a high eminence, overlooking the loch and surrounded by trees, and you drive up through evergreens and trees of all kinds. Half an hour brought us to the door of the house, *Invertrossachs*, which is small and comfortable. At the entrance is a nice little hall in which there is a small billiard-table ; to the left, beyond that, a very nice well-sized dining-room with one large window. To the right of the hall is the drawing-room, very much like the one at *Invermark* (Lord Dalhousie's) ; altogether the house is in that style, but larger. The staircase is almost opposite the hall-door, and there is a narrow passage which goes on to the left and right, along which are Louise's, Baby's (Beatrice's), my sitting-room (a snug little room), and my bedroom (very good size); and out of that, two little rooms which I use as dressing and bath-rooms, and Emilie Dittweiler's. Further on, round a corner as it were, beyond Louise's, are Lady Churchill's, her maid's and Colonel Ponsonby's rooms, all very fair-sized and comfortable. Close to my dressing-rooms is a staircase which goes up stairs to where Brown and our other people live. The rooms are very comfortably and simply furnished, and they have put down new carpets everywhere. In the absence of poor Kanné, whom we are so sorry for, Jungbluth, the cook, acts as steward, and showed us over the rooms.

We took tea and rested a little, and at twenty minutes to six drove out with the two girls (sweet Beatrice very happy and very good, the first time she had been without a govern-. ess) and Lady Churchill. We drove along the loch, which has always to be done, as there is no road on the *Invertrossachs* side further than *Invertrossachs* itself, and crossed over the bridge at *Coilantogleford* celebrated in the "Lady of the Lake," then to the right down a steep hill and over the bridge by *Kilmahog*, where there are a few cottages and a turnpike, on through the *Pass of Leny*, which is now (like every other burn and river) nearly dry, overhung by beautiful trees with very grand hills, reminding me much of *Switzerland* from their greenness, the rugged rocks, and the great amount of wood which grows at their base and a good way up. It reminded Louise and me very much of *Pilatus* with its meadows

and fine trees on the way to *Hergessvyl.* We went as far
as the beginning of *Loch Lubnaig,* a very fine wild, grand-
looking loch; turning there and going back the same way.
The view of *Loch Vennachar,* with the beautiful deep blue of
Ben Venue and the other hills, was lovely. We came in at
half-past seven.

Darling Beatrice took her supper on coming in, but she
came and sat with us while we were at dinner for a short
while. Only four at dinner. We went out for a moment
afterwards. Very mild and starlight. Louise went to bed.
Jane read a little to me in the drawing-room, but I went up
stairs soon, as I was tired.

Thursday, September 2.

A very fine, bright, warm morning. We decided to go on
an expedition, but not to *Loch Lomond,* as we should have to
start so early. Breakfasted in the drawing-room with Louise
and Beatrice. Then writing, etc. At twenty minutes to
twelve I started in the sociable with Louise, Beatrice, Jane
Churchill, and Colonel Ponsonby and Brown on the box, and
drove (excellent post-horses, always only a pair) to *Callander,*
but turned to the right short of it, and went on some little
way. On coming to the top of a hill we saw *Ben Ledi,* a
splendid hill; to the north *Ben Voirlich,* and to the east the
heights of *Uam Var,* a pink heathery ridge of no great eleva-
tion; and in the distance, rising up from the horizon, *Dun
Myat,* and the *Wallace Monument* on the *Abbey Craig,* near
Stirling. We went across a moor, and then soon passed
Loch Ruskie, quite a small lake. The country about here is
rather lowland, but as we proceeded it was extremely pretty,
with very fine trees and cornfields, and harvesting going on;
and soon after, descending a hill, we came upon the Loch of
"*Menteith*" (the only loch in Scotland which is ever called
lake). It reminds one very much of *Loch Kinnord* near
Ballater, and very low blue and pink hills rise in the distance.
There are two or three islands in it; in the large one *Inchmahome,* you perceive amongst the thick woods the ruins of the
ancient priory. Queen Mary lived there once, and there are
monuments of the Menteiths to be seen on it. To the right
we passed the ruin of *Rednock Castle,* and to the left the
gates of the Park of *Rednock,* with very fine large trees, where
Mr. Graham, the proprietor, was standing. We went on and
passed the *Clachan of Aberfoyle* (renowned in Sir Walter

Scott's "Rob Roy"), and here the splendid scenery begins
—high, rugged, and green hills (reminding me again of
Pilatus), very fine large trees and beautiful pink heather, interspersed with bracken, rocks, and underwood, in the most
lovely profusion, and *Ben Lomond* towering up before us with
its noble range. We went on perhaps a quarter of a mile,
and, it being then two o'clock, we got out and lunched on
the grass under an oak at the foot of *Craig More.* It was
very hot, the sun stinging, but there were many light white
clouds in the blue sky, which gave the most beautiful effects
of light and shade on this marvellous coloring. After luncheon and walking about a little, not finding any good view
to sketch, we got into the carriage (our horses had been
changed), but had not gone above a few yards when we came
upon *Loch Ard*, and a lovelier picture could not be seen.
Ben Lomond, blue and yellow, rose above the lower hills,
which were pink and purple with heather, and an isthmus of
green trees in front dividing it from the rest of the loch. We
got out and sketched. Only here and there, far between,
were some poor little cottages with picturesque barefooted
lasses and children to be seen. All speak Gaelic here.
Louise and I sat sketching for half an hour, Beatrice running about merrily with Jane Churchill while we drew. We
then drove on, and certainly one of the most lovely drives I
can remember, along *Loch Ard*, a fine long loch, with trees
of all kinds overhanging the road, heather making all pink;
bracken, rocks, high hills of such a fine shape, and trees
growing up them as in *Switzerland;* the road rough and bad,
with very steep bits of hill (but the post-horses went remarkably well) overhanging the loch, which reminded me very
much of the drive along the *Lake Zug* in *Switzerland.* Altogether, the whole drive along *Loch Ard*, then by the very
small *Loch Dow* and the fine *Loch Chon*, which is very long,
was lovely. The heather in full bloom, and of the richest
kind, some almost of a crimson color, and growing in rich
tufts along the road. One can see, by the mounds or
heaps of stone, all along *Loch Chon*, where the *Glasgow
Waterworks* are carried, but they have not disfigured the
landscape.

Emerging from this road we came upon the *Loch Lomond
Road*, having a fine view of *Loch Arklet*, on the banks of
which Helen MacGregor is said to have been born. The
scene of our drive to-day is all described in "Rob Roy."

Loch Arklet lies like *Loch Callater*, only that the hills are higher and more pointed.   Leaving this little loch to our left, in a few minutes we came upon *Loch Katrine*, which was seen in its greatest beauty in the fine evening light.   Most lovely !   We stopped at *Stronachlachar*, a small inn where people stay for a night sometimes, and where they embark coming from *Loch Lomond*, and *vice versa*.   As the small steamer had not yet arrived, we had to wait for about a quarter of an hour.   But there was no crowd, no trouble or annoyance, and during the whole of our drive nothing could be quieter or more agreeable.   Hardly a creature did we meet, and we passed merely a very few pretty gentlemen's places, or very poor cottages with simple women and barefooted, long-haired lassies and children, quiet and unassuming old men and laborers.   This solitude, the romance and wild loveliness of everything here, the absence of hotels and beggars, the independent simple people, who all speak Gaelic here, all make beloved *Scotland* the proudest, finest country in the world.   Then there is that beautiful heather, which you do not see elsewhere.   I prefer it greatly to *Switzerland*, magnificent and glorious as the scenery of that country is.

It was about ten minutes past five when we went on board the very clean little steamer " Rob Roy "—the very same we had been on under such different circumstances in 1859 on the 14th of October, in dreadful weather, thick mist and heavy rain, when my beloved Husband and I opened the *Glasgow Waterworks*.   We saw the spot and the cottage where we lunched.

We took a turn and steamed a little way up the bay called *Glen Gyle*, where there is a splendid glen beautifully wooded, which is the country of the MacGregors, and where there is a house which belonged to MacGregor of *Glen Gyle*, which, with the property, has been bought by a rich Glasgow innkeeper of the same clan.   We turned and went on, and nothing could be more beautiful than the loch, wooded all along the banks.   The rugged *Ben Venue*, so famed in the "Lady of the Lake " (which we had with us, as well as several guidebooks, of which we find Black's far the best), rises majestically on the southern side of the lake, and looking back you see the *Alps of Arrochar*, which well deserve the name, for they are quite pointed and most beautiful; their names are *Ben Vean, Ben Voirlich, Ben Eim*, and *Ben Crosh*.   Next came the well-known "*Silver Strand.*" "*Helen's Isle,*" which is most lovely, and the narrow creek so beautifully wooded below the splendid high hills, and the little wooden landing-place which I remembered so well; and very melancholy and yet sweet were my feelings when I landed and found on the path some of the same white pebbles which my dearest Albert picked up and had made into a bracelet for me. I picked up and carried off a handful myself.

We had taken our tea on board on deck. We now entered two hired carriages, the girls and I in the first, with Brown on the box, and Jane Churchhill and Colonel Ponsonby in the second. The evening was lovely, and the lights and pink and golden sky as we drove through the beautiful *Trossachs* were glorious indeed—

> So wondrous wild, the whole might seem
> The scenery of a fairy dream—

and along *Loch Achray*—the setting sun behind *Ben Venue,* which rose above most gloriously, so beautifully described by Sir W. Scott :

> The western waves of ebbing day
> Rolled o'er the glen the level way.
> Each purple peak, each flinty spire
> Was bathed in floods of living fire.

We passed the fine *Trossachs Inn* where Louise had stopped with Alice and Louis in 1865, and a lovely little church in a most picturesque position, and lastly the *Brig of Turk.* It is a long way round *Loch Vennachar* to *Invertrossachs :* you see the house for three-quarters of an hour before you can get to it. Home at eight. The drive back was lovely, for long after the sun had set the sky remained beautifully pink behind the dark blue hills. A most successful day. Dinner as yesterday. I felt very tired.

Friday, September 3.

A very dull. dark thick morning, and the hills beyond *Callander* hardly visible. Still, no rain. Went up to my room and wrote a little, and at twelve took a walk in a very pretty wood quite close below the house, from several points of which there are beautiful views, but the atmosphere was too thick to see them to-day. . . . We lunched all together. . . . At half-past three we started again (just as yesterday), and drove up the noble *Pass of Leny* past *Kilmahog*, where a little boy tried to give me a nosegay which was fixed to a pole, and

in trying to catch it Colonel Ponsonby let it fall. The little
boy screamed " Stop, stop ! " and ran in such an agony of disappointment that I stopped the carriage and took it from him
to his mother's great delight. On our way we saw on a
hill among woods *Leny House* (belonging to Mr. Buchanan
Hamilton), where Sir W. Scott lived when he wrote " Rob
Roy."

We went along that truly beautiful *Loch Lubnaig*, driving
along its windings like the *Axenstrasse* on the *Lake of
Lucerne*, the high, jagged, and green hills rising precipitously
from it. It is four miles long, and very romantic. There is
a railway unfinished, only a single line, on the western side,
and as it ran along the loch it again reminded me of the
Axenstrasse at the points where it goes low near the water.
The road leads under beautiful sycamore trees. We passed
on the right a farmhouse called *Ardhullary*, where formerly
the Abyssinian traveller Bruce used to live, and next entered
Strathyre, a fine broad open strath, wooded and with cornfields, the heather on the hills quite pink. The village of
Strathyre is composed of a row of a few peasants' houses,
with very poor people, and a nice well-built little inn. A little way on again you come to a picturesque little inn called
the *King's House*, covered with creepers and convolvulus,
and here you turn short to the left and go up *Balquhidder*,
another most lovely glen, with a beautiful view of *Loch Voil*
with its beautiful sweeping green hills, the *Braes* of *Balquhidder*,
the strath itself very rich with its fine trees and cornfields,
the small river *Balvaig* running through it. We drove about
two miles, passing some pretty cottages covered with creepers like the inn I mentioned, and stopped outside a neat-
looking little village, the *Kirkton of Balquhidder* (twelve
miles from *Callander*), composed of only a few cottages. We
got out and walked up a steep knoll overhanging the road, on
which, under a splendid plane tree (we passed some most
beautiful limes just before), is the old kirkyard with the ruins
of the old church. We went at once to look at the tomb of
Rob Roy—a flat stone on which is carved a figure in a kilt,
and next to it a stone where his wife is buried, and on which
a sword is rudely carved.* His son's tomb is next to his,
but looks far more modern. We went on to look at a very
curious old font, and then at two or three other tombstones.
On one of these were some verses, which Mr. Cameron, the

---

* These stones are supposed to be very ancient, and carved centuries before
they were adapted to their present use.

schoolmaster, an intelligent young man, recited, and afterwards wrote out for me.*

We afterwards went into the pretty new church, which is close to the old ruin. Nothing can surpass the beauty of the position of this spot, for it overlooks *Loch Voil* and a glen, or rather mere ravine or corry, with a hill rising behind it. We walked down again and re-entered our carriage, driving back the same way, and passing about half a mile from the *Kirkton*, on our road back, the present burial-place of the MacGregors (whose country this is, or, alas! rather was), which is a chapel standing in a wood, the whole enclosed by a wall and iron gateway. We drove past the *King's House* a very short way, and then got out, scrambled up the hillside, sat down on a bank overhanging a burn, kindled a fire, and had our tea. This was on Lord Breadalbane's property. We got home from this very interesting and beautiful drive by a quarter-past eight. The day had not been bright—dark and dull, but quite clear enough to see everything in this truly beautiful country.

Dinner as before. We always sit in the drawing-room, and Jane read out the newspaper to us.

Saturday, September 4.

Up by half-past seven, and breakfasting at a quarter to eight. Got on my pony Sultan † at nine, the others walking, and went through the wood to the loch's edge, where we three got into a small boat and were rowed across to the other side by the keeper and underkeeper, Brown sitting in the bow, Colonel Ponsonby and Jane Churchill going across in another very small boat rowed by one man. Here we got

---

* The words of the inscription are:—

ISABEL CAMBELL.

SPOUSE TO MR. ROBERT KIRK, MINISTER,

DIED 25 DECEMBER, 1680.

SHE HAD TWO SONS, COLIN AND WILLIAM.

HER AGE 25.

Stones weep tho' eyes were dry;
Choicest flowers soonest die :
Their sun oft sets at noon,
Whose fruit is ripe in June.
Then tears of joy be thine,
Since earth must soon resign
To God what is divine.

Nasci est ægrotare, vivere est sæpe mori, et mori est vivere.

LOVE AND LIVE.

† I rode him up to the top of the Righi (near Lucerne), 5000 feet high, in 1868.

into our carriage as before.   Dear Beatrice enjoys it all very much, and is so good and cheerful.

We drove on through the beautiful *Trossachs* to *Loch Katrine*.   It was a very dark thick morning, no distance to be seen at all, and *Ben Venue* very imperfectly.   We embarked by ten o'clock on board the steamer "Rob Roy," and steamed off for *Stronachlachar*.   No distant view was visible, and the color of the sky was really that of a thick November fog.   However, by the time we reached *Stronachlachar*, it was much lighter to the left, towards where we were going.

Here we got into two hired carriages again, Jane and Colonel Ponsonby preceding us this time.   We drove along *Loch Arklet*, a lovely drive with pink heathered hills to the right, and gradually the mist cleared off, and allowed us to see rugged peaks above and in front of us.   We met (as we had done from the first) several large coaches, but with only out-side seats, full of tourists.   This reminded me, as did the whole tour this day and on Thursday, of *Switzerland* and our expeditions there, especially now when we suddenly came upon *Loch Lomond,* and drove down a very steep hill to *Inversnaid*, where there is only one house (a small inn), and saw high mountains, looking shadowy in the mist (dry mist), rising abruptly from the loch.   We went at once on board the fine steamer " Prince Consort " (a pleasant idea that that dear name should have carried his poor little wife, alas! a widow, and children, on their first sail on this beautiful lake which he went to see in 1847).   She is a fine large vessel, a good deal larger than the " Winkelried " (in which we used to go on the *Lake of Lucerne*), with a fine large dining-cabin below, a very high upper deck, and a gallery underneath on which people can stand and smoke without incommoding the others above.   The following people were on board : Mr. A. Smollett, late M.P., Mr. Wylie, factor to Sir T. Colquhoun, and Mr. Denny, the auditor, and Mr. Young, the secretary.

We steamed southward, and for the first half nothing could be finer or more truly Alpine, reminding me much of the *Lake of Lucerne;* only it is longer—*Loch Lomond* being twenty-two miles long.   We kept close to the east shore, passing under *Ben Lomond* with its variously called shoulders —*Cruachan, Craig a Bochan,* and *Ptarmigan*—to *Rowaid-ennan* pier, where there is a pretty little house rented from the Duke of Montrose (to whom half *Loch Lomond* belongs) by a Mr. Mair, a lovely spot from whence you can ascend *Ben Lomond,* which is 3192 feet high, and well wooded part of the way, with cornfields below. After you pass this, where there are fine mountains on either side, though on the west shore not so high, the lake widens out, but the shores become much flatter and tamer (indeed to the east and south completely so); but here are all the beautifully wooded islands, to the number of twenty-four. Some of them are large ; on *Inchlonaig Island* the firs are said to have been planted by Robert Bruce to encourage the people in the use of archery. Another, *Inch Cailliach*, is the ancient burial-place of the Mac Gregors.

On the mainland we passed *Cornick Hill*, and could just see *Buchanan House*, the Duke of Montrose's, and to the right the island of *Inch Murrin*, on which the Duke has his deer preserve. The sun had come out soon after we went on board, and it was blowing quite fresh as we went against the wind. At two o'clock we stopped off *Portnellan* for luncheon, which we had brought with us and took below in the handsome large cabin, where fifty or sixty people, if not more, could easily dine. Colonel Ponsonby also lunched with us. . . . This over, we went to the end of the lake to *Balloch*, and here turned. It became very warm. To the left we passed some very pretty villas (castles they resembled) and places, amongst others *Cameron* (Mr. Smollett's), *Arden* (Sir J. Lumsden's, Lord Provost of Glasgow), *Ross-Dhu* (Sir J. Colquhoun's), the road to *Glen Fruin*, the islands of *Inch Connachan, Inch Tavanach*, the point of *Stob Gobhlach, Luss*, a very prettily situated village, the mountain of *Ben Dubh*, and the ferry of *Inveruglas*, opposite *Rowardennan*. Then *Tarbet*, a small town, where dearest Albert landed in 1847, and here began the highest and finest mountains, with splendid passes, richly wooded, and the highest mountains rising behind. A glen leads across from *Tarbet* to *Arrochar* on *Loch Long*, and here you see that most singularly shaped hill called the *Cobbler*, and a little further on the splendid *Alps of Arrochar*. All this and the way in which the hills run into the lake reminded me so much of the *Nasen* on the *Lake of Lucerne*.

The head of the lake with the very fine glen (*Glen Falloch*), along which you can drive to *Oban*, is magnificent. We (Louise and I) sketched as best we could, but it is most difficult to do so when the steamer keeps moving on ; and we were afterwards much vexed we had not asked them to go more slowly, as we had to wait again for the "Rob Roy" steamer at *Stronachlachar*. From the head of *Loch Lomond* (where is the *Hotel of Inverarnan*) we turned; we were shown a hole in the rock, on the east side, which they called *Rob Roy's Cave*, and landed at *Inversnaid*. The people (quite a small crowd) threw bunches of heather as we passed. Heather is everywhere the decoration, and there is indeed no lovelier, prettier ornament. It was in such full bloom. The mountains here are peculiarly fine from the sharp serrated outline and wonderful clothing of grass and trees. It was a very bright warm evening, and the drive back, which we had to take slowly, not to arrive too soon, was extremely pretty. At *Stronachlachar*, both on embarking and disembarking, there were a few people collected. On board we had again our tea, and Mr. Blair, the very obliging gentlemanlike host of the *Trossachs Inn* (and possessor of the *Loch Katrine* steamer), who was in attendance each time, gave us some clotted cream.

It was a splendid sail over this most lovely loch, and delightful drive back by the *Trossachs*. We got into the boat again where we left it this morning, and rowed across; but this time it was most unpleasant, for it blew and was very rough, and the little boat rolled and danced. The second smaller one with the two others shipped water. Rode back and got up to the house by half-past seven. This was the only *contretemps* to our most successful, enjoyable day. How dearest Albert would have enjoyed it !

Dinner just as before, Jane reading the newspapers. This day year we went to the *Brünig Pass*.

Sunday, September 5.

A dull muggy morning. Decided not to go to kirk, as it would have been very public. So at eleven rode (on Sultan) with dear Beatrice (on her little Beatrice) for an hour, first up at the back of the farm, and then a little way on the beautiful pink heathery and bracken hills just behind the house, and saw *Loch Drunkie* almost dry from the drought, and looked over to the *Brig of Turk*, then back by the stables to the house. Read the collect, epistle, and gospel, and the second lesson for the day, with the two girls, Beatrice reading the last-named.

While we were at luncheon it rained, but it soon ceased, and the afternoon became quite fine and was very warm. At half-past five walked out with Louise, Beatrice, and Jane Churchill, stopping at the lodge where McIsaacs, the keeper, and his wife live. Walked some way on, and then drove with Beatrice round a short way on the *Trossachs Road*, coming home at half-past seven.

Monday, September 6.

Misty early, then beautiful and clear and very hot. Got up with a bad headache. At five minutes to eleven rode off with Beatrice, good Sharp going with us and having occasional "collie-shangies"* with collies when we came near cottages (A. Thomson and Kennedy following). We rode out the same way we came back yesterday, and then up the same hill overlooking *Loch Drunkie*—which really is nearly dry—and on down the other side of the hill, as fast as we could go along a rough but very pretty road, which brought us, over perfumed pink heather interspersed with bracken, to a spot where you get a lovely glimpse of *Loch Achray* and *Ben Venue*. We then continued along a wood past a few miserable cottages, but as private as if I were riding at *Balmoral*, out into the high road just at the *Brig of Turk*, and stopped at what is called "*Fergusson's Inn*," but is in fact the very poorest sort of Highland cottage. Here lives Mrs. Fergusson, an immensely fat woman and a well-known character, who is quite rich and well dressed, but will not leave the place where she has lived all her life selling whisky. She was brought out and seemed delighted to see me, shaking hands with me and patting me. She walks with a crutch, and had to sit down. We only stopped a very few minutes, and then went home as fast as we came, and got back by one. But Brown and the other two men were as hot as the day we went up the *Righi*, and it was indeed very hot. Our ride must have been eight miles altogether. My head still aching,

At three, after luncheon, we started just as yesterday, and drove the same way as last Friday up the *Pass of Leny* by *Loch Lubnaig, Strathyre* and the *King's House:* here, instead of turning to the left to *Balquhidder*, we went straight on for four miles, till we came to *Loch Earn Head.* It was a beautiful and very hot afternoon. We stopped at the inn, which is quite a small place commanding a beautiful view of *Loch Earn*, which was splendidly lit up, the loch deep blue and the hills all lilac and violet. Sir Malcolm † and Lady Helen MacGregor with their two little children received us at the door and took us up stairs. They have got a very

---

* A Scotch word for quarrels or "rows," but taken from fights between "collies."

† He died in 1879.

pretty little drawing-room (looking on to the loch), which they have arranged nicely and comfortably. The two little girls are dear little things, Malvina four and Margaret two years old. Sir Malcolm wore the kilt. He is a captain in the Navy, and showed us some curiosities brought home from *New Zealand*, also a bottle which is said to have belonged to Rob Roy, and was given to Lady Helen by an old man in the parish, and a silver quaich out of which Prince Charles Edward had drunk, and which had belonged to Sir Malcolm's great-great-grandfather. Lady Helen is the late Lord Antrim's only child. Both were most kind and gave us some tea, and at half-past five we left on our return. There was a small friendly crowd collected at the door, who cheered both when we arrived and when we left. We changed horses here, or at least very near, in 1842 on our way back from *Taymouth*. They said I mentioned the circumstance in my book.* We drove through the grounds of *Edinchip*, which belongs to Sir Malcolm MacGregor (but was then let), on the way home, and came back the same road, reaching home by half-past seven.

My headache, which had been very bad all day, got much better just before we got home.

Tuesday, September 7.

Received a letter from Colonel Elphinstone, dated 22d from *Halifax*, with excellent accounts of dear Arthur. The passage had been a very good one ; he had mixed with every one on board, and been a general favorite—three hundred emigrants on board. Walked, and rode a little, while the others walked. Tired and feeling ill. It turned wet and continued so, all the evening. We however, determined to go to *Loch Katrine*, having ordered the steamer, and boats to row to the *Silver Strand.* So off I went with the girls and Lady Churchill just as on the other days, but when we got there it was too wet to do anything ; so we only went on board the steamer, took our tea in the cabin below, and then drove back again by half-past seven.

Wednesday, September 8.

A very bad night from a violent attack of neuralgia in my leg. I only got up after nine, and could hardly walk or stand, but was otherwise not ill. I took a little, but very little, breakfast, alone. I remained at home reading, writ-

* "Our Life in the Highlands," p. 31.

ing, and resting on the sofa or in an arm-chair. I came
down to luncheon, Brown helping me down and up, but took
it alone with the children in the drawing-room. Rested
afterwards, and at twenty minutes to four took a quiet but
enjoyable drive with Jane Churchill. It was not very bright,
nor the distance very clear, but there were occasional gleams
of bright sunshine which lit up the fine scenery. We drove
to *Loch Menteith,* just the same way as on Thursday, and
were surprised to find how short the distance was. After
passing the gate of *Rednock Castle* we turned to the left and
drove a short way close along the lochside past the kirk and
small village (composed of only two or three houses) of *Port
Menteith,* getting a good view of *Inchmahome* on the way.
We stopped to take our tea (which had been made before we
went out, but was quite hot still) outside *Rednock* grounds,
and then drove back again, but took another turn through
Callander, and then along a road (above which a number of
pretty villas are built, and where you have a very pretty
view) which comes out at *Kilmahog Turnpike.* Then home
by a quarter past seven. Found Sir William Jenner, whom
we had sent for, arrived. I dined below (hobbling along a
little better and down stairs without help) in the drawing-
room with Louise and Jane Churchill.

Thursday, September 9.

I had a really very fair night, and on getting up found I
could walk much better, for which I was most thankful. I
went down to breakfast as usual. Received again letters
from dear Arthur and Colonel Elphinstone with excellent and
favorable accounts of the good his presence had already done.
At half-past eleven drove with Louise and Beatrice up the
Pass of Leny as far as the commencement of *Loch Lubnaig,*
intending to sketch, but it was too late. We met first two
large coaches covered with people on the narrowest part of
the bridge going to *Kilmahog,* and then endless droves of
wild-looking, and for the most part extremely small, shaggy
Highland cattle with their drovers and dogs—most wild and
picturesque—going to *Falkirk* Tryst. They stop for nights
on the road—we saw some droves grazing on the lower parts
of the hills on our way to *Loch Earn Head*—and the drovers
get shelter with friends in the cottages and villages about.
Home at half-past one. Planted two (very small) trees in
front of the house, as did Louise and Beatrice also. Luncheon as yesterday, only with the children. My leg very stiff,

so that, with great regret, I had to give up going to *Loch Katrine* for the last time, which I had so much wished. However, I did drive with Beatrice as far as the *Trossachs Inn* and back, and got a glimpse of the beautiful *Trossachs* and *Loch Achray*, with *Ben Venue* rising gloriously above it. I even made a slight outline of it, and returned, quite pleased at this, by half-past seven, stopping to make and take our tea not far from home, I remaining in the carriage. Felt better altogether, and was able to come to the usual dinner, to which also Sir W. Jenner came. Dear Beatrice sat with us during part of the dinner, as she had done almost every night. Brown (the only upper servant in attendance, as I brought no page), who waited at all my meals, and did all the outdoors attendance on me besides, with the greatest handi-dess, cheerfulness, and alacrity, and the three very good foot-men, Blake, Cannon, and Charlie Thomson (one of seven brothers, two of whom are also in my service, and one a gillie at *Balmoral*), did all the waiting at dinner and luncheon. Good Sharp was always in the dining-room, but remained quietly lying down.

Friday, September 10.

Raining early, which made me feel I had done right in giving up going by the *Spital*, as I had intended up to yester-day afternoon. Felt, however. better, and could walk with much greater ease. At half-past eleven we left *Invertrossachs* the recollection of the ten days at which—quiet and cozy—and of the beautiful country and scenery I saw in the neighbor-hood, though the last two days were spoilt by stupid indis-position, will ever be a very pleasant one. The two girls and I drove in a *Callander* carriage. with Brown on the box, perched up alarmingly high, Jane Churchill and the two gen-tlemen having preceded us to the station at *Callander*. All our luggage, ponies and all, went with our train. We stopped outside *Perth* for luncheon for a few minutes—and Jane Churchill came in again at *Aberdeen* for our tea—to enable Brown to come and help us. When we reached *Ballater*, where we got into two carriages, it began to rain.

Reached *Balmoral* at half-past six.

SHEEP CLIPPING, 1870.

BALMORAL, *Monday, June* 13, 1870.

DROVE off at half-past eleven on past J. Thomson's house. Here, in the nearest adjoining field, close to the wall, all the sheep (mine) were in a pen, and James Brown, the shepherd, and Morrison, my grieve at *Invergelder*, assisted by others (one, a brother of the Morgans), took them out one by one, tied their legs together, and then placed them on the laps of the women who were seated on the ground, and who clipped them one after the other, wonderfully well, with huge scissors or clippers. Four were seated in a sort of half-circle, of whom three were Mrs. Durran, Mrs. Leys (both these did their work admirably), and Mrs. Morrison, who seemed rather new at it, and had some difficulty with these great heavy sheep, which kick a good deal. The clippers must take them between their knees, and it is very hard work. Four other women were sitting close under the wall, also clipping. Then the sheep were all marked; and some, before being clipped, had to have their horns sawn to prevent them growing into their heads. It was a very picturesque sight, and quite curious to see the splendid thick wool peel off like a regular coat.

BETROTHAL OF PRINCESS LOUISE TO THE MARQUIS OF LORNE, OCTOBER 3, 1870.

BALMORAL, *October* 3, 1870.

THIS was an eventful day! Our dear Louise was engaged to Lord Lorne.

The event took place during a walk from the *Glassalt Shiel* to the *Dhu Loch*. She had gone there with Janie Ely, the Lord Chancellor (Lord Hatherley), and Lorne. I had driven with Beatrice and the Hon. Mrs. Ponsonby to *Pannanich Wells*, two miles from *Ballater*, on the south side of the *Dee*, where I had been many years ago. Unfortunately almost all the trees which covered the hills have been cut down.

We got out and tasted the water, which is strongly impregnated with iron, and looked at the bath and at the humble but very clean accommodation in the curious little old inn, which used to be very much frequented. Brown formerly stayed there for a year as servant, and then quantities of horses and goats were there.

The same perfectly cloudless sky as on the two preceding days. We got home by seven. Louise, who returned some time after we did, told me that Lorne had spoken of his devotion to her, and proposed to her, and that she had accepted him, knowing that I would approve. Though I was not unprepared for this result, I felt painfully the thought of losing her. But I naturally gave my consent, and could only pray that she might be happy.

COMMUNION SUNDAY AT CRATHIE, 1871.

BALMORAL, *Sunday, November* 13, 1871.

A VERY bright morning with deep snow. At twelve o'clock I went to the kirk with my two ladies (the Duchess of Roxburghe and Lady Ely), Lord Bridport being also in attendance. At the end of the sermon began the service of the Communion, which is most touching and beautiful, and impressed and moved me more than I can express. I shall never forget it.

The appearance of the kirk was very striking, with the tables in the cross seats, on either side facing the pulpit, covered with a white cloth. Neither Brown, though he came with us, nor any of our Scotch servants sat behind us, as usual, but all below, as every one does who intends taking the sacrament at the "first table." A table, also covered with a white cloth, was placed in front of the middle pew, directly facing the pulpit.

The service was the same as that on ordinary Sundays until after the sermon, excepting that every psalm and prayer had reference to the Lord's Supper, and the sermon was on the *perfect obedience of the Son* (Hebrews ii. 10).

The prayer after the sermon was very short, after which Dr. Taylor delivered an address from the pulpit, in which he very beautifully invited all true penitents to receive the communion, the hardened sinner alone to abstain. It was done in a very kind and encouraging tone. Dr. Taylor adopted part of one of the English prayers, only shortened and simplified. . . . After this address—"the Fencing of the Tables," as it is called—the minister came down to the small table in front of the pulpit, where he stood with the assistant minister,

and the elders on either side, and while the 35th Psalm was
being sung the elders brought in the Elements, and placed
them on the table, viz., the bread cut into small pieces, and
two large plates lined with napkins, and the wine in four
large silver cups. The minister then read the words of the
institution of the Lord's Supper, from 1 Corinthians xi. 23,
and this was followed by a short but very impressive prayer
of consecration.

This done, he handed the bread first, and then the wine,
right and left to the elders, Francis Leys (Brown's uncle),
Symon "the merchant," Hunter, and Dr. Robertson, to dis-
pense ; himself giving both to one or two people nearest to
him, who were in the middle pew, where the Thomsons all
sit generally, and in which, on this occasion, were old Donald
Stewart and his wife (eighty-six and eighty-one, looking so
nice and venerable), the young Donald Stewarts, the Thomsons, old Mr. and Mrs. Brown (he eighty-one and very much
bent, and she seventy-one). Old John Brown and old Donald Stewart wore large plaids ; old Smith of *Kintore* was likewise in this pew. The bread was then reverently eaten, and
the wine drunk, sitting, each person passing it on one to the
other ; the cup being replaced by each on the table before
them after they had partaken of the wine, and then the elder
carried it on to the next pews, in which there were tables, until
all those in that portion of the church prepared for the Lord's
Supper, had communicated. After which the elders replaced
the Elements on the table before the minister, who delivered
a short address of thankfulness and exhortation. He then
gave out the 103d Psalm, which was sung while the commu-
nicants were leaving the tables, to be occupied in turn by
others.

We left after this. It would indeed be impossible to say
how deeply we were impressed by the grand simplicity of the
service. It was all so truly earnest, and no description can
do justice to the perfect devotion of the whole assemblage.
It was most touching, and I longed much to join in it.* To
see all these simple good people in their nice plain dresses
(including an old woman in her mutch), so many of whom I
knew, and some of whom had walked far, old as they were,
in the deep snow, was very striking. Almost all our own
people were there. We came home at twenty minutes before
two o'clock.

---

* Since 1873 I have regularly partaken of the Communion at Crathie every au-
tumn, it being always given at that time.

THE "SPATE," 1872.

Tuesday, June 11, 1872.

BROWN came in soon after four o'clock, saying he had been down at the waterside, for a child had fallen into the water, and the whole district was out to try and recover it—but it must be drowned long before this time. I was dreadfully shocked. It was the child of a man named Rattray, who lives at *Cairn-na-Craig*, just above where the new wood-merchant has built a house, and quite close to the keeper Abercrombie's house, not far from *Monaltrie Farmhouse* in the street. At a little before five, set off in the wagonette with Beatrice and Janie Ely, and drove along the north side of the river. We stopped a little way beyond *Tynebaich*, and saw the people wandering along the riverside. Two women told us that two children had fallen in (how terrible!), and that one "had been gotten—the little een" (as the people pronounce "one"), but not the eldest. They were searching everywhere. While we were there, the old grandmother, Catenach by name, who lives at *Scutter Hole*, came running along in a great state of distress. She is Rattray's mother. We drove on a little way, and then turned round.

We heard from the people that the two boys, one of ten or eleven and the other only three, were at *Monaltrie Burn* which comes down close to the farmhouse and below Mrs. Patterson's shop, passing under a little bridge and running into the *Dee*. This burn is generally very low and small, but had risen to a great height—the *Dee* itself being tremendously high—not a stone to be seen. The little child fell in while the eldest was fishing; the other jumped in after him, trying to save his little brother; and before any one could come out to save them (though the screams of Abercrombie's children, who were with them, were heard) they were carried away and swept by the violence of the current into the *Dee*, and carried along. Too dreadful! It seems, from what I heard coming back, that the poor mother was away from home, having gone to see her own mother who was dying, and that she purposely kept this eldest boy back from school to watch the little one.

We drove back and up to Mrs. Grant's, where we took tea, and then walked up along the riverside, and heard that nothing had been found and that the boat had gone back; but as we approached nearer to the castle we saw people on the banks and rocks with sticks searching; amongst them was the poor father—a sad and piteous sight—crying and looking so anxiously for his poor child's body.

Wednesday, June 12.

Drove up to the *Bush* to warn Mrs. William Brown never to let dear little Albert run about alone, or near to the burn, of the danger of which she was quite aware. She said her husband, William, had started off early at three this morning. Some people went down to *Abergeldie* and as far as the *Girnoch* to search, and others were up and below the castle.

No word of the poor child being found. All were to start early to search.

Thursday, June 13.

At half-past ten drove out in the wagonette with Beatrice and Janie Ely, and drove beyond Mrs. Patterson's "shoppie" a little way, and turned up to the right off the road behind the wood-merchant's new cottage, and got out just below Abercrombie the keeper's house, and walked a few paces on to the small cottage called *Cairn-na-Craig*, at the foot of *Craig Noerdie*, in a lovely position, sheltered under the hill, yet high, with a beautiful view of *Lochnagar*. Brown went in first, and was received by the old grandmother: and then we went in, and on a table in the kitchen covered with a sheet, which they lifted up, lay the poor sweet innocent " bairnie," only three years old, a fine plump child, and looking just as though it slept, with quite a pink color, and very little scratched in its last clothes—with its little hands joined—a most touching sight. I let Beatrice see it, and was glad she should see death for the first time in so touching and pleasing a form.

Then the poor mother came in, calm and quiet, though she cried a little at first when I took her hand and said how much I felt for her, and how dreadful it was. She checked herself, and said, with that great resignation and trust which it is so edifying to witness, and which you see so strongly here, " We must try to bear it; we must trust to the Almighty."

The poor little thing was called Sandy. She herself is a thin, pale, dark, very good, and respectable-looking woman. She had no wish to go away that day, as the old grandmother told us, but her husband wished her to see her mother. She has one boy and two girls left, and the eldest and youngest are taken.

They were playing at the burnside, but some way above the road, where there is a small bridge. As we were leaving I gave her something, and she was quite overcome, and blessed me for it.

We walked down again, and then drove back, and walked at once past the stables to the riverside, where, on both sides every one was assembled, four in the boat (Donald Stewart and Jemmie Brown amongst them), and all with sticks, and up and down they went, searching under every stone. They had been up to the boat pool and back, but nothing appeared. I remained watching till one o'clock, feeling unable to tear myself away from this terrible sight. The poor father was on our side, William Brown amongst the others on the other side. I sat on the bank with Janie Ely for some time (Beatrice having gone in earlier than I), Grant as well as Brown standing near me. When they came to that very deep pool, where twenty-two years ago a man was nearly drowned when they were leistering for salmon, they held a piece of red cloth on a pole over the water, which enabled them to see down to the bottom. But all in vain. The river, though lower, was still very high.

At four took a short drive in the single pony carriage with Janie Ely, and back before five. Saw and talked to the schoolmaster, Mr. Lubban, a very nice little man, and he said that this poor child, Jemmie, the eldest, was such a good, clever boy. Every one shows so much feeling and kindness. It is quite beautiful to see the way in which every one turned out to help to find this poor child, from the first thing in the morning till the last at night—which, during these long days, was very hard work—and all seemed to feel the calamity deeply. We heard by telegraph during dinner that the poor boy's body had been found on an island opposite *Pannanich*, below *Ballater*, and that steps would be taken at once to recover it.

Saturday, June 15.

After luncheon, at a quarter to three, drove with the two children up as far as the *West Lodge*, and then just descried the sad funeral procession slowly and sadly wending its way along the road ; so we drove back again, catching glimpses of it as we went along, and drove on a little way beyond the bridge, when, seeing the first people not far off, we turned and drove back, stopping close to the bridge, and here we waited to see them pass. There were about thirty people, I

Beatrice

should say, including the poor father, Jemmie and Willie Brown, Francie's brother, Alick Leys, Farmer Patterson, etc. The poor father walked in front of one of the coffins ; both covered with white, and so small. It was a very sad sight. Dr. Taylor walked last with another gentleman. He had of course been up to the house and performed the service there, as is always done throughout *Scotland* by all the Protestant denominations except the Episcopalian, and no service whatever near the grave.* We watched the sad procession as long as we could, and drove home again.

VISIT TO HOLYROOD AND EDINBURGH, AUGUST 13, 1872.

Tuesday, August 13.

AT six I left sweet *Osborne* with Leopold and Beatrice, Marie Leiningen, and the Duchess of Roxburghe, Flora Macdonald,† Colonels Ponsonby and De Ros, Mr. Collins, and Fräulein Bauer. It was very warm. The yachts, which were out, had a very pretty effect. At *Gosport*, where we had to wait about ten minutes before landing, as we arrived too soon, I took leave of dear Marie Leiningen, who was to return to *Germany* next day. We had our own usual large travelling railway carriages, which are indeed charming.

It was a splendid night. Sir W. Jenner joined us at *Basingstoke*, and at *Banbury* at half-past ten we stopped for refreshments, and lay down before twelve.

Wednesday, August 14.

I had a good deal of rest, and was up and dressed by eight, or a little past. But we had already passed *Melrose*, and there was so much fog, and the air so thick, that we could see very little. The last station (not in a village or town) was *Fountainhall*, where old Mr. Lawson, the former Lord Provost of *Edinburgh* and famous seedsman, came up to the carriage, and some little girls presented Baby (as Beatrice is always called by us still) with a nosegay. We passed *Portobello*, and a few minutes more brought us to the very station —the private one, outside *Edinburgh*—which for eleven years my beloved Albert and I had always arrived at, and

* A change has taken place since this was written, and now (1883) a prayer is sometimes said as well at the grave.
† The Hon. Flora Macdonald, Maid of Honor, now Bed-chamber Woman.

where we left it together eleven years ago.   There it was, all
unaltered, and yet all so altered !

The general, Sir J. Douglas,* the Lord Provost, and other
official people received us there, and we got into our carriage.
The two children and the Duchess of Roxburghe went in
the carriage with me.

It was a dull, gloomy, heavy morning, but a great many people were out, and all most enthusiastic, reminding me forcibly
and sadly of former days.   We had an escort of the Scots
Grays.   We drove up to the door of the old, gloomy, but historical Palace of *Holyrood*, where a guard of honor with a band
of the 93d Highlanders were stationed in the quadrangle of
the court.   We got out, walked up the usual stairs, and passed
through two of the large gloomy rooms we used to occupy,
and then went past some passages up another and very steep
staircase to the so-called "*Argyll rooms*," which have been
arranged for me, with very pretty light paper, chintz, and carpets (chosen by Louise).   There is a suite, beginning with a
dining-room (the least cheerful) at the farthest end, and then
my sitting-room, a large and most cheerful room, the nicest
of all, with very light paper ; next to this the bedroom, almost
too large a room, and out of this the dressing-room.   All
open one out of the other, and have, except the dining-room,
the same pretty carpets and chintzes (red geraniums on
a white ground).   The page's room and a wardrobe and
dresser's room are just opposite, across a small passage.

We three took breakfast directly in the dining-room.   Our
rooms are above the old rooms, and have the same look-out.

It cleared up, and though still thick and hazy, the sun
shone out brightly, and at a quarter to twelve I went out into
the garden, going through our old rooms, which looked sadly
deserted : all open and some few things removed from them ;
the gloomy bedroom with its faded tapestry and green silk
bed, and the wretched little dark box-room in which I un-
dressed at night, all full of many recollections.   I went
through the long picture gallery, down the small steps into
the garden, where I met Beatrice, who walked with me.   We
walked about the garden, which is improved, but terribly
overlooked, and quite exposed to public view on the side
looking towards the street.   We walked about the fine old
chapel with its beautiful window and its tombstones, and then
went in—Beatrice and I with Brown (who was much interested by all)—conducted by the keeper, an intelligent sensi-

* Commanding the forces in Scotland.

ble man called Anderson, and visited the rooms of Queen
Mary, beginning with the Hamilton apartments (which were
Lord Darnley's rooms) and going up the old staircase to
Queen Mary's chamber. In Lord Darnley's rooms there are
some fine old tapestry and interesting portraits of the Royal
family, and of the Dukes and Duchesses of Hamilton.
There are some other curious old pictures in this room.

We saw the small secret staircase which led up in the
turret to Queen Mary's bedroom, and we went up another
dark old winding staircase at the top of which poor Rizzio
was so horribly murdered—whose blood is still supposed to
stain the floor. We entered the Presence Chamber, the ceiling of which, in panels, is from the time of Queen Mary, and
contains her mother's and her own initials and arms as
Dauphine of France and Queen of Scotland, with Darnley's
initials. Here is the bed provided for Charles I. when he
came to *Holyrood* to be crowned King of Scotland. Thence
we were shown into poor Queen Mary's bedroom, where are
the faded old bed she used, the baby-basket sent her by
Queen Elizabeth when King James I. was born, and her
work-box. All hung with old tapestry, and the two little turret rooms ; the one where she was supping when poor Rizzio
was murdered, the other her dressing-room. Bits of the old
tapestry which covered the walls at the time are hung up in
frames in the rooms. Beatrice is immensely interested by
all she sees, and delighted with everything.

At half-past five drove off in the open landau and four with
Beatrice, Leopold, and the Duchess of Roxburghe, the two
equerries riding. We drove up through the *Canongate*, that curious old street with its very high-storied houses, past *Knox's
House* and quaint old buildings, with the lowest, poorest people about, down *Bank Street*, and eastward along *Princes Street*,
that splendid street with its beautiful shops, hotels, etc., on
one side, and its fine monuments on the other, the gardens
and institutions and other parts of the town rising above it
and crowned by the picturesque *Castle*; then by *Saint Andrew Street*, across *Saint Andrew Square* (where Lord Melville's statue is), along *George Street*, a fine wide street, at the
end of which is *Charlotte Square*, where my dear one's Monument is to be placed, and where I was to have stopped to
look at the site. But the crowd, which was very great everywhere and would run with us (facilitated by the great steep-
ness and slipperiness of the streets), as well as the great
number of cabs and vehicles of all kinds which would drive

6

along after us everywhere, made this impossible. We turned to the left with some difficulty—one or two carriages coming in contact with ours—and went on by *Hope Street, Queen's Ferry Street,* where we took a wrong turn, and went by *Clarendon Crescent* and *Forres Street* till we got to the *Water of Leith,* where we found we could not go on.

We had to turn, with considerable difficulty, owing to the narrowness of the road, and go back again by *Moray Place, Heriot Row,* and thence down by *Pitt Street* on to *Inverleith Row* (outside the town), past the *Botanic Garden,* then along the *Queen's Ferry Road, Pilrig Street,* and *Leith Walk* (which I remembered from our having taken the same drive in 1861), then along a broad street, under the *Calton Hill,* and *Regent Terrace,* past *Holyrood,* into the beautiful *Queen's Drive,* right round *Arthur's Seat* with its fine grass, its rocks and small lochs. Unfortunately, however, no clear distant view could be obtained on account of the fog. Home to *Holyrood* at half-past seven. It was a fatiguing drive.

The crowds were very great, but the people behaved remarkably well; only they kept cheering and shouting and running with us, for the postilions drove very slowly whenever there was the slightest descent, and there were many in the town, and one long one coming down home from the *Queen's Drive.* A good many flags were out, but there were hardly any decorations. The equerries kept extremely well close up to the carriage, which was no easy task.

Thursday, August 15.

Again a very foggy morning. Breakfasted at half-past nine. Beatrice and Leopold started to go and see *Roslin Chapel.* Walked a little in the garden at half-past ten, and then sat for half an hour under the only tree which afforded shade and was not overlooked by the street, a thorn, with very overhanging long branches, on a small grassy mound or " hillock." Here I read out of a volume of Poems by the " Ettrick Shepherd," full of beautiful things (which Brown had given me some years ago), and wrote till half-past twelve.

At half-past five I started as yesterday with Beatrice, Leopold, and the Duchess of Roxburghe, the two equerries riding, and took a very long—rather too long—drive. It would have been quite beautiful and most enjoyable from the very fine scenery with rich vegetation, fine trees, and hills, and dales, with the *Pentlands* in the distance, had it not been for a dark, heavy, leaden fog and sky like November, but

warmer, which obscured all the distance in the most provoking way, and at one time even came down in a rather heavy
shower. We went out by the *Queen's Drive,* going to the
right as we left *Holyrood.* Numbers of people surrounded the
entrance, and, as there is a long ascent part of the way, some
of them, especially boys, ran along with us. We proceeded
by the *Liberton Road,* on past the villages of *Straiton, Lass-
wade* (very picturesque, and which I well remember from
1842), and *Bonnyrigg,* to *Dalhousie Castle,* where we had visited the late Marquis and Marchioness from *Dalkeith* in 1842
(the Duchess of Buccleuch drove me over), an old Scotch castle in red stone, where, however, we did not get out. It had
been raining, but we did not shut the carriage, and just as
we had thought of doing so the rain ceased. From here we
drove under a very fine viaduct along the *South Esk,* past
Newbattle (not into the grounds)—where there is an arch
which was built for George IV. to drive through, but he never
went there—on through the small town of *Dalkeith,* where
many people, as indeed in almost every other place, had collected, into the *Park of Dalkeith.* Here, as well as everywhere in the neighborhood, there are beautiful trees, especially some very fine sycamores. We drove up to the house,
and got out, as I wished the children to see the rooms where
we had lived. The staircase and the gallery where I held
the Drawing-room I remembered well, as also the dining-
room. Our former rooms were shown us ; but though the
bed and even the washing-basin still exist, the rooms which
had been arranged for us are altered.

We visited it last in September, 1859. The population of
Dalkeith and of all the villages about here are colliers and
miners, and are very poor. We came home straight, coming
into the same road as we started by, and going down the hill
of the *Queen's Drive.* We collected again a goodly and most
good-humored crowd, and saw the little boys and girls rolling down the steep hill, and people pouring in from the town
to get a sight of us.

Friday, August 16.

A thoroughly wet day. At half-past eleven I walked out
with Flora Macdonald (whose name attracted great attention
in *Edinburgh*), right across the court to the stables. which are
very good, and saw all belonging to them—harness-room,
coach-house, etc. Then I looked into the guard-room next
door, where the guard, who were called out and drawn up

thinking I was coming by, did not know us. I went in behind them, and I found a sergeant (I think) of the 93d in
full dress, with four medals, and I asked him his years' service, which were twenty, and where he came from—"*Perth-
shire.*" Two other men, who were cooking and had their
coats off, were in the room where they also slept. The newspapers have reported an absurd conversation of mine with
them, but none took place. We then walked back through
the house into the garden, and finally came home through the
chapel at half-past twelve.

It was raining hard, but nevertheless we started at half-
past four in the open landau, Beatrice and the two ladies with
me, the two equerries riding. We drove by way of *Princes
Street*, which overlooks the *Mound* with its gardens and
fine buildings, and is always so animated and full of people on foot and in carriages; crossed the *Dean Bridge*, which
commands a most beautiful view, though then it was obscured
by the pelting rain; passed *Stewart's Asylum*, a fine new
building, getting from the road a good view of another fine institution, *Fettes College*, built only within the last few years;
and so on to the edge of *Barnton Park*, where we turned back to
Granton. By this time it had begun to blow most violently,
in addition to the rain, and the umbrellas dripped and the carriage became soaked. Our road lay close to the sea, past
Granton Pier where we had landed in 1842; *Trinity* came
next, a place with some good houses, and then *Newhaven*—
where we saw many fishwives who were very enthusiastic, but
not in their smartest dress—and then *Leith*, where there were
numbers of people looking out for us in spite of the dreadful
rain; but indeed everywhere the poor people came out and
were most loyal. We took a wrong turn here, and had to
come back again to go to the *Albert Docks*—new and very
splendid large docks, with the ships all decked out. We stopped
a moment to speak to the Provost of *Leith*, who said the
people were very grateful for my coming; and I have since
had repeated expressions of thanks, saying the good people
felt my coming out in the rain more than anything. We
drove on along the shore, with a distant view of the *Island of
Inchkeith*, by *Leith Links*, the *London Road*, the *Cavalry Barracks*, *St. Margaret's Station* and *Queen's Park*, home. We
got home by ten minutes past seven. We were all more or
less wet, and had to change our things. The waterproofs
seemed not to have done their work. After dinner, at
twenty minutes past eleven, we left *Holyrood;* a gardener

presented me with a bouquet, and said it was " the proudest
day in his life." It did not rain, so we had the carriage open.
The two children and the Duchess of Roxburghe were in our
carriage, and we had an escort. Numbers of people were
out. The whole way was splendidly lit up by red, blue, and
yellow lights from *Salisbury Crags* and *Arthur's Seat*, and the
effect was most dazzling and beautiful. There were besides
some torches near the station, which was the same we arrived
at. The Provost hoped I " was leaving well," and I thanked
him for the very kind reception which I had met with, and for
the beautiful illuminations.

Saturday, August 17.

Did not sleep much or well—it was so very hot, and I was
too much excited, and then we had to be roused up and to
dress hurriedly before seven, by which time we were at *Ballater.* There were many people out, and so there were at
Balmoral, where we arrived at a quarter to eight. The
heather beautiful, but not completely out yet. The air sweet
and soft.

Beloved Mama's birthday! That dear, dear mother! so
loving and tender, so full of kindness! How often I long
for that love! She frequently spent this day at *Abergeldie,*
but we were not here then.

VISIT TO DUNROBIN, 1872.

Friday, September 6, 1872.

A DULL but fair morning. Breakfasted with the children
before nine o'clock, and at half-past nine I left dear *Balmoral* in the open landau and four with Beatrice and Leopold,
Jane Churchill, Fräulein Bauer, and Lord Granville. and
drove to *Ballater,* where Colonel Ponsonby, Sir W. Jenner,
and Mr. Collins met us. Besides Brown, who superintends
everything for me, Emilie Dittweiler, Annie Macdonald,
Jemmie Morgan, my second piper Willie Leys. Beatrice's,
Leopold's, and Lady Churchill's attendants, three footmen
and Goddard went with us. We passed into the station at
Aberdeen, which was immensely crowded. An address and
the keys were presented by Provost Leslie; then Lord Kintore (who gave me a nosegay and some fruit) and young
Lord Aberdeen were presented. The day was becoming fine,

and it was excessively hot. From *Aberdeen* we went by a line totally new to me—past *Inverurie*, close past the hill of *Benachie*, and got a good sight of the *Buck of Cabrach* and the surrounding hills, past *Huntly* and the ruined *Castle of Huntly* to *Keith*, where the *Banff* Volunteers were drawn up and there were many people close to the station, but no one on the platform. Here we were delayed by one of the doors, from the bedroom into the little dressing-room. refusing to open. Annie had gone through shortly before we got to *Keith*, and when she wanted to go back, the door would not open, and nothing could make it open. Brown tried with all his might, and with knives. but in vain, and we had to take in the two railway men with us, hammering and knocking away as we went on. till at last they forced it open. We were at *Keith* at 1.20, and at *Elgin* at 1.58. The station here was beautifully decorated ; there were several arches adorned with flowers and heather, and a platform with raised seats for many ladies. The Provost and the Duke of Richmond and Lord March were there. The Provost presented an address, and then I spoke to the Duke of Richmond, who told me that dear Uncle Leopold had received the freedom of the city when he was staying in the neighborhood in 1819. The ruins of the Cathedral are said to be the finest in *Scotland*, and the town is full of ancient recollections. No British sovereign has ever been so far north. The Provost's daughter presented me with a nosegay.

We stopped here about ten minutes. It was broiling hot. The corn and oats looked ripe, and were cut in many places. After this we took our luncheon (cold), and as we were sitting at the small table we suddenly found ourselves passing slowly, without stopping, the station of *Forres*, near which is the wild " muir " which Shakespeare chose as the scene of Macbeth's meeting with the witches. *Nairn* lies very prettily on the shore of the *Moray Frith*. We passed *Culloden*, and the moor where that bloody battle, the recollection of which I cannot bear, was fought. The heather beautiful everywhere, and now the scenery became very fine. At half-past three we were at *Inverness*, the capital of the *Highlands*, the position of which is lovely. We stopped here for ten minutes, but outside the station. There was an immense crowd, but all very well managed, and no squeeze or crush. There were numbers of seats in galleries filled with ladies, among whom I recognized Mrs. Cluny Macpherson. Cluny Macpherson himself was in command of the Volunteers. On the platform to the left (the Volunteers and the galleries with seats were to the right) was the Provost, Dr. Mackenzie, a fine-looking old man in a kilt, with very white hair and a long white beard, who presented an address. Lord Seafield, the Master of Lovat, Mr. Baillie of *Dochfour*, and his son Mr. Evan Baillie, were all there, and I said a word to each. The Provost's granddaughter presented a bouquet. There was an immense crowd at the back of the platform.

As our train proceeded, the scenery was lovely. Near the ruins of the old *Priory of Beauly* the river of the same name flows into the *Beauly Frith,** and the frith looks like an enormous lake with hills rising above it which were reflected on the perfectly still water. The light and coloring were rather gray, but had a charming effect. At twenty minutes to four we reached *Dingwall,* where there were Volunteers, as indeed there were everywhere, and where another address was presented and also flowers. Sir J. Matheson, Lord Lieutenant of the county, was named to me, also the Vice-Lieutenant; and some young ladies gave Beatrice nosegays. The position of *Dingwall,* in a glen with hills rising above it, is extremely pretty, and reminds me of a village in *Switzerland.* The head of the *Cromartie Frith* appears here. After this and passing slowly *Tain* and *St. Duthus* (called after the Cathedral there), we thought, as we did not stop, and were not to do so, that we would take our tea and coffee—which kept quite hot in the Norwegian kitchen—when suddenly, before we had finished, we stopped at *Bonar Bridge,* and the Duke of Sutherland came up to the door. He had been driving the engine (!) all the way from *Inverness,* but only appeared now on account of this being the boundary of his territory, and the commencement of the *Sutherland* railroad. He expressed the honor it was to him that I was coming to *Dunrobin.* Lord Ronald L. Gower also came up to the carriage-door. There was a most excited station-master who would not leave the crowd of poor country-people in quiet, but told them to cheer and "cheer again," another "cheer," etc., without ceasing.

Here the *Dornoch Frith,* which first appears at *Tain,* was left behind, and we entered the glen of the *Shin.* The railway is at a very high level here, and you see the *Shin* winding below with heathery hills on either side and many fine rocks, wild, solitary, and picturesque. The Duchess of Sutherland's own property begins at the end of this glen.

* Beauly, so called from the French " Beau lieu."

At six we were at *Golspie* station, where the Duchess of Sutherland received us, and where a detachment of the *Sutherland* Volunteers, who look very handsome in red jackets and Sutherland tartan kilts, was drawn up. I got into the Duchess's carriage, a barouche with four horses, the Duke riding, as also Lady Florence and their second son Lord Tarbat, and drove through the small town—one long street like *Dufftown*—which is inhabited chiefly by a fishing population, and was extremely prettily decorated with heather and flowers, and where there were many triumphal arches with Gaelic inscriptions (which I annex) and some very pretty English ones.

" Ar Buidheachas do 'n Bhuadhaich."
" Our gratitude to Victoria."

" Na h-uile lath chi's nach fhaic, slainte duibh 'is solas."
" Health and happiness, far or near."
(Literally—" Every day see we you, or see we not,
health to you and happiness.")

"Ceud mile failte do Chattaobh."
" A hundred thousand welcomes to Sutherland."

" Failte do 'n laith Buidhe."
" Hail to the lucky day."

" Better lo'ed you canna' be ;
Will you no come back again ? "

Everywhere the loyalty and enthusiasm were very great. In about ten minutes we were at *Dunrobin Castle.* Coming suddenly upon it as one does, or rather driving down to it, it has a very fine imposing appearance with its very high roof and turrets, a mixture of an old Scotch castle and French château. Constance Westminster (the Marchioness of Westminster, the Duke's youngest sister) was at the door, and Annie Sutherland's little girl in the hall, which is, as also the staircase, all of stone, with a sort of gallery going round opening into a corridor. But I will describe this and the rooms to-morrow.

The Duchess took me to my rooms, which had been purposely arranged and handsomely furnished by the dear late Duke and Duchess for us both, and consist of a sitting-room next to the drawing-room, with a little turret communicating by a small passage with the dressing-room, which opens into the bedroom and another room which is my maid's room, and was intended for dearest Albert's dressing-room. I went to see Beatrice's room, which is close by, down three steps in the same passage. Fräulein Bauer, and Morgan, her dresser, are near her. Brown lives just opposite in the room intended for Albert's valet. It was formerly the prison.

Rested a little while, for I felt very tired. Dined at half-past eight alone in my sitting-room with Beatrice and Leopold, Brown waiting. Shortly afterwards Annie Sutherland came to see us for a little while, and later Jane Churchill. The children went early to bed.

DUNROBIN, *Saturday, September* 7.

I will now describe my rooms. They are very high ; the bedroom is the largest and very handsome, with a beautiful bed with white and gold flowers and doves at each corner (just like one at *Clieveden*), with light blue furniture, and gold and white round the cornice of the ceiling; pale blue and white panels ; blue satin spangled with yellow leaves (which look just like gold) on the walls ; and furniture and carpet to match. The dressing-room the same, but pale blue and pink silk fluted, on the walls. The sitting-room pale sea-green satin, with the cyphers of the late Duke and Duchess and their daughters on the ceiling. The furniture of light wood, and the sofas, chairs, tables, etc., remind me greatly of *Clieveden* and *Stafford House.* The little boudoir has a small domed ceiling, spangled with golden stars, and the same furniture. There are some pretty pictures in the sitting-room and prints in the other rooms. At half-past nine we breakfasted in the sitting-room, and soon after saw the Duchess. At twenty minutes to eleven, 1 walked out with the Duchess and Beatrice to the steps, of which there are several flights, leading down to the garden, which is very pretty, and where there are fountains, and from here straight on to the sea, which is closer to the house, by half a mile I should say, than at *Osborne.* We walked along here, and then up and into the pretty byre for Ayrshire cows, and a little farther on to the dairy, a very nice, cool round one. The Duchess told Brown to open the sitting-room, and we found it occupied by a policeman in bed, which we were not at all prepared for, and which caused much amusement. Florence, Jane Churchill, and Fräulein Bauer had joined us here, and shortly after the Duke did so too. We walked back through the kitchen garden, which is very well kept, and the Duke also showed us where he has a quantity of young salmon which are artificially hatched, and also a new apparatus for watering grass. We came home by the steps again. There is plenty of shade, but rather too many trees. The old part of the Castle is as old as the twelfth century. The late Duke enlarged it and added on the towers, and finished the new part in 1849–50.

In at a quarter to twelve. A dull muggy day. We lunched as we breakfasted. Afterwards reading, etc., and at twenty minutes past four drove out in the wagonette (Bourner* driving, as I had sent my own carriage and ponies) with the Duchess, Constance Westminster, and Jane Churchill. We drove past the monument of the late Duke, which faces the Castle and is outside the gates, close to which is the Duke's private little station, used only by the family; rather near, for it cannot be above five hundred yards from the house, but it is very well managed, so as to be but little seen. We drove by the four cross-roads, turning to the left through *Dunrobin Wood*, which is really very pretty, with fine Scotch firs and other trees of all kinds, beech, oak, ash, and birch, above and below the drives, with quantities of lovely pink heather and ferns—some parts of the drive are rather steep —on to *Bacchies*, then by the *Dutch Cottage*, on to *Benabhraghie Drive*, and stopped at the four cross-roads to take our made tea and coffee, the warmth of which surprised Constance and Annie very much. We saw some deer. Drove on by the same drive (*Benabhraghie*, the name of the hill on which the old Duke's very colossal statue stands). We stopped a little farther on to look at a fine view of the Castle and village, and to the right the hills which are seen farther inland, and the blue distant hills above the coast of *Ross-shire;* then came out at *Culmallie Lodge* and passed through the village of *Golspie* with all its pretty decorations, and stopped at two cottages outside, when Annie called out a nice-looking girl who makes beautiful Shetland shawls in the one, and an oldish woman, a character, who worked me a book-marker and lives in the other (a double cottage under one roof). We drove through the *Golspie Burn* and dairy park, along the grass drive on the sea-shore below the woods, as far as *Strath-*

* My coachman and postilion, who has been thirty-eight years in my service. —1883.

stephen, and looking back had one of the finest views of the Castle, with the hills of *Cambusmore* rising behind, and, turning up into the *Caithness* high road, came back to the Castle.

Home at half-past six. A dull evening. Tried to sketch a bit of sea-view. At a quarter-past eight we had dinner in the dining-room with the Duke and Annie (between whom I sat), Leopold, Constance Westminster, the Granvilles, Jane Churchill, and Ronald. I felt strange—such a dinner in a strange place for the first time without my dear one! Brown waited on me, and did so at all meals, attending on me indoors and out of doors, most efficiently and indefatigably. Then went for a short time into the drawing-room, which is next my sitting-room. Here we were joined by Mrs. Sumner (Miss Kingscote by birth, half-sister to Colonel Kingscote and niece to Lord Bloomfield), a great friend of the Duchess's and who is staying in the house with her husband, who is a great friend of the Duke's; Constance Pitt, a younger sister of Mary Pitt, and travelling with her uncle and Lady Granville; Dr. Fayrer (a distinguished physician, who was for two years in *India*),* Mr. Sumner, and Mr. Edwin Lascelles, brother to Mary. I remained for a few minutes, and then went to my room.

Sunday, September 8.

A fine bright morning. Breakfast as yesterday. Directly after it, at a quarter-past ten, walked with Beatrice along the *Lady's Walk*, as it is called, which commences near the Castle and goes for a mile and a half entirely amongst trees, very shady, and overlooking the sea, and with paths leading down to the sea, and seats commanding lovely views of the sea and distant coast. It was very warm, and the thickness of the adjoining woods made the air feel close. We walked back the same way, and got home at a quarter-past eleven. At twelve there was quite a short service performed by Dr. Cumming in the gallery which runs round the staircase, Dr. Cumming being opposite to us. It was over by a quarter to one. Annie then took me up to her room, which is a very pretty one; long, but not high, and very light, with a very fine view above all the trees; very simply furnished. Her dressing-room and bedroom equally nice and airy, like those they have at *Stafford House*. The Duke's dressing-room is very simply and plainly furnished; he is wonderfully plain and simple in his tastes. The Duchess took me along the

---

* He travelled with Alfred, and has written a remarkable book on snakes.

passage to where Florence lives, and to the nursery where
we saw little Alix in her bed, and then by a staircase, which
belongs to the very old ,part of the Castle, to the rooms
which were the dear late Duke's and Duchess's, though the
last time she came here she lived in my rooms.   Everywhere
prints of ourselves and of people I know. After this came
down again.   Luncheon as yesterday.

At twenty minutes past four walked to the nearest seat in
the *Lady's Walk,* and sketched the view, and about half-past
five drove out in the wagonette with Beatrice and Lady
Granville.   We drove through the *Uppat Woods,* along the
big burn drive, past the *Pictish Tower* up to Mr. Loch's Memorial, which has the following inscription on it by the late
Duchess :—

TO THE HONORED MEMORY OF

JAMES LOCH,

WHO LOVED IN THE SERENE EVENING OF HIS LIFE TO LOOK AROUND
HIM HERE.

May his children's children gather here, and think of him whose life
was spent in virtuous labor for the land he loved and for the friends he
served, who have raised these stones, A.D. 1858.

OBIIT JUNII 28° 1855.

The heather is very rich all round here.   We got out and
went into it, and there is a very fine view looking up *Dunrobin Glen* and over the sea, and *Birk Head,* which is the
extreme point of the land which runs into the sea.   You also
get a very pretty glimpse of the Castle at the end of a path cut
through the wood.   We drove down again, and before we
were out of the lower wood, which is close down upon the
sea-shore, we stopped to take our tea and coffee, but were
half devoured by midges.   We then came out upon the high
road, and got into the sea-shore road, about half a mile
beyond where we went yesterday, and drove along it and in
by the Dairy—home at seven.   Resting, writing.   Dined in
our sitting-room with our two children and Annie.   Afterwards we went into the drawing-room where the ladies and
gentlemen were, but I only stayed a short time.

Monday, September 9.

Raining a little early in the day.   After breakfast drove
in the wagonette with Beatrice and Jane Churchill to the
Kennel, a remarkably nice and clean one to the left, and

rather farther on than the stables, which are close to the railway station. Mr. Macdonald, the head keeper (who is brother to our poor Macdonald, Albert's late Jäger), whom I saw at *Windsor* two years ago, showed us over them. There are fine deer-hounds and pointers and setters. We visited the Macdonalds in their nice house, and saw their daughters, three of whom are very good-looking and remind me of their cousins. He is not the least like his brother. From here we went to the stables, which are small, where my ponies were, and where we also saw some of Annie's ponies and horses. Then walked home, meeting the Duke and Ronald on the way. Two splendid Highland beasts, which are being fattened for the Christmas show, were brought up to the road for me to see. We passed the herd they belong to yesterday, when driving. These beasts really are beautiful, and most picturesque, with their rough coats, shaggy heads, and immense spreading horns; the greatest number are dun and mouse-colored. At twenty-five minutes past twelve I started with the two children and Annie for the laying of the first stone of the Memorial to be raised by the clansmen and servants to the memory of my dear Duchess of Sutherland, who was adored in *Sutherland.* We drove in the barouche and four. The rain had quite ceased. Every one else had gone on before; the Duke waited to help us in, and then ran on followed by MacAlister, his piper, valet, and confidential servant—a short stout man of sixty, I should say—an excellent man, and first-rate piper. We got out, and I went up on a platform, which was covered over and close to the stone, with the children, Annie, the Duke, Constance, and Jane Churchill. All the others, and many spectators, stood around. Mr. Joass, the minister there, offered up a short prayer, and after it presented (but did not read) the Address. I then answered what I had thought over, but spoke without reading:

" It gives me great pleasure to testify on this occasion my love and esteem for the dear Duchess, my valued friend, with whose children I am happy to be now staying, and I wish also to express my warm thanks for the loyal and hearty welcome I have met with in *Sutherland.*"

This made me very nervous, but it was said without hesitating. Then the usual ceremony of spreading the mortar and of striking the stone with a mallet was gone through. The Duke gave me a drawing of the intended Memorial, which is to be an Eleanor cross, with a bust of the dear Duchess, and a medal of her which Ronald L. Gower had

struck.   After this we got into the carriage again, amid the
cheers of the people, and drove back.   Only Leopold walked,
and Constance took his place in the carriage.   We were in,
before one.   Almost directly afterwards Beatrice and I went
into the ante-room (where all the company who afterwards had
luncheon were assembled) with Annie and the Duke, who
presented some people to me ; amongst others a very old lady,
Mrs. Houston by name, who is between eighty and ninety,
and was a great friend of the dear Duchess and of the Duchess of Norfolk.   She was quite overcome, and said, " Is that
my dear Queen," and, taking the Duke's hand, " and my
darling Duke ? "
     Luncheon as usual.   After it saw Lord Granville.   At a
quarter-past four drove out in the wagonette, drawn by four
of the Duke's horses, with Beatrice, Annie, and Constance.
It was fine though not very bright weather, and windy.   We
drove to the top of *Benabhraghie,* or the *Monument Hill,* on
which is the very colossal statue of the Duke's grandfather,
the first Duke, who married the Countess of Sutherland, from
whom this enormous property came.   She died in 1839, and
I remember her quite well as a very agreeable, clever old lady.
We drove through part of the wood by the way we went
the previous days, up the big burn drive and through *Bacchies,*
looking up *Dunrobin Glen,* which is very wild ; and the pink
heathery hills, though not very high, and the moor, with
distant hills, were very pretty.   It is a long pull upwards on
a grass drive, which makes it very hard work for the horses.
Halfway up we stopped to take tea and coffee ; and before
that, Brown (who has an extraordinary eye for it, when driving quite fast, which I have not) espied a piece of white
heather, and jumped off to pick it.   No Highlander would
pass by it without picking it, for it is considered to bring
good luck.   We got a very extensive view, though not quite
clear, of endless hills between this and the west coast—all
the Duke's property—where the Westminsters have two if
not three forests of the Duke's.
     In fine weather seven counties are to be seen in the other
direction, looking towards *Ross-shire* and the *Moray Frith,*
but it was not clear enough for this.   We saw distinctly *Ben
Rinnes,* a highish hill that rises in the distance above a long
stretch of low land extending into the sea which belongs to
the Duke of Richmond.   We drove down the hill the same
way, but afterwards took a different turn into the high-road,
and home by *Golspie* and the Lodge by seven.   The dear

pretty little girl came to see me. Beatrice brought in Lilah Grosvenor, who had just arrived. Dined at a quarter-past eight in the dining-room, as on Saturday. The same people exactly, with the addition of Colonel Ponsonby. We had some sheep's head, which I tasted for the first time on Sunday, and think really very good. Remained a little while in the drawing-room, and the Duke presented Mr. Stanley, the discoverer of Livingstone. He talked of his meeting with Livingstone, who he thinks will require eighteen months to finish the work on which he is bent. Sir Henry Rawlinson was also there.

Then went to my room and Jane read.

Tuesday, September 10.

Very fine. Our usual breakfast. At half-past ten got on my pony Maggie, Annie and Jane Churchill walking, and went to see the *Golspie Burn Falls.* We made two mistakes before we got right. We went out by the usual approach down to the mill, and past the mill under the great arch for the railway, over some very rough stones in the river, and then along a path in the wood full of hazel bushes and trees of all kinds, till the glen narrows very much, and we came to a wooden bridge, where I got off and walked to the head of the falls—over several foot-bridges, along a small path overhung by high rocks and full of rich vegetation. It is extremely pretty, reminding me of *Corriemulzie*, only on a much smaller scale. I mounted my pony again, and rode home the same way about twelve. Very warm. We had a few drops of rain, but it remained very fine all day.

At ten minutes to four started with the two children and Annie Sutherland in my wagonette for *Loch Brora*, which is nine miles off. We drove past the stables out on the main *Caithness* road, through the small fishing village of *Brora*, where all the people were out, and where they had raised a triumphal arch and decorated the village with heather. We turned sharp to the left, and came into a wild moor country, stopping for a moment at a place where one of the new coal mines which the Duke has found is being worked. One of these, near the sea, we had passed on Sunday. Then on, till we came very soon to the commencement of *Loch Brora*, which is seven miles in length, very narrow at first, and out of which the *Brora* flows into the sea. The hills heighten as the loch widens, and to the left as we drove along the *Carrol Hill* rises very finely with bold rocks up above the

loch. An hour's drive took us to the Fishing Cottage, a
small wooden house, built like a châlet, which is just off the
road, on the grass. Here we got out. The Duke drove his
break, four horses in hand. They had never been together
before, and it was not easy to drive them, for the road is full
of turnings and rather narrow. Lord Granville sat on the
box with him; and Constance Westminster, Jane Churchill,
the Duchess de San Arpino (who had just arrived, and is a
great friend of the Duchess) and Lady Granville were inside,
and two grooms sitting behind. The three young ladies,
and Mr. Collins, and Colonel Ponsonby followed in the wagonette. They had started before us, but we caught them
up at *Brora*. MacAlister had broiled some fish and got tea
ready for us in a very small room up stairs in this little cottage, where there was a fire. I had my coffee. We ladies
and Leopold all squeezed into this room. It was a very
merry tea. The tea over, we all went down to see a haul of
fish. It was very successful; quantities of brilliantly red
char, trout, and two salmon, both of which had to be put
back again. After this haul I went up and sat sketching on
the balcony while there were several more hauls, which Macdonald the keeper superintended, and some walked, and
others rowed. The view, looking towards the *Carrol Hill*,
was lovely, and the coloring beautiful.

The ladies and gentlemen rowed across, having sent the
carriages round, but I preferred *terra firma*, and drove round
the loch to where the *Black-Water*, runs into *Loch Brora*,
and is literally black; we drove over it. The Duchess told
us that there was a fine drive into a wild country up that
glen. We drove along the loch side, really a beautiful drive,
under the *Carrol Rock* or *Hill*, through the *Carrol Wood;* the
trees seem to grow remarkably well there. We saw some
deer on the very top of the hills. As we drove along the
loch, some high hills were seen rising up behind the low ones
on the opposite side, one of which, called *Ben Arlmin*, is in
the Duke's nearest deer-forest.

We turned to the right, passing by moors which the Duke has
cultivated wonderfully with the steam plough, and came back
through *Uppat* stopping near Mr. Loch's place, *Uppat*, where,
in early days, the late Duke and Duchess used to live when
they were Lord and Lady Gower. Mr. Loch's father was the
commissioner for the late Duke, and the present Mr. Loch
(whom I remember in a similar capacity at *Worsley*, Lord
Ellesmere's in 1851) is commissioner to the present Duke.

Mrs. Loch, and her daughter, and little granddaughter, who gave me a nosegay, were there. And the *Dol* schoolchildren were drawn up outside the school. We got home through the woods at twenty minutes past seven. Dinner was at half-past eight in the dining-room, the same as before, only with the addition of the Duchess of San Arpino and Sir Henry Rawlinson, and the omission of Lord Ronald L. Gower and Colonel Ponsonby.

I must now describe the dining-room. It is not a very large room, but a pretty one; with wood panelling and a portrait of the first Duchess's father, the Earl of Sutherland, at one end, and a beautiful chalk drawing, by Landseer, of two deer in the snow, one having been killed by the other. Stags' heads are round the room, and behind one (a very fine one) gaspipes have been introduced, which light up each point. In each panel along the sides of the room are paintings after Thorwaldsen's statues. By daylight the room is dark. We had some haggis at dinner to-day, and some sheep's head yesterday. MacAlister had walked round the table each of the previous days playing, but to-day it was my piper,* Willie Leys ; and afterwards they played together in the next room. Went again for a little while into the drawing-room, which is handsome, and about the size of the dining-room, and cheerfully arranged with tables and ornaments. The paper on the walls is dark red. There is a little turret at one end of it, and windows on two sides, and it opens into the ante-room, which again opens into the library. There is a full-length picture of me in the ante-room. The dining-room is a detached room on the other side ; and the billiard-room is close opposite to my sitting-room. Jane Churchill again read to me in my room.

Wednesday, September 11.

A dull morning. The military manœuvres in the South seem to be going on very satisfactorily, and every one praises dear Arthur, his indefatigable zeal and pains. It is very gratifying. At a quarter to eleven walked with Jane Churchill and the Duke down to the small museum in the garden, which is very nicely arranged, and where there is a very interesting collection of Celtic ornaments, some of which are quite perfect, and have been very well imitated, and of all sorts of odd and curious Celtic remains, weapons, utensils, etc., and a very fine large collection of all the birds found at or near

* He left my service in 1876.

7

Dunrobin. Mr. Joass, the minister, was there to explain
everything to us.

We took a short turn, and came home at half-past eleven,
as it rained. We met little Alix on her wee pony. We also
saw the Duchess's Norwegian cariole and pony. (Busy
choosing presents to give away ; and after our usual luncheon
there was some more arranging about these presents.)
Painting the view of the sea from my window. At ten
minutes to four started in the wagonette, with the two children and Annie. The Duke, the other ladies, Ronald L.
Gower, Colonel Ponsonby, and Sir Henry Rawlinson had
gone on in the drag. We drove out by the *West Lodge,* through
Golspie, on the road (on part of which we had come before)
under the *Silver Hill,* a very pretty wooded road, and turned
to the right across the Mound, an embankment constructed
by the first Duke to make a communication across an arm of
the sea, called *Loch Fleet,* which comes in there. This
Mound " spans *Strathfleet.*" Near it is a railway station.

We then drove through a very pretty glen, with fine hills,
to *Dornoch,* along the shore of *Dornoch Frith,* past *Cambusmore* (though not near the house, which lies up in the wood
at the foot of the fine hill of that name), on through woods
for some way, till we suddenly emerged on lower ground and
saw the steeple of *Dornoch Church,* formerly a cathedral.

We turned sharp to the left, and went into *Dornoch ;* quite
a small place, but the capital of *Sutherland,* now much out
of the world, as the railway does not go near it. It is a small
fishing town, smaller than *Golspie.* There was an arch with
a Gaelic inscription, and the houses were decorated with
flowers, heather, and green boughs, and many people out.
We drove to the door of the so-called cathedral; though I
had not intended doing it, I got out there, and walked up the
large kirk. The late Duke's father and mother are buried
there, as were sixteen Earls of Sutherland; and there is a
statue of the old Duke in marble. The cathedral was built
by Gilbert de Moravia, Bishop from 1223 to 1260, at his own
expense. St. Gilbert was related to the Sutherlands, who
had then recently acquired that vast territory, " the Southern
land of *Caithness,*" which now gives the title to their descendant, the present and third Duke. In a very ancient stone
sarcophagus are the bones of Richard Murray, brother to
the Bishop. We only remained a few minutes in the church,
and then went out by another door, where we got into the
carriage. There is a curious old tower opposite the church,

which was part of the Bishop's Palace. The people were very enthusiastic, and an old fish-wife, with her creel on her back, bare legs and feet, and very short petticoat (we met many such about *Dunrobin*), begun waving a handkerchief, and almost dancing, near the end of the place as we drove away. Brown motioned to her to come on, and threw her something, which the poor old thing ran to pick up. We stopped when we had regained the wood to take our tea and coffee, and were joined by the Duke's drag just as we had finished.

We changed our road, going by *Embo* and *Skelbo*, the model farm of the late Duke, and drove up to *Cambusmore*, the pretty little cottage of Mr. and Mrs. Bateson. There is a small garden in front. The two children got out, and so did all the others, but I begged to remain in the carriage, as I was tired. However, I afterwards got out; and certainly the little cottage is most charmingly fitted up with deer's heads, pretty prints, and pretty things of all kinds. They asked me to write my name in a book, which I did, sitting in the carriage.

From here we drove back again the same way; and the evening was very fine, and the sky beautiful, red and every possible bright color. As we drove along, before reaching *Cambusmore* we saw the high land of *Caithness*, a good way beyond *Brora*. Back by seven. Dined with the two children in my own room, and then went for a short while into the drawing-room; then wrote, and at half-past eleven left *Dunrobin*, with the two children and Annie, in the Duke's carriage, the Duke (in the kilt) helping us in, and then walking, with MacAlister after him, up the approach, straight to the private station, which is about five hundred yards from the house.

There were many people out, and the whole was brilliantly illuminated by Egyptian and red and blue lights. At the station all the ladies and gentlemen were assembled, and I wished them all good-by, and then got into the train, having kissed Annie, and Constance, and the two girls, and shaken hands with the Duke, who, as well as the Duchess, had been most kind.

It was half-past twelve before I lay down. Beatrice did so sooner.

Thursday, September 12.

I had not slept much, but the journey was very quiet. At eight we were at *Ballater.* A splendid morning. We drove off at once, Beatrice, Leopold, and I in one carriage, and reached dear *Balmoral* safely at a quarter to nine A.M.

Felt as though all had been a dream, and that it was hardly possible we should have been only last night at *Dunrobin,* and dined there.

DR. NORMAN MACLEOD.

[MARCH, 1873.—I am anxious to put on record all my recollections of my dear and valued friend Dr. Norman Macleod, who has been taken from us, and whose loss is more deeply felt every day.

I have therefore made the following extracts from my journal since the year 1861, when my heavy misfortune brought me into very close contact with him.]

BALMORAL, *Sunday, May* 11, 1862.

Hurried to be ready for the service which Dr. Macleod was kindly going to perform. And a little before ten I went down with Lenchen and Affie (Alice being still in bed unwell) to the dining-room, in which I had not yet been. The ladies and gentlemen were seated behind me, the servants, including Grant and some of the other Highlanders, opposite. And never was service more beautifully, touchingly, simply, and tenderly performed. There was the opening prayer, then the reading from Scripture, which was most beautifully selected as follows : the twenty-third chapter of Job, the forty-second Psalm, the fourteenth chapter of St. John, some of the first verses, and then from the twenty-third verse to the end, and the seventh chapter of Revelations to the end. All so applicable. After this came another prayer, and then the sermon, entirely extempore, taken from the twelfth chapter of the Epistle to the Hebrews to the thirteenth verse, also alluding to the tenth chapter, and occasionally turning to the Corinthians. The sermon was admirable, all upon affliction, God's love, our Saviour's sufferings, which God would not spare Him, the blessedness of suffering in bringing us nearer to our eternal home, where we should all be together, and where our dear ones were gone on before us. He concluded with another prayer, in which he prayed most touchingly for me. The children and I were much affected on coming up stairs.

Monday, May 12.

On coming home in the afternoon, Dr. Macleod came to see me, and was so clever, agreeable, kind and good. We talked of dear Albert's illness, his readiness to go hence at all times, with which Dr. Macleod was much struck, and said what a beautiful state of mind he must always have been in —how unselfish—how ready to do whatever was necessary; and I exemplified this by describing his cheerfulness in giving up all he liked and enjoyed, and being just as cheerful when he changed to other circumstances, looking at the bright and interesting side of them ; like, for instance, going from here to *Windsor* and from *Windsor* to *London*, leaving his own dear home, etc., and yet being always cheerful, which was the reverse with me. He spoke of the blessing of living on with those who were gone on before. An old woman, he said, whom he knew, had lost her husband and several of her children, and had had many sorrows, and he asked her how she had been able to bear them, and she answered : " Ah! when *he* went awa' it made a great hole, and all the others went through it." * And so it is, most touchingly and truly expressed, and so it will ever be with me.

BALMORAL, *Sunday, August* 24, 1862.

At ten service was performed by Dr. Macleod down stairs, again very beautifully. His selections were very good : the hundred and third Psalm, part of the eleventh chapter of Isaiah, and then before his sermon, the fourth chapter of Philippians, sixth verse, which was the text · " Be careful for nothing, but in everything by prayer and supplication with thanksgiving let your requests be made known unto God," and part of the eleventh chapter of St. Luke, fifth verse : " Which of you shall have a friend, and shall go unto him at midnight, and shall say unto him, Friend, lend me three loaves ? " As usual, it made a deep impression.

After dinner, in the evening, I went over to Mrs. Bruce's room, and there Dr. Macleod joined us, and was so kind, so comforting, and so cheering. He expressed great admira-

* I since hear that this poor woman was not personally known to Dr. Macleod, but that her remark was related to him by Dr. Black, his predecessor in the Barony Parish, Glasgow. Her words were : " When *he* was ta'en, it made sic' a hole in my heart that a' other sorrows gang lichtly through."

tion of my dearest Albert's statue (the cast of which was standing in the vestibule below). His eyes were full of tears, and he said his loss was felt more and more. I showed him a drawing of the mausoleum, and he said, "Oh! *he* is not there," which is so true ; and again, when admiring the photograph of the reclining statue by Marochetti, he added, "But I think *he* is more like the statue below," which is a beautiful and a true idea. He looks so truly at the reality of the next life.

Sunday, May 24, 1863.

My poor birthday !

At a quarter-past ten service was performed by Dr. Macleod. All the children but Baby there. He read the ninetieth and hundred and third Psalms ; part of the twenty-fourth chapter of St. Matthew, ninth verse : " All hail." His sermon very fine, but he read it, not having had time to prepare one by thinking the subject over, or even by the help of mere notes. I saw him in the evening, and he was most kind and sympathizing.

Sunday, October 9, 1864.

At four, went to kirk with Lenchen and Augusta Stanley. Dr. Macleod performed the service admirably, and gave us a very striking sermon, all extempore, and appealing very strongly to the people's feelings. Saw good Dr. Macleod afterwards, and was much upset in talking to him of my sorrows, anxieties, and overwhelming cares ; and he was so kind and sympathizing, so encouraging and full of that *faith* and *hope* which *alone* can comfort and sustain the broken heart. In his sermon he spoke of there being *peace without happiness*, and *happiness without peace*, which is so true.

BALMORAL, *Sunday, June* 11, 1865.

At twelve, went (a great effort) to the kirk with the girls and the Duchess of Athole. I had only been once at the end of our stay last year in October, in the afternoon, and it made me very nervous. Still, as no one expected me to go, it was better so. Dr. Macleod performed the service most impressively. His sermon was from 1 Thessalonians iv. 10. No one reads the Bible better than he does, and his prayers were most beautiful. In the one for me, which he always words so expressively and touchingly, he prayed for Alix and her dear babe very beautifully. The singing and the whole service brought tears to my eyes. I felt so alone ! All reminded me of former blessedness.

BALMORAL, *Saturday, October* 14, 1865.

After dinner Dr. Macleod gave us a long account of that dreadful Dr. Pritchard,* and his interviews with him. Never in his life had he seen anything so dreadful as this man's character and his wonderful untruthfulness.

Dr. Macleod afterwards came up stairs, and read to Lenchen and me of Burns most beautifully.

Sunday, October 15, 1865.

At twelve we went to the kirk, where dear Dr. Macleod performed the service more beautifully than I ever heard it. The sermon was touching, and most striking and useful. It touched and struck all. The text was from Genesis iii. 13 : " And the Lord God said unto the woman, What is this that thou hast done ? "

And then he showed how we all had a secret life which no one knew but God, and showed the frightful danger of living a life of deception till you deceived yourself, and no longer knew wrong from right. I wish I could repeat *all* he said, but it was admirable. Then in his beautiful prayers he brought in a most touching allusion to Lord Palmerston,† and prayed for him.

BALMORAL, *Sunday, June* 17, 1866.

We went at twelve to the kirk, and Dr. Macleod gave us a beautiful sermon from St. Mark ix. 38, etc. It was very fine, so large-minded and charitable, much against party spirit and want of charity, and showed how thoroughly charity in its highest form, existed in our Saviour.

. . . The Duchess of Athole and Dr. Macleod dined with me. He was so amiable, and full of sympathy ; he also suffers much from constant work and worry, and must go abroad for relaxation. Told him how much I required it, and that I came here for it, and had had a hard fight for it. He said he quite felt this, and entreated me—" as you work for us " —always to insist upon coming here. I said my dearest Albert had injured himself by never giving himself enough rest ; and we spoke of the absolute necessity of complete relaxation occasionally, and of the comfort of it.

* He had poisoned his wife and his wife's mother, and Dr. Macleod attended him in prison.
† He was dying, and expired on October 18.

BALMORAL, *Sunday, September* 16, 1866.

The church was very full and the atmosphere very close. Dr. Macleod preached admirably, especially the latter part of the sermon, when he preached extempore, and spoke of our responsibilities which made us work out our salvation. God wished us all to be saved, but we must work that out ourselves. And we might by our own fault not be saved. The first part was read, he having told me the night before that he felt nervous, and must read it.

BALMORAL, *Thursday, September* 20, 1867.

Good Dr. Macleod (who arrived yesterday, for two nights) came to talk to me for some little time while I was sitting out. He spoke most kindly, and said enough to show how shocked he was at my many worries, but said also that he was convinced of the great loyalty of the nation, and that I should take courage.

On the next day, the 21st, he came to take leave of me, as he was going to *India*, sent by the General Assembly to look after the missions. He is only going for six months; still, his life is so valuable that it is a great risk. He was much affected in taking leave of me, and said, " If I should not return, I pray God to carry your Majesty through all your trials."

BALMORAL, *Saturday, October* 10, 1868.

Mr. Van de Weyer and good Dr. Macleod, who is looking ill, and rather broken, and with a long beard, dined with us.*

Sunday, October 11.

All to kirk at twelve. Christian and Franz † sat in the *Abergeldie* pew. Dr. Macleod performed the service, and I never heard a finer sermon or more touching prayer for me. The text, St. Luke ix. 33 : " Peter said unto Jesus, Master, it is good for us to be here . . . not knowing what he said."

Saw Dr. Macleod, who talked, as also last night, of *India*, and of the disturbance in the Church.

BALMORAL, *Sunday, June* 6, 1869.

To kirk with Louise, Leopold, Baby (Beatrice), and Christian. Dr. Macleod (who arrived last night) performed the service, and admirably, speaking so much to the heart. The

---

* He had only lately returned from India.

† The Prince and Princess Christian of Schleswig-Holstein and the Prince and Princess of Teck were on a visit.

prayers were beautiful, and so was the sermon. It was so full of truth and simple good advice, telling us to act according to the spirit of what is told us, and according to what we felt was right. The text from 1 Peter iv. 21. Afterwards saw dear Dr. Macleod, whom I find a good deal altered and aged. He is Moderator of the General Assembly for this year, and spoke with much pleasure of the unanimity prevailing, and of the good feeling shown towards him; and regretted much this Irish Church Bill.

BALMORAL. *Sunday, October* 3, 1869.

At twelve, went with our children to the kirk. Dr. Macleod preached a fine sermon, and gave us two beautiful prayers as usual. The text was from Matthew xxvi. 30.

I saw Dr. Macleod before dinner. He is greatly alarmed for the Established Church of Scotland, as he fears that an attempt will be made to pull that down also: though, thank God, there is no difference of form or doctrine there, and were this to happen, the Free Church and United Presbyterians, with the present Established Church, would become one very strong Protestant body. I also asked him about Lord Lorne, and he said he had a very high opinion of him; that he had long known him, and had prepared him for confirmation, that he thought very highly of him, and had a great respect for him, and that he had fine, noble, elevated feelings.

Sunday, October 2, 1870.

A very fine morning after a frost. The sun intensely hot. Dear Leopold breakfasted with us out of doors. Sat out for a short while. To the kirk at twelve. It was not so stifling. Dr. Macleod gave us such a splendid sermon on the war, and without mentioning *France*, he said enough to make every one understand what was meant (when he pointed out how God would punish wickedness, and vanity, and sensuality; and the chapters he read from Isaiah xxviii., and from Ezekiel, Amos, and one of the Psalms, were really quite wonderful for the way in which they seemed to describe *France*). It was all admirable and heart-stirring. Then the prayers were beautiful in which he spoke of the sick, the dying, the wounded, the battlefield, and my sons-in-law and daughters. We all came back deeply impressed.

Monday, October 3.

Dr. Macleod came to wish me good-by. He yesterday again told me what a very high opinion he had of Lord Lorne, how good, excellent, and superior he thought him in every way, and the whole family so good.

BALMORAL. *June* —, 1871.

Dear Dr. Macleod was unable to come during my present stay here, having been unwell in the winter. He has gone abroad to *Ems.*

BALMORAL, *Sunday, November 5,* 1871.

At a little before twelve, went to kirk with Baby and Janie Ely, for the first time after a very severe illness—a great pleasure to me who am so fond of going to the dear little church here. Brown helped me up and down the steep stair-case, but I found no great difficulty. Dr. Macleod (who arrived yesterday evening at the Castle) performed the service, which he made purposely rather short for me. He gave us a beautiful sermon, the text from St. Matthew vi. 9 : " Our Father, who art in heaven ; " and he preached upon the great importance, as well as comfort, of our looking on God as a Father, and not as a judge or " magistrate," to use a homely phrase. He also gave an admirable explanation of the Sacrament, which he announced was to be given next Sunday, explaining that it was not a miracle, which people often consider it to be. Back by a quarter-past one, much edified.

He came to see me before dinner.

Monday, November 6, 1871.

Had a long and satisfactory talk with Dr. Macleod after luncheon to-day again.

BALMORAL, *Sunday, May 26,* 1872.

To kirk at twelve, with Baby and the ladies, etc. Dr. Macleod preached a very fine sermon, full of love and warm feeling, upon future life and hope. The text was from St. Matthew v. 9, " Thy kingdom come." But I was grieved to see him looking ill.

After luncheon saw good Dr. Macleod, who was very depressed and looking very ill, and willingly sat down at my request. He said he was quite broken down from hard work, and would have to give up his house in *Glasgow* (where he has not a moment's rest), and his Indian mission work, etc.

He feels all this much, but it is unavoidable. He did too
much. He has never recovered from the effects of his visit
to *India*. He is, however, going to *America* for some months,
and has refused everything in the way of preaching and lect-
ures. He talked much of a future life, and his certainty of
there being a continuation there of God's educational pur-
poses, which had commenced in this world, and would work
on towards the final triumph of good over evil, and the ex-
tinction of sin.

Balmoral, *Monday, May* 27, 1872.

Saw and wished good Dr. Macleod good-by, with real regret and anxiety. Towards the end of dinner, yesterday, he
cheered up, having hardly talked at all during the course of it.

Balmoral, *Sunday, June* 16, 1872.

We had come home at five minutes past eight; I had
wished Brown good-night, and was just going to my dressing-
room, when he asked to come in again and say a few words
to me. He came in, and said, very kindly, that he had seen
Colonel Ponsonby, and that there was rather bad news of Dr.
Macleod, who was very ill, in fact that they were afraid he
was *dead!* Oh! what a blow! How dreadful to lose that
dear, kind, loving, large-hearted friend! My tears flowed
fast, but I checked them as much as I could, and thanked
good Brown for the very kind way he broke this painful and
most unexpected news to me. I sent for and told Leopold,
who was quite stunned by it, and all my maids. Every one
was most deeply grieved—the Duchess of Athole, Janie Ely,
Miss MacGregor, Colonel Ponsonby, and Dr. Taylor, who
was so overcome as hardly for some time to be able to speak.
The loss, he and we all felt, was quite irreparable. Dr.
Taylor knew (which I did not) that he had been very ill for a
week, and that he might die at any moment, and that the
long and most admirable speech which he made in the
Assembly had been far too much for him. That was on the
30th. Still we all hoped that rest would have restored him.
How thankful I felt that I had seen him so lately! When
the Duchess came up stairs, we could speak of little else.
After she left, and I was alone, I cried very bitterly, for this
is a terrible loss to me.

Monday, June 17.

When I awoke the sad truth flashed upon me, which is
doubly painful, as one·is unaware of the reality on first waking.

After breakfast, when I thought of my dear friend Dr. Macleod, and all he had been to me—how in 1862–63–64 he had cheered, and comforted, and encouraged me—how he had ever sympathized with me, and how much I always looked forward to the few occasions I had of seeing him when we went to *Balmoral*, and that this too, like so many other comforts and helps, was forever gone—I burst out crying.

Yesterday evening we heard by telegraph from Mr. Donald Macleod (for the first news came from the *Glasgow* telegraph clerk to Warren *) that his dear brother had died at twelve that morning.

I telegraphed to all my children, and could think of nothing else. I try to dwell on all he said, for there was no one to whom in doubts and anxieties on religion I looked up with more trust and confidence, and no one ever reassured and comforted me more about my children. I remember that he expressed deep satisfaction at hearing such good accounts of them. . . . And then he seemed so full of trust and gratitude to God. He wrote a beautiful letter to Janie Ely on his birthday (June 3), in answer to my inquiries after him, of which I annex the copy. His words seemed almost prophetic!

June 3, 1872.

Dear Lady Ely,—Whether it is that my head is empty or my heart full, or that both conditions are realized in my experience, the fact, however, is that I cannot express myself as I feel in replying to your Ladyship's kind—far too kind—note, which I received when in the whirlwind or miasma of Assembly business.

Thanks deep and true to you, and to my Sovereign Lady, for thinking of me. I spoke for nearly two hours in the Assembly, which did me no good, nor, I fear, to any other.

I was also to preach yesterday. As I have nice summer quarters, I much hope to recruit, so as to cast off this dull, hopeless sort of feeling.

I ought to be a happy, thankful man to-day. I am to-day sixty, and round my table will meet my mother, my wife, and all my nine children, six brothers, sisters, and two aunts—one eighty-nine, the other seventy-six; and all these are a source of joy and thanksgiving! Why such mercies to me, and such sufferings as I often see sent to the rest on earth?

* My own telegraph clerk.

God alone knows! I don't see *how* He always acts as a wise, loving, and impartial Father to all His children. What we know not now, we shall know hereafter. Let us trust when we cannot trace.

God bless the Queen for all her unwearied goodness! I admire her as a woman, love her as a friend, and reverence her as a Queen; and you know that what I say I feel. Her courage, patience, and endurance are marvellous to me.

(Signed) N. MACLEOD.

March, 1873.

Dear Dr. Macleod likewise came to *Balmoral*, and preached there, on the following occasions: October 11, 1863, May 24, 1864 (my birthday, after his visit to the *Holy Land*), on May 27, 1867, and on May 29, 1869.

When I last saw him I was greatly distressed at his depression and sadness, and instead of my looking to him to cheer and encourage *me*, I tried to cheer *him*. He said he had been ordered to give up all work, and to give up his house at *Glasgow*, merely continuing to preach at the *Barony Church;* and that then they gave him hopes of a recovery, but it was not at all certain. He must give up the Indian Mission, which was a great sorrow to him; and he meant to take the opportunity of resigning it in person, to say what he felt so strongly, though others might not be pleased. He meant to go to *America* in August, merely to recruit his health and strength; and he had refused every invitation for dinners, or to lecture or preach. He had not much confidence, he said, in his recovery, but he might be wrong. All was in God's hands. "It is the nature of Highlanders to despond when they are ill," he added. He hoped God would allow him to live a few years longer, for his children, and to be able to go on with "Good Words." He dwelt then, as always, on the love and goodness of God, and on his conviction that God would give us, in another life, the means to perfect ourselves and to improve gradually. No one ever felt so convinced, and so anxious as he to convince others, that God was a loving Father, who wished all to come to Him, and to preach of a living personal Saviour, One who loved us as a brother and a friend, to whom all could and should come with trust and confidence. No one ever raised and strengthened one's faith more than Dr. Macleod. His own faith was so strong, his heart so large, that all—high and low, weak and strong, the erring and the good—could alike find sympathy, help, and consolation from him.

How I loved to talk to him, to ask his advice, to speak to him of my sorrows, my anxieties!

But, alas! how inpossible I feel it to be to give any adequate idea of the character of this good and distinguished man! So much depended on his personal charm of manner, so warm, genial, and hearty, overflowing with kindness and the love of human nature ; and so much depended on himself, on knowing and living with him, that no one who did not do so can truly portray him. And, indeed, how can any one alas, who has not known or seen a person, ever imagine from description what he is really like?

He had the greatest admiration for the beauties of nature, and was most enthusiastic about the beautiful wild scenery of his dear country, which he loved intensely and passionately. When I said to him, on his last visit, that I was going to take some mineral waters when I went south, he pointed to the lovely view from the windows, looking up the glen of the *Dee*, and said : "The fine air in these hills, and the quiet here, will do your Majesty much more good than all the waters." His wife, he said, had urged him to come, though he felt so ill. "It always does you good to go to *Balmoral*," she told him. He admired and loved the national music of his country, and wrote the following description of it, most kindly, as a preface to a book of Pipe Music published by my head piper, William Ross :—

THE BAGPIPE AND ITS MUSIC.

BY THE REV. DR. NORMAN MACLEOD.

THE music of the *Highlands* is the pibroch of the great war-pipe, with its fluttering pennons, fingered by a genuine Celt, in full Highland dress, as he slowly paces a baronial hall, or amidst the wild scenery of his native mountains. The bagpipe is the instrument best adapted for summoning the clans from the far-off glens to rally round the standard of their chiefs, or for leading a Highland regiment to the attack amidst the roar of battle. The pibroch is also constructed to express a welcome to the chief on his return to his clan, and to wail out a lament for him as he is borne by his people to the old burial-place in the glen or the sainted *Isle of Graves*. To those who understand its carefully composed music there is a pathos and depth of feeling suggested by it which a Highlander alone can fully sympathize with ; associated by him as it always is with the most touching memories of his home and country: recalling the faces and forms of the departed: spreading forth before his inward eye panoramas of mountain, loch, and glen, and reviving impressions of his early and happiest years. And thus, if it excites the stranger to laughter, it excites the Highlander to tears, as no other music can do, in spite of the most refined culture of his after life. It is thus, too, that what appears to be only a tedious and unmeaning monotony in the music of the genuine pibroch, is not so to one under the magic influence of Highland associations. There is, indeed, in every pibroch a certain monotony of sorrow. It pervades even the "welcome," as if the young chief who arrives recalls the memory of the old chief who has departed. In the "lament" we naturally expect this sadness; but even in the "summons to battle," with all its fire and energy, it cannot conceal what it seems already to anticipate, sorrow for the slain. In the very reduplication of its hurried notes, and in the repetition of its one idea, there are expressions of vehement passion and of grief—"the joy of grief," as Ossian terms it, which loves to brood upon its own loss, and ever repeats the one desolate thought which fills the heart, and which in the end again breaks forth into the long and loud agonizing cry with which it began. All this will no doubt seem both meaningless and extravagant to many, but it is nevertheless a deliberately expressed conviction.

The characteristic poetry of the *Highlands* is Ossian, its music the pibroch; and these two voices embody the spirit and sing the praises of "Tir na'm Beann, na'n Gleann's na Gaisgeach" ("the land of the mountains, the glens, and the heroes ").

I said I was sure he would rejoice to think that it was a Highlander who had seized O'Connor,* and he replied, " I was deeply thankful to hear it."

He possessed a keen sense of wit and great appreciation of humor, and had a wonderful power of narrating anecdotes. He had likewise a marvellous power of winning people of all kinds, and of sympathizing with the highest and with the humblest. and of soothing and comforting the sick, the dying, the afflicted, the erring and the doubting. A friend of mine told me that if she were in great trouble, or sorrow, or anxiety, Dr. Norman Macleod was the person she would wish to go to! And so it was! One felt one's troubles, weaknesses, and sorrows would all be lovingly listened to, sympathized with, and entered into.

I detected a sign of illness in dear Dr. Macleod's accepting, contrary to his ordinary usage, my invitation to him to sit down, saying he could not stand well; and I afterwards heard he had complained greatly of fatigue in walking back from the kirk. I said I feared *India* had done him harm. He admitted it. but said, " I don't regret it." I expressed an earnest hope that he would be very careful of himself, and that on his return at the end of October he would take *Balmoral* on his way.

When I wished him good-by and shook hands with him, he said, " God bless your Majesty," and the tears were in

---

* The young man who rushed up to my carriage with a petition and a pistol in Buckingham Palace Garden on February 29, 1872, was seized by Brown.

his eyes.   Only then did the thought suddenly flash upon me,
as I closed the door of my room, that I might never see this
dear friend again, and it nearly overcame me.   But this
thought passed, and never did I think, that not quite three
weeks after, his noble, pure spirit would be with the God and
Saviour he loved and served so well!   I have since heard that
he mentioned to several at *Balmoral* that he thought he
should never come there again.

   I will here quote from my Journal some part of an account of
my conversations at *Balmoral* on August 24 and 25, 1872, with
Dr. Macleod's excellent and amiable brother, the Rev. Donald Macleod, about his dear brother Norman :—

   " He (Norman) was a complete type in its noblest sense of
a Highlander and a Celt, which, as Mr. Donald Macleod and
I both observed, was peculiarly sympathetic, attaching, and
attractive.   I said that since my great sorrow in 1861, I had
found no natures so sympathetic and so soothing as those of
the Highlanders. . . . He (Donald Macleod) said, ' I went to
him for everything ; he was like a father to me (he is twenty
years his junior) !   His indefatigable kindness to every one
was unequalled, and his patience was so great and he was so
good.'   His acts of kindness to people whom he did not
know were frequent and unknown even to his family.   His
sense of humor and fun was unbounded, and enabled him
to win the confidence of persons of the greatest diversity of
character.   Mr. Donald Macleod thinks, however, that it
was a mercy his dear brother was taken when he was, for that
a life of inactivity, and probable infirmity, would have been
unbearable to him. . . . His health had been unsatisfactory
already before he went to *India,* but, no doubt, that journey
had done him great harm ; still he never would have spared
himself, if he thought there was a work given to him to do. . . .
His wife and children bore up wonderfully, because he had
taught them to look on the future state so much as a reality,
and as one of such great happiness, that they felt it would be
doing wrong not to rejoice in his joy. His faith was so strong
that it held others in a marvellous manner, and he realized
the future state and its activity, as he believed, in a most remarkable way.

VISIT TO INVERLOCHY, 1873.

Tuesday, September 9, 1873.

GOT up at ten minutes to seven, and breakfasted with Beatrice at twenty minutes past seven. The morning was splendid. At five minutes past eight I left *Balmoral* with Beatrice and Jane Churchill in the landau and four (Brown on the rumble) for *Ballater*, whither General Ponsonby and Dr. Fox had preceded us. We had our own comfortable train ; Jane Churchill came with us. Emilie Dittweiler, Annie Macdonald, Morgan, and Maxtead (Jane's maid) went in the dresser's compartment, and Francie with dear Noble,* with Brown next to me. After crossing the *Bridge of Dun,* where we were at half-past eleven, we had some cold luncheon, and by a quarter to one we were at *Stanley Junction,* where we left the main line from *Aberdeen* to the south, and turned into the Highland Railway. Here, alas ! the distance became indistinct, the sky gray, and we began fearing for the afternoon. At one we passed the really beautiful valley of *Dunkeld,* catching a glimpse of the cathedral and the lovely scenery around, which interested Beatrice very much, and made me think of my pleasant visits and excursions thence ; then passed opposite *St. Colme's,* the Duchess's farm, by *Dalguise,* and saw the large Celtic cross at *Logierait,* put up to the late Duke of Athole ; then *Pitlochry,* after which we passed through the magnificent *Pass of Killiekrankie,* which we just skirted in our long drive by *Loch Tay* and *Loch Tummel,* in 1866. The dull leaden sky which overhung *Dunkeld* continued, and soon a white veil began to cover the hills, and slight rain came down.

We passed close by *Blair,* which reminded me much of my sad visit there in 1863, when I came by this same line to visit the late Duke ; and I could now see the great improvements made at the Castle. From here the railway (running almost parallel with the road by which *we* went so happily from *Dalwhinnie* the reverse way in 1861) passes *Dalnaspidal Station*—a very lonely spot—then up *Drumouchter,* with *Loch Garry* and *Loch Ericht,* fine and wild, but terribly desolate and devoid of woods and habitations, and so veiled by mist and now beating rain as to be seen to but very little advantage. Next comes *Dalwhinnie Station,* near the inn where we slept in 1861, having ridden over from *Balmoral* to

* Another favorite and splendid collie.

Glen Fishie, and thence down by *Newton More:* consequently,
the distance across the hill is comparatively nothing, though,
to avoid posting in uncertain weather, we had to come all
this way round.   At thirty-five minutes past two we reached
Kingussie.   The station was decorated with flowers, heather,
and flags, and the Master of Lovat (now Lord Lieutenant of
Inverness-shire) and Cluny Macpherson (both of course in
kilts) were there.   We waited till all our things were put into
our carriage, and then got out, in heavy rain at that moment.
We three went in the sociable, General Ponsonby and Brown
on the box, Dr. Fox and my maids in the wagonette, the
other maids and Francie with the dog, and the remainder following in two other carriages.   We passed through the village of *Kingussie*, where there were two triumphal arches and
decorations, and some of Cluny's men drawn up, and then
turned sharp to the left up amongst the hills, through the
very poor long village of *Newton More* (which Annie Macdonald, whose late husband came from there, had never
seen, but which *we* had driven through in 1861) and on
amongst desolate, wild, heathery moors.   The road skirts the
Spey, which meanders through a rich green valley, hills rising
grandly in the distance and on either side.   We passed the rock
of *Craig Dhu*, and a castle amongst trees, where there was
an arch, and the owner and his family standing near it, and
where a nosegay was presented to me.   Next we came to
Cluny Castle, at the gate of which stood Mrs. Macpherson
with her family.   We stopped after we had gone past and she
came and presented me with a nosegay.

From here the road was known to me, if I can call going once
to see it in 1847 knowing it.   Very few inhabitants, and not
one village after *Newton More*, only miserable little cottages
and farmhouses, with a few people, all very friendly, scattered about here and there.   We changed horses first at *Laggan Bridge*, having crossed the *Spey* over a large stone bridge,
which I well remember; it is near *Strathmashie*.   Here we
stopped a few minutes; and a little girl presented me with a
nosegay, and the innkeeper gave Brown a bottle with some
wine and a glass.   We were preceded the whole way by the
postmaster of *Banavie*, who supplied the horses; he was
called McGregor, and wore a kilt.   We had only a pair of
horses all along and after the first stage—excellent ones.
The roads admirable—hardly any hills, though we drove
through such a hilly, wild country.   The rain had ceased,
and only occasional showers came on, which did not prevent

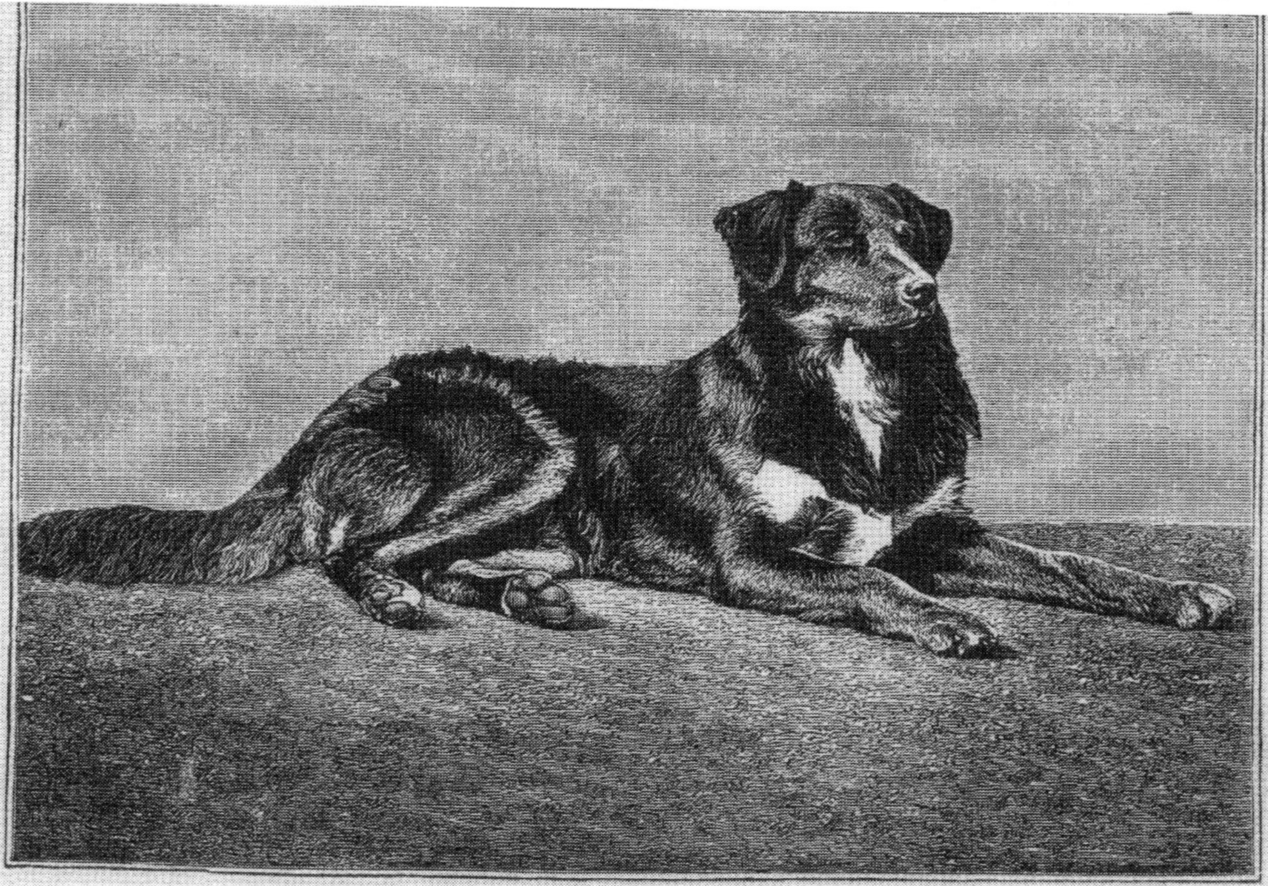

NOBLE.

our seeing the very grand scenery, with the high finely pointed and serrated mountains, as we drove along. Shortly after changing horses we left the river and came to the beautiful *Loch Laggan,* seven miles in length, along which the drive goes under birch, mountain-ash laden with bright berries, oak, alders in profusion, and is really beautiful. I was quite pleased to see the loch again after twenty-five years—recognized it and admired its beauty, with the wooded promontories, its little bays, and its two little islands, its ferry (the only communication to the other side) and the noble hills, the two *Ben Alders.*

We stopped, soon after passing the ferry, in a very secluded spot at five, and had our (made) tea in the carriage, which was very refreshing. We at length came opposite *Ardverikie,* which I so well remember, recalling and relating, as we now drove along, many of the incidents of our month's stay there, which was as wet as this day. Sir John Ramsden, who has bought the property, was standing with some other people by the roadside. At the head of the loch is *Moy Lodge,* a pretty little place in the style of *Ardverikie,* at which Mr. Ansdell, the artist, is staying. A little beyond this we changed horses at *Moy* (only a single house), and drove along through *Glen Spean,* which is very fine and grand in some parts, the road looking down upon the rapid, rushing, gushing river, as it whirls along imbedded in rocks and overhung with wood, while high ranges of hills, fine and pointed in shape, are seen in the distance rising peak upon peak. Along this road I had driven, but I had forgotten it. Before coming to the *Bridge of Roy* Inn, we saw some of the celebrated *Parallel Roads* quite distinctly, which are more clearly seen farther on, and which are very interesting to all geologists as being supposed to mark the beaches of an inland lake, which was pent back by a great glacier in *Glen Spean,* and subsided to different levels, as the glacier sank or broke away at three successive periods.

The rain ceased, and we walked a little before coming to the *Bridge of Roy,* where we changed horses for the last time, and directly afterwards passed a triumphal arch with heather and inscriptions, pipers playing, etc., and Highlanders as well as many other people drawn up, but we unfortunately drove past them too quickly. There was an inscription in Gaelic on one side, and on the other " Loyal Highlanders welcome their Queen." The papers say that it was put up by Mrs. McDonell of *Keppoch.*

About three miles farther on we reached *Spean Bridge*, and it was already getting dark. Here there is only an inn, and Lord and Lady Abinger and their tenantry met us. Lord Abinger said he had been requested to express the people's thanks for my honoring their country with a visit, and his little girl presented me with a large nosegay in the name of the tenantry. We then drove on through rather desolate moors, and the rain began to fall again very heavily. It became quite dark, and we could just descry mountains under which we drove. At ten minutes past eight we arrived at *Inverlochy*, entering by a lodge, which was lit up and looked cheery enough. The house is entered through a small, neat-looking hall, and I have three nice rooms up stairs, with the maids close by, and Beatrice and Morgan also, just at the other side of the passage. My sitting-room is very nice. It was nine before we got to dinner, which I took with Beatrice and Jane, Brown waiting on us as well as Cannon * (the footman). The drawing-room is a large, rather handsome and well-finished room. We soon went up to our rooms, and all were glad to go to bed.

INVERLOCHY CASTLE, *Wednesday, September* 10.

Mist on all the hills and continuous rain ! Most disheartening, but the views from the house beautiful, especially from my sitting-room, which has a bow-window, with two small ones on either side, looking towards *Ben Nevis* (which is close in front of it), and commands a lovely view of *Fort William* (farther to the right), and of *Loch Linnhe*, etc., a portion of *Loch Eil* (pronounced *Loch Eel*) which runs up a long way, nearly twelve miles, with the fine *Moidart* range, close to *Glen Finnan*, as a background ; and this, with *Banavie* and the hotel, close to the *Caledonian Canal*, is distinctly seen from the other window. This very pretty little room does not open into any other ; next to it is Emilie Dittweiler's, next to that my dressing-room, and Annie's room, all narrow and long, and next again is a really large and also long room, my bedroom, in which I had my own bed, which has been to *Switzerland, Invertrossachs, Sandringham,* and *Baden*. Downstairs is the dining-room. a good-sized room (in which the gentlemen dine), also the drawing-room, and a small library, in which *we* take our meals. No room in the house opens into another. Though some of the bedrooms are larger than

* He left my service in 1879.

those at *Invertrossachs*, the servants are not so well off. After breakfast (which, as well as luncheon, Beatrice and I always took alone) at half-past nine, went up stairs again and looked at Brown's room, which is a few steps lower than mine, in fact, only a very small bathroom. Beatrice is just opposite where I am, or rather round the corner. Jane Churchill and the two gentlemen, up stairs, have also good rooms. As the rain did not cease, Beatrice, Jane Churchill, and I walked out in the grounds to the stables, which we looked at, then out at the lodge and as far as the farm, where, however, no beasts were at the time, and on coming home we went through the house and kitchen, servants' hall, etc., and were in at a quarter to one. There were short gleams of sunshine which lit up the splendid scenery, and I sketched from my window looking up to *Banavie.*

Played with Beatrice on the piano. The day seemed better, but again and again the sunshine was succeeded by heavy showers; still we determined to go out. So at twenty minutes to five we three started in the sociable. Brown on the box, with a pair of horses and a postilion who drove extremely well. We drove past the distillery (between this and *Fort William*), then turned to the right over the suspension bridge to *Banavie*, about a mile farther, where there is a good hotel, quite close to the *Caledonian Canal*, which we crossed by a bridge, and drove through *Corpach*, a very small village, where the horses made a halt and turned another way, and Brown said nearly put us into a ditch! but we soon got all right again, having to go on a little way to turn. We went along the upper part of *Loch Eil*, the sea loch, on which *Fort William* stands. It is very narrow at first, and then widens out into a large broad loch as you approach the head of it, beyond which is the very fine range of the *Moidart* Hills, high and very serrated and bold. These are close to *Glen Finnan.* The road is excellent and not hilly, though it skirts the hills the whole time and is very winding, with much wood, so that you drive a good deal under trees, ash, oak, alder, and the mountain ash, which is now laden with red berries. The bright heather, growing in tufts of the richest color mixed with a great deal of high tall bracken which is beginning to turn, has a lovely effect. Here and there were some very poor little huts, most miserable, of stone, wretchedly thatched with moss and grass, and weeds growing on the roofs, very dirty and neglected-looking, the little fields full of weeds choking the corn, and neglected bits of garden, bushes and brambles growing into the very window; and yet generally the people who looked most poor had a cow!

We passed *Fassifern*, which belonged to the father of the Colonel Cameron killed at *Quatre Bras*, now merely a farmhouse, and surrounded by fine trees. I think the drive to near the head of the loch must have been nearly ten miles! It was a beautiful drive, in spite of the frequent very heavy showers of rain.

We came home at twenty minutes to eight. Good accounts of Leopold, but the weather has been bad. Dined as yesterday. Played on the piano with Beatrice in the drawing-room, and then we went up stairs.

Thursday, September 11.

A pouring wet morning after a pouring wet night. Could not go out all the morning. It, however, cleared up in the afternoon, and became very bright and fine. Just as we decided to go out at a quarter past four, it began raining again; however, as I left with Beatrice and Jane in the sociable, it cleared, and was very fine for some time. We drove out the way we came on Tuesday as far as *Spean Bridge*, and then turned sharp to the left along the *Spean*, under fine trees which abound in the valleys, and in view of scattered birches which creep up the hills. We changed horses after passing *High Bridge* and an old neglected-looking churchyard, from which a funeral party was evidently returning, as we met "a good few" (i.e. a good many) farmers in black, and saw the gate open and a spade near it. The road ascends to *High Bridge*, commanding a very fine view over the *Ben Nevis* range and the hills above *Loch Lochy*, of which, as we approached the *Caledonian Canal* and came to a lock, we caught a glimpse. We changed horses at *Gairlochy* before crossing the canal, by the side of which flows the *Lochy*. The road ascends and goes along the western side high above the canal and river, commanding a splendid view of *Ben Nevis* and the surrounding range of hills, "*the Grampians.*" The road is, as all the roads here are, very good and most picturesque, winding through trees, with small and wretched but picturesque cottages with little bits of fields dotted here and there and with Highland cattle grazing about. It was again rainy and showery after we came to *Gairlochy*. We came down again to *Banavie*, the hotel at which seems excellent, and were at home by a quarter-past six. Beatrice and Jane took some tea in the dining-room, and then took a short walk in the grounds, coming in at seven. Wrote. It was still raining, but not blowing. Played after dinner on the piano with Beatrice, and then went up stairs, and Jane Churchill read.

Friday, September 12.

A most beautiful bright sunshiny day. After breakfast Mr. Newton, the artist, brought some lovely sketches. Sketched and painted, for the views are quite lovely, from my room. At eleven drove in the wagonette with Beatrice and Jane Churchill, General Ponsonby being on the box with Brown, to and through *Fort William*, which is three miles and a half from *Inverlochy*, passing the celebrated *Ben Nevis Distillery*, which is two miles from here, and through a triumphal arch, just beyond the bridge over the *Nevis Burn*, by an old, very neglected graveyard, to the right, in which is an obelisk to McLachlan, a poet, and past the *Belford Hospital*, a neat building, built by a Mr. and Mrs. Belford; then a little farther on, entered the town, where there was a triumphal arch, the fort, now private property, belonging to Campbell of *Monzie.* Here Glencoe came to take the oath to King William III.

The town of *Fort William* is small, and, excepting where the good shops are, very dirty, with a very poor population, but all very friendly and enthusiastic. There are four churches (Established, Free Church, Episcopalian, and Roman Catholic). We drove on along *Loch Eil* (called *Loch Linnhe* below *Corran* ferry) a mile, and turned at *Achintee,* and down to old *Inverlochy Castle*, which is nearer to *Fort William* than the new castle. We got out to look at the ruin, but it is uninteresting, as there is so little of it and literally nothing to see. About a quarter of a mile from the house we got out and walked; home by half-past twelve.

Friday, September 12.

At a quarter-past three, the day being most splendid, started with Beatrice and Jane Churchill, the two gentlemen following in the wagonette (with Charlie Thomson on the box), and drove by *Banavie*, the same road we came home yesterday, as far as where we crossed the canal at *Gairlochy*— only, instead of going down to it, we kept above, and went to the left: it is a beautiful road, coming in sight of *Loch Lochy*, which, with its wooded banks and blue hills, looked lovely. Leaving the main road, we turned into a beautiful drive along the river *Arkaig*, in Lochiel's property, reminding one very much of the *Trossachs.*

As you approach *Achnacarry*, which lies rather low, but is surrounded by very fine trees, the luxuriance of the tangled woods, surmounted by rugged hills, becomes finer and finer till you come to *Loch Arkaig*, a little over half a mile from the house.   This is a very lovely loch, reminding one of *Loch Katrine*, especially where there is a little pier, from which we embarked on board a very small but nice screw steamer which belongs to Cameron of *Lochiel*.

He received us (wearing his kilt and plaid) just above the pier, and we all went on board the little steamer.   The afternoon was beautiful, and lit up the fine scenery to the greatest advantage.   We went about half way up the *Loch* (which is fourteen miles long), as we had not time to go farther, to the disappointment of Lochiel, who said it grew wilder and wilder higher up.   To the left (as we went up) is the deer forest; to the right he has sheep.

Both sides are beautifully wooded all along the lower part of the fine hills which rise on either side, and the trees are all oaks, which Cameron of *Lochiel* said were the "weed of the country," and all natural—none were planted.   A good many grow up all the hollows and fissures of the hills and rocks.   Right ahead, where we turned, was seen a fine conical-shaped hill called *Scour-na-nat*, and to the left *Glenmally*, to the north *Muir Logan,* and *Giusach* and *Gerarnan* on either side.   Before we came to the turning we three had our tea, which was very refreshing.   I tried to sketch a little, but the sun shone so strongly that I could not do much.

Mr. Cameron, who was with Lord Elgin in *China*, came and explained everything, and talked very pleasantly.   His father had to let this beautiful place, and Lord Malmesbury had it for fifteen years.   The Cannings used to go there, and I often heard Lady Canning speak of its beauties, and saw many pretty sketches which she made there.   Thirteen years ago his father died, and he has lived there ever since. Alfred was there in 1863.

It was, as General Ponsonby observed afterwards, a striking scene.   "There was Lochiel," as he said, "whose great-granduncle had been the real moving cause of the rising of 1745—for without him Prince Charles would not have made the attempt—showing your Majesty (whose great-great-grandfather he had striven to dethrone) the scenes made historical by Prince Charlie's wanderings.   It was a scene one could not look on unmoved."

Yes; and *I* feel a sort of reverence in going over these

scenes in this most beautiful country, which I am proud to call my own, where there was such devoted loyalty to the family of my ancestors—for Stuart blood is in my veins, and I am *now* their representative, and the people are as devoted and loyal to me as they were to that unhappy race.

We landed at the little pier, but walked over the small bridges (the carriages following)—on which a piper was playing—a few hundred yards to a gate (on the side opposite to that by which we came), where we got into the carriages again. We drove through a beautiful road called the *Dark Mile*—dark from the number of very fine trees which overhang it, while on the left it is overshadowed by beetling rocks with a rich tangled undergrowth of bracken and heather, etc. The heather grows very richly and fully in these parts, and in thick tufts. We saw here the cave in which Prince Charles Edward was hid for a week. We came out of this road at the end of *Loch Lochy*, which looked lovely in the setting sun, and drove along the water's edge till nearly where we joined the road by which we had come. It is all Lochiel's for a long way—a splendid possession.

And now came the finest scene of all—*Ben Nevis* and its surrounding high hills, and the others in the direction of *Loch Laggan*, all pink and glowing in that lovely after-glow *Alpenglühen*), which you see in the *Alps*. It was glorious. It grew fainter and fainter till the hills became blue and then gray, and at last it became almost quite dark before we reached *Banavie*, and we only got home at a quarter-past eight. As we drove out I sketched *Ben Nevis* from the carriage.

Quantities of letters. The post comes in after eight and goes out at ten, which is very inconvenient.

Our usual little dinner only, about nine.

Saturday, September 13.

Another splendid morning, of which we were very glad, as we meant to go to *Glencoe*, which was the principal object of our coming here. Our nice little breakfast as usual. Sketching.

At eleven we started, just as yesterday. Francie Clark * and Cannon going on the box of the second carriage. We drove through *Fort William*, on as we did yesterday morning by *Achintee*, and down the eastern side of *Loch Eil*, which was beautifully lit, the distant hills intensely blue. The cot-

---

* My Highland servant since 1870, and cousin to Brown.

tages along the roadside here and there hardly deserve the name, and are indeed mere hovels—so low, so small, so dark with thatch, and over-grown with moss and heather, that if you did not see smoke issuing from them and some very ragged dirty old people, and very scantily clothed, dishevelled children, you could not believe they were meant for human habitations.   They are very picturesque and embedded in trees, with the heathery and grassy hills rising above them, and reminded me of *Switzerland.*   There were poor little fields, fuller of weeds than of corn, much laid by the wet, and frequently a " calvie " or " coo " of the true shaggy Highland character was actually feeding in them.

The road, which runs close above the loch, commands an excellent view of the fine noble hills on the opposite side of the loch.   At *Corran Ferry** (eleven miles) are seen across the loch *Conaglen,* and *Ardgour,* Lord Morton's, at the entrance of a very fine glen.   He has bought a large property in these parts, which formerly belonged to the Macleans. South of *Corran Ferry* the loch is called *Loch Linnhe,* and the road turns inland westwards, soon after passing up along the shore of *Loch Leven,* which is, in fact, also an arm of the sea. After three miles we passed a few cottages called *Onich,* the high hills of *Glencoe* beginning already to show.   All was so bright and green, with so much wood, and the loch so calm, that one was in perpetual admiration of the scenery as one went along.   Four miles more from *Corran Ferry* brought us to *Ballachulish* at a little before one o'clock.   The situation of the hotel—the large one—on the opposite side, at the foot of the hills close to the ferry, is extremely pretty.   There was a smaller and less handsome inn on the north side, by which we had come.   Here we got out, after all our things—cloaks, bags, luncheon baskets, etc.—had been removed from the carriage, which we had to leave, and walked down to the boat.   The small number of people collected there were very quiet and well behaved.   Beatrice and Jane Churchill and I, with General Ponsonby and Brown, got into the boat, and two Highlanders in kilts rowed us across to the sound of pipes.   On the opposite side there were more people, but all kept at a very respectful distance and were very loyal.   A lady (a widow), Lady Beresford, who owns the slate quarries, and her daughter, in deep mourning, were at the landing-place, and one of them presented me with a bouquet.   We got at once into two carriages (hired, but very fair ones),

* Here Alfred got his very favorite Skye terrier Corran.

Beatrice, Jane, and I in a sort of low barouche, Brown on the box. We had a pair of horses, which went very well. The two gentlemen occupied the second carriage. The drive from *Ballachulish*, looking both ways, is beautiful, and very Alpine. I remember Louise, and also Alice, making some sketches from here when they went on a tour in 1865.

We went on, winding under the high green hills, and entered the village of *Ballachulish*, where the slate quarries are, and which is inhabited by miners. It was very clean and tidy—a long, continuous, straggling, winding street, where the poor people, who all looked very clean, had decorated every house with flowers and bunches or wreaths of heather and red cloth. Emerging from the village we entered the *Pass of Glencoe*, which at the opening is beautifully green, with trees and cottages dotted about along the verdant valley. There is a farm belonging to a Mrs. Mac-Donald, a descendant of one of the unfortunate massacred MacDonalds. The *Cona* flows along the bottom of the valley, with green " haughs," where a few cattle are to be seen, and sheep, which graze up some of the wildest parts of this glorious glen. A sharp turn in the rough, very winding, and in some parts precipitous road, brings you to the finest, wildest, and grandest part of the pass. Stern, rugged, precipitous mountains with beautiful peaks and rocks piled high one above the other, two and three thousand feet high, tower and rise up to the heavens on either side, without any signs of habitation, except where, halfway up the pass, there are some trees, and near them heaps of stones on either side of the road, remains of what once were homes, which tell the bloody, fearful tale of woe. The place itself is one which adds to the horror of the thought that such a thing could have been conceived and committed on innocent sleeping people. How and whither could they fly? Let me hope that William III. knew nothing of it.

To the right, not far on, is seen what is called *Ossian's Cave;* but it must be more than a thousand feet above the glen, and one cannot imagine how any one could live there, as they pretend that Ossian did. The violence of the torrents of snow and rain, which come pouring down, has brought quantities of stone with them, which in many parts cover the road and make it very rough. It reminds me very much of the *Devil's Bridge, St. Gothard,* and the *Göschenen Pass,* only that is higher but not so wild. When we came to the top, which is about ten miles from *Ballachulish*, we stopped and got out, and we three sat down under a low wall, just below the road, where we had a splendid view of those peculiarly fine wild-looking peaks, which I sketched.

Their Gaelic names are *Na tri Peathraichean* (*the Three Sisters*), but in English they are often called "*Faith, Hope, and Charity.*"

We sat down on the grass (we three) on our plaids, and had our luncheon, served by Brown and Francie, and then I sketched. The day was most beautiful and calm. Here, however—here, in this complete solitude, we were spied upon by impudently inquisitive reporters, who followed us everywhere : but one in particular (who writes for some of the Scotch papers) lay down and watched with a telescope and dodged me and Beatrice and Jane Churchill, who were walking about, and was most impertinent when Brown went to tell him to move, which Jane herself had thought of doing. However, he did go away at last, and Brown came back saying he thought there would have been a fight : for when Brown said quite civilly that the Queen wished him to move away, he said he had quite as good a right to remain there as the Queen. To this Brown answered very strongly, upon which the impertinent individual asked, " Did he know who he was ? " and Brown answered he did, and that " the highest gentlemen in *England* would not dare to do what he did, much less a reporter "—and he must move on, or he would give him something more. And the man said, " Would he dare say that before those other men (all reporters) who were coming up ? " And Brown answered " Yes," he would before " anybody who did not behave as he ought." More strong words were used ; but the others came up and advised the man to come away quietly, which he finally did. Such conduct ought to be known. We were there nearly an hour, and then began walking down a portion of the steep part.

The parish clergyman, Mr. Stewart, who had followed us up, and who had met us when we arrived at *Ballachulish*, explained the names of the hills, and showed the exact place of the dreadful massacre. He also said that there were many Episcopalians there from the old Jacobite feeling, and also Roman Catholics.

There was seldom frost in the glen, he said, but there was a good deal of snow.

A short distance from where Ossian's cave is shown there is a very small lake called *Loch Treachtan*, through which the

Cona flows; and at the end of this was a cottage with some cattle and small pieces of cultivated land. We drove down on our return at a great pace. As we came through *Ballachulish* the post-boy suddenly stopped, and a very respectable, stout-looking old Highlander stepped up to the carriage with a small silver quaich, out of which he said Prince Charles had drunk, and also my dearest Albert in 1847, and begged that I would do the same. A table, covered with a cloth and with a bottle on it, was on the other side of the road. I felt I could hardly refuse, and therefore tasted some whiskey out of it, which delighted the people who were standing around. His name, we have since heard, is W. A. Cameron.

We drove to the same small pier where we had disembarked, and were rowed over again by two Highlanders in kilts. The evening was so beautiful and calm that the whole landscape was reflected in the lake. There is a high, conical-shaped hill, the commencement of the *Pass of Glencoe*, which is seen best from here; and the range of hills above *Ardgour* and *Corran Ferry* opposite was of the most lovely blue. The whole scene was most beautiful. Three pipers played while we rowed across, and the good people, who were most loyal and friendly, cheered loudly. We re-entered our carriages, and drove off at a quick pace. When we were on the shores of *Loch Eil* again, we stopped (but did not get out) to take tea, having boiled the kettle. The setting sun cast a most glorious light, as yesterday, on *Ben Nevis* and the surrounding hills, which were quite pink, and gave a perfectly crimson hue to the heather on the moor below. The sky was pink and lilac and pale green, and became richer and richer, while the hills in the other direction, over *Fort William*, were of a deep .blue. It was wonderfully beautiful, and I was still able to make, or at least begin, a sketch of the effect of it, after we came home at a quarter to seven, from Beatrice's window.

Resting and writing. Leopold has had far less fine weather for his excursion than we have had.

Sunday, September 14.

It was dull, and there had been some rain, but it cleared, and the day was fine, though not bright.

At twenty minutes past eleven walked out with Beatrice. We walked first to look at the kitchen garden, which is large, and has some very nice hot-houses with good grapes. From here we went out by the lodge, meeting not a soul, and past the farm, going down a road on the left to a small burn, over

which there is a foot-bridge.   Finding, however, that it only
led to a keeper's house, Brown advised us to return, which
we accordingly did, coming by the back and the stables, and in
at ten minutes to one o'clock.   Rested, wrote, and then read
prayers with Beatrice, and part of Mr. Campbell's * sermon,
which Beatrice was so pleased with that she copied it entirely.
Luncheon as usual.   Painted and finished the view looking
towards *Fort William.*

At five drove out with Beatrice and Jane Churchill in the
wagonette.   We drove past the distillery; and then just beyond the bridge, which must be very little over two miles
from *Inverlochy,* we turned off the main road.   We drove up
for four miles along the *Nevis,* a fine rapid burn rolling over
large stones and almost forming cascades in one or two places,
under fine trees with very steep green hills rising on either
side, and close under and along the base of *Ben Nevis,* which
rose like a giant above us.   It was splendid!   Straight before
us the glen seemed to close; halfway up we came to a large
farm, the drive to which is under an avenue of ash trees.   But
there is no other habitation beyond this of any kind; and
soon after the trees become fewer and fewer, though still a
good many grow at the burnside and up the gullies of the
hills.   Sheep were grazing at a great height.   The road became so rough and bad that we got out and walked almost a
mile, but could go no farther.   We were delighted with the
solemn solitude and grandeur of *Glen Nevis;* it is almost
finer than *Glencoe.*   There was no one when we first entered
the glen, but as we walked back we met several people coming out to look.   After getting into the carriage again, I
stopped a little to take a rough sketch.

The farm belongs to Mrs. Campbell of *Monzie,* only
daughter of the late Sir Duncan Cameron of *Fassifern,* who
owns a good deal of *Ben Nevis.*   Every hill has a name, but
I cannot remember them, though I have them written down
by the keeper at *Inverlochy.*   As it was still a little too early
to go home, we drove as far as the Fort and turned back,
coming in at a quarter past seven.   Writing.   The post comes
in at a most inconvenient hour, a little past eight.

Dinner as usual.   My favorite collie Noble is always down
stairs when we take our meals, and was so good, Brown making him lie on a chair or couch, and he never attempted to
come down without permission, and even held a piece of cake
in his mouth without eating it, till told he might.   He is the

* The newly appointed minister at Crathie.

most "biddable" dog I ever saw, and so affectionate and kind; if he thinks you are not pleased with him, he puts out his paws, and begs in such an affectionate way.

Jane Churchill read.

Monday, September 15.

The mist hung about the hills, but the sun struggled through. It was very mild and became beautiful. We decided to go up *Glenfinnan* and to lunch out. Painted and finished two other sketches looking up *Loch Eil* and towards *Banavie*, and then wrote, after which at a quarter to twelve took a short turn in the grounds with Beatrice.

At twenty minutes to one started with Beatrice and Jane Churchill in the sociable (Brown going each day of course with us on the box), the two gentlemen following (with Francie Clark and Charlie Thomson), and drove past *Banavie* through *Corpach* and up *Loch Eil.* When we had come to the head of the loch, the road turned towards the right, winding along through verdant valleys, with that noble range of *Moidart* before you, rather to the left. In one valley, which became very narrow after passing a large meadow in which they were making hay, we turned into a narrow sort of defile, with the stream of the *Finnan* flowing on as slowly as an English river, with trees and fir trees on the rocks, and unlike anything I had seen in *Scotland*, and then you come at once on *Loch Shiel* (a freshwater loch), with fine very high rugged hills on either side. It runs down twenty miles.

At the head of the loch stands a very ugly monument to Prince Charles Edward, looking like a sort of lighthouse surmounted by his statue, and surrounded by a wall. Here it was that he landed when he was brought by Macdonald of *Borradale*—whose descendant, now Macdonald of *Glenaladale*, has a house here (the only habitation to be seen)—to wait for the gathering of the clans. When Prince Charlie arrived at the spot where the monument stands, which is close to the loch and opposite to *Glenfinnan* (the road we came going past it and on up a hill to *Arisaig*, twenty-five miles farther on), he found only a dozen peasants, and thought he had been betrayed, and he sat down with his head in his hands. Suddenly the sound of the pipes aroused him, and he saw the clans coming down *Glenfinnan.* Soon after the Macdonalds appeared, and in the midst of a cheering host the Marquis of Tullibardine (Duke of Atholc but for his attainder) unfurled the banner of King James. This was in

August, 1745. In 1746 poor Prince Charles was a fugitive hiding in the mountains on the sides of *Loch Arkaig* and *Loch Shiel.* As we suddenly came upon *Loch Shiel* from the narrow glen, lit up by bright sunshine, with the fine long loch and the rugged mountains, which are about three thousand feet high, rising all around, no habitation or building to be seen except the house of *Glenaladale*, which used to be an inn, and a large picturesque Catholic church, reminding one, from its elevated position to the right and above the house, of churches and convents abroad, I thought I never saw a lovelier or more romantic spot, or one which told its history so well. What a scene it must have been in 1745! And here was *I*, the descendant of the Stuarts and of the very king whom Prince Charles sought to overthrow, sitting and walking about quite privately and peaceably.

We got out and scrambled up a high hillock off the road where I lunched with Beatrice and Jane Churchill and then sketched, but did not attempt to color. We walked about a little, and then came down to the road to speak to Mr. Macdonald of *Glenaladale*, whom General Ponsonby had been to speak to, and who had never seen me. He is a stout, robust-looking Highlander of about thirty and a widower. He is a Catholic, as are all the people in this district. The priest is his uncle, and lives with him. He showed me some curious relics of Charles Edward. An old-fashioned, strange silver snuff "mull" which had been given by him to Macdonald's ancestor, with the dates 1745 and 1746 engraved on it, for at *Borradale* Prince Charlie slept for the last time in *Scotland;* a watch which had belonged to him, and a ring into which some of his fair hair had been put, were also shown.

This is the district called *Moidart*, and from the highest hills the *Isle of Skye* is seen distinctly. Lord Morton's property comes up close to *Loch Shiel*, and to the right are *Lochiel*, etc., and Macdonald of *Glenaladale's* in front, at the head of the loch. The family used to live at *Borradale* near *Arisaig*, but acquired *Glenaladale* from the former Macdonalds of *Glenaladale* who emigrated to *Prince Edward's Island* after the Forty-five.

Beatrice, Jane Churchill, and Brown went up with Mr. Macdonald to the top of the monument, but said the ascent was very awkward and difficult. General Ponsonby had been into the church, and said it was very expensively and handsomely decorated, but we have since heard there are only about fifty people in the neighborhood. We left this beautiful spot about half-past four, having spent two hours there. The evening was not so bright as on Friday and Saturday, and there was no after-glow on the hills, *Ben Nevis* having its top covered with mist, as it often has. The horses were tired, and went rather slowly. I observed a flower here, which I have not seen with us at *Balmoral*, viz., instead of the large white daisies *—"Marguerites," as the French call them, and of which such numbers are seen in the fields in *England*—there is a large yellow one,† just the same in form, only the petals are bright yellow.

The heather, as I before observed, is of a very full and rich kind, and, as we drove along, we saw it on the old walls, growing in the loveliest tufts. We met those dreadful reporters, including the man who behaved so ill on Saturday, as we were coming back. We got home at twenty minutes past six. Had some tea. Wrote and put everything in order. All had been settled about money to be given, etc. Our last nice little dinner, which I regretted. Came up directly after and wrote.

Tuesday, September 16.

Had to get up by seven, and Beatrice and I breakfasted at a quarter to eight. The morning was fine.

The real name of the place used to be *Torlundy*, which is the name of the "lochie," or "tarn," below the house, in the middle of which there is a little island on which there are ducks. The property, which is very large, sixty-four miles in extent, was purchased from the late Duke of Gordon by the late Lord Abinger, who began a house, but it was burnt down; the present Lord built this one, in fact, only ten years ago, and added to it since. He has called it *Inverlochy Castle*, after the old fortress, which is supposed to have belonged to the Pictish kings, but the present ruin is thought to date from the time of Edward I. The Marquis of Montrose defeated the Marquis of Argyle there in 1645, an incident described in Sir Walter Scott's "Legend of Montrose."

At a quarter-past eight we left *Inverlochy Castle*, where we had spent very pleasant days. The gentlemen had gone on before.

We drove to *Banavie*, where a good many people were assembled, and stepped on board the steamer which was on the *Caledonian Canal*. Here were Lord and Lady Abinger, whom I thanked very much for their kindness. I left an

---

* *Chrysanthemum Leucanthemum*, White ox-eye daisy.
† *Chrysanthemum segetum*, Yellow ox-eye or corn marigold.

9

illustrated copy of my book and prints of Albert's and my portraits at *Inverlochy* for Lord Abinger.   She is an American lady from the *Southern States*, a Miss Macgruder, and they have five children, of whom one only is a boy.   They left the steamer, and we began moving.   The steamer is called the "Gondolier."   It is built on the same principle as the one we had on *Loch Lomond*, with a fine large cabin with many windows, almost a deck cabin (though it is down one flight of steps), which extends through the ship with seats below, open at the sides far forward.   In this large cabin sixty-two people can dine.   We remained chiefly on deck.   We steamed gently along under the road by which we had driven from *Gairlochy* and *Achnacarry*, Lochiel's to the left or west, and Lord Abinger's to the right.   *Ben Nevis*, unfortunately, was hid in the mist, and the top invisible, which we hear is very generally the case.

We came to one lock, and then shortly afterwards to *Gair-lochy*, after which you enter *Loch Lochy*.   The *Caledonian Canal* is a very wonderful piece of engineering, but travelling by it is very tedious.   At each lock people crowded up close to the side of the steamer.   As the river rises from *Banavie* to *Loch Oich* (which succeeds *Loch Lochy*), the canal has to raise the vessels up to that point, and again to lower them from *Loch Oich* to *Inverness*.   The vessel, on entering the lock from the higher level, is enclosed by the shutting of the gates.   The sluices of the lower gates are raised by small windlasses (it was amusing to see the people, including the crew of the steamer, who went on shore to expedite the operation, which is not generally done, run round and round to move these windlasses), and holes are thus opened at the bottom of the lower gates, through which the water flows till the water in the lock sinks to the lowest level.   The lower gates are then opened, as the water is on the lowest level, while the upper gates keep back the water above.   The same process raises the ships in the lock which ascend.   About five or six feet can be raised or depressed in this manner at each lock.   (I have copied this from an account General Ponsonby wrote for me.)

As we entered *Loch Lochy*, which looked beautiful, we saw where *Loch Arkaig* lay, though it was hid from us by high ground.   The hills which rise from *Loch Lochy* are excellent pasture for sheep, but the lower parts are much wooded. After eight miles' sail on *Loch Lochy* we came to *Loch Oich*, which is entered by another lock at *Laggan*.   Here Mr. and

Mrs. Ellice (who is a first cousin of the Greys) were waiting, and came on board. They had wished me to get out and drive round their fine place, *Invergarry*, to rejoin the steamer at the next lock, but I declined, preferring to remain quietly on board, though the process of going through the locks is slow and necessarily tedious. It is nervous work to steer, for there is hardly a foot to spare on either side. Mrs. Ellice went on shore again, having given us some fine grapes, but Mr. Ellice remained on board till the next lock, *Cullochy*. A road much shaded runs along the side of the loch, and here we passed the small monument by its side, put over the well into which a number of heads of some of the Mac-Donalds, who had murdered two of their kinsmen of *Keppoch*, were thrown after they had been killed in revenge for this act, by order of MacDonald of the Isles. It was erected in 1812. We next came to the old ruined castle of *Invergarry*, embosomed in trees, close to which, but not in sight, is Mr. Ellice's new house. He has an immense deal of property here on both sides. The hills rise high, and one con-ically shaped one called *Ben Tigh* towers above the rest. At *Cullochy* Mr. Ellice left the steamer. Mr. Brewster, formerly Lord Chancellor of *Ireland* and nearly eighty years old, was standing on the shore here. Francie and one of the police-men got out with good Noble, and walked to meet us again at *Fort Augustus*. While we were stopping to go through one of the locks, a poor woman came and brought us a jug of milk and oat-cake, which with their usual hospitality the country people constantly offer.

After this, and at about ten minutes past twelve, Beatrice, Jane Churchill, and I went below and had some hot luncheon. The people from the locks looked down upon us, but it was unavoidable. We had now reached *Fort Augustus*, where there was again some delay and a great many people, and where there was a triumphal arch. Here on this very day thirty-six years ago my beloved Albert passed, and he saw poor Macdonald the Jäger here, and took a liking to him from his appearance, and, being in want of a Jäger, inquired after him and engaged him. He was keeper to Lord Digby and Colonel Porter then, and brought some game for dearest Albert from them, and Albert was greatly struck by his good looks. He was very handsome, especially in the kilt, which he habitually wore.

There had been a heavy shower, but it was over when we came up on deck again. We entered *Loch Ness* here. It is twenty-four miles long and broad, the banks wooded, with many pretty places on them. We passed *Invermorriston* in *Glen Morriston*, the seat of Sir G. Brooke Middleton, formerly Grant property. (So many of the finest, largest estates in the *Highlands* have passed into English hands, chiefly by purchase, but also often by inheritance.) *Foyers*, the celebrated falls, which are much visited, could just be seen, but not the falls themselves. Everywhere, where there were a few houses or any place of note, people were assembled and cheered.

Next, to the left comes the very fine old ruin of *Castle Urquhart*, close upon the *Lochan Rocks*, where there were again a great many people. The Castle has stood several sieges, and one in particular in the fourteenth century in the reign of Edward 1. It belongs to Lord Seafield (head of the Grants), who has a very large property here, and whose own shooting-place, *Balmacaan*, is up in the glen just beyond. The fine mountain of *Mealfourvonie* rises above it. It is two thousand seven hundred feet high, but the peak alone is seen from here. I tried to sketch a little, but in vain, the wind in my face was so troublesome.

At about twenty minutes to four (or half-past three) we passed *Dochfour House*, Mr. Baillie's, which I think stands rather low, and in which Albert passed this night twenty-six years ago. A few minutes more brought us to *Dochgarroch*, quite a quiet place, but where a good many people had assembled. We waited to see every one and all our luggage landed and packed in and off before we stepped on shore. It was an amusing sight. There must have been two or three carriages besides ours. The last to drive off was the one in which Morgan, Maxted, and Lizzie Stewart * got, with Francie Clark and Noble on the box. Mr. Baillie and Lady Georgiana, whom I had not seen for long, were at the end of the landing platform, as well as Mr. Evan Baillie and Mrs. Colville, their son and daughter. Two little girls put down bunches of flax for me to walk upon, which it seems is an old Highland custom. There is a small village where we landed. Lady Georgiana Baillie is quite an old lady, aunt of the Duke of Manchester, and granddaughter of the celebrated Duchess of Gordon.

Beatrice, Jane, and I got into a hired (not very beautiful) open landau (on the rumble of which Brown sat, as in crowds it is much safer to have a person close behind you) with a

* My second wardrobe maid since 1879, a native of Balmoral.

pair of post-horses and a postilion. In the second carriage went General Ponsonby, Emilie Dittweiler (sitting next to him), Dr. Fox, and Annie, every available place being necessary. We were escorted by the 7th Dragoon Guards, which was thought better on account of the great crowds in *Inverness*, where no Sovereign had been seen since my poor ancestress Queen Mary.

The mixture of half state and humble travelling (we being in our common travelling dresses) was rather amusing.

The evening was beautiful, and *Inverness* looked extremely well on the blue *Moray Frith*. We passed a magnificent building, which is the country Lunatic Asylum. We had to drive six miles to the town, through a small portion of which only we passed, and had to drive quickly, as it was late. The streets were full of decorations and arches, and lined with volunteers. Great order prevailed, and the people were most enthusiastic. The fine-looking old Provost was there, and the Master of Lovat, who walked up along the station with us. A great squeeze, which Brown, having a great heap of cloaks etc. to carry, had some difficulty in getting through. But every one, including the dog, got safe in, and we travelled by train as before. We went the same way as last year, but never stopped till we got to *Keith*, where last time our door got wrong. After this, about six, we had some warm tea and cold meat, which was very refreshing. A fine evening.

We reached *Ballater* at five minutes to nine, and started at once in the open landau and four, preceded by the outrider with the lamp. There were a few drops of rain, but very slight. At twenty minutes to ten we reached *Balmoral* safely, very thankful that all had gone off so well.

HOME-COMING OF THEIR ROYAL HIGHNESSES THE DUKE AND
DUCHESS OF EDINBURGH, AUGUST, 1874.

Saturday, August 29, 1874.

AT a quarter to two started in the landau and four with Beatrice and Lady Abercromby, Brown in full dress on the rumble. It was raining, so we kept the carriage shut, but there were decided symptoms of clearing, and by the time we reached *Ballater* the sun began to shine, and the rain ceased as I got out.

The train with Alfred and Marie had already arrived, and Marie got out as I advanced. Alfred was already out of the carriage. I kissed them, and then, with Marie, Alfred, and Beatrice, got in again, the carriage being open, and it was very fine. Marie wore a brown travelling dress with a hat. When we reached the bridge we went slowly. The *Ballater* company of volunteers, to the number of thirty (kilted in Farquharson tartan), were next it, and from here to the arch, and beyond it, stood all our people in full dress with their families, and all the tenants of the three estates with theirs, also the ladies and gentlemen. The pipers walked in front playing, and our keepers and others, who wore full dress, on either side (Brown remaining in his place on the carriage), followed by all the other people.

In this way we proceeded through the arch up to *Balmoral*, just as when Helena arrived, only then there were fewer people. Leopold was in his carriage. We got out at the door of the Castle, and then Dr. Robertson proposed the health of Alfred and Marie, which was drunk by all with cheers. Then two reels were danced, after which we took Marie and Alfred to their rooms down stairs, and sat with them while they had tea.

VISIT TO INVERARAY, SEPTEMBER, 1875.

Tuesday, September 21, 1875.

WE had a family dinner at twenty minutes to nine. At a quarter past ten left *Balmoral* with Beatrice and Jane Church‑ill, Brown on the rumble. We reached *Ballater* by eleven, when we took the railroad. General Ponsonby and Sir W. Jenner met us there. Emilie, Annie, Morgan (for Beatrice), Francie Clark, and the footmen, Cannon, Charlie Thomson, and Heir, went in attendance, as well as Baldry and three men of the police. The horses (six) with Bourner, Hutch‑inson, and Goddard with the luggage, had gone on in ad‑vance. We started immediately, and very soon after lay down. We went steadily and slowly, but I did not sleep very well.

INVERARAY, *Wednesday, September* 22.

At eight we reached *Tyndrum*, a wild, picturesque. and desolate place in a sort of wild glen with green hills rising around. Here we breakfasted in the train, Brown having had the coffee heated which we had brought made with us, and some things coming from the nice-looking hotel. The morning was beautiful, just a little mist on the highest hills, which cleared off. There are a few straggling houses and a nice hotel at this station, where we got out and where Lord and Lady Breadalbane met us, as this is his property. The day was beautiful.

We got into the sociable (that is, Beatrice, Jane Churchill, and I) with a pair of posthorses, Brown and Francie Clark on the box, the two gentlemen and four maids in a wagonette following, and further behind the unavoidable luggage with the footmen, etc. The road lay up a broad glen, with green hills on either side, on one of which are lead mines belonging to Lord Breadalbane. It was very winding, very rough, and continually up and down, and we went very slowly. Looking back, behind *Tyndrum* was a fine range of hills which are in the forest of the *Black Mount*. Passed the entrance of a broad glen with many trees called *Glenorchy* (the second title of Breadalbane), and saw all along where the railway is being made. A small stream flows at the bottom. To the left we saw *Ben Luie*; then as we descended, the country became more and more beautiful, with trees and copsewood sprinkled about, till we came to *Dalmally*, lying embosomed in trees, with *Ben Cruachan* and its adjacent range rising close before us, with the bluest shadows and tints on all the heights, and the sky pure and bright with a hot sun, though a good deal of air. Looking back we still saw the other green hills from which we had come.

As it approaches *Dalmally* the road goes under trees till you reach the inn, which stands quite alone. The church is beautifully situated at the bottom of the glen, and is surrounded by trees. There was no large crowd here, and the people behaved very well. *Dalmally* is thirteen miles from *Tyndrum*. Four horses were put on here to drag us up the first hill, which was long and high, and brought us in view of *Loch Awe*, which looked beautiful. Here the leaders were taken off. *Loch Awe* extends back a good way, and we could just see *Kilchurn Castle*, of historic celebrity, and the beautiful head of the loch with high hills on the right, and the islands of *Innishail* and *Ardchone*, besides many smaller ones. On the first-named of these is said to be buried an ancestor of the Argylls. The loch is thirty miles in length, and as it stretches out and widens, the hills become much flatter. We drove quite round the head of *Loch Awe*, then passed *Cladich*, and here the ground became very broken, and high hills were seen in the background, towering above the nearer ones. Bracken, with birch and oak, etc., grow profusely among the green hills and rocks, much as they do near *Inverlochy, Loch Eil,* etc. Here and there were small knots of people, but not many. About five or six miles before *Inveraray,* at a place called *Crais-na-Schleacaich,* at the foot of *Glen Aray,* where the Duke's property begins, four of our own horses were waiting, and here dear Louise and Lorne met us, looking pleased and well. Lorne rode, and dear Louise got into her pony-carriage and drove after us. We soon after came to an arch with a Gaelic inscription—" Ceud mille Failte do'n Bhan Rhighinn do Inerara " (A hundred thousand welcomes to the Queen to *Inveraray*). A very stout tenant's wife, Mrs. McArthur, presented me with a nosegay, which a child she held in her arms gave me.

On we went along *Glen Aray,* the road as we approached *Inveraray Castle* being bordered on either side by trees. When we reached the gate there were two halberdiers, whilst others were posted at intervals along the approach, dressed in Campbell tartan kilts with brown coats turned back with red, and bonnets with a black cock's tail and bog-myrtle (the Campbell badge). With them were also the pipers of the volunteers. In front of the house the volunteers in kilts and red jackets, and the artillery volunteers in blue and silver, of whom Lorne is the colonel, were drawn up, and a good many spectators were assembled. The Duke and Duchess of Argyll and their six girls were at the door; the outside steps are now under glass and made into a sort of conservatory.

The Duke and Duchess took us up stairs at once to our rooms, part of which are Louise's; very comfortable, not large but cheerful, and having a beautiful view of *Loch Fyne.* It was one when we arrived, and we lunched at two, only Louise, Beatrice, and Lorne, in a nice room (in fact the Duchess's drawing-room) with tapestry, at the foot of the stairs. Brown (who has attended me at all the meals since we came here) waited, helped by two or three of the Duke's people. After lunch we went into the large drawing-room, next door to where we had lunched in 1847, when Lorne was only two years old. And now I return, alas! without my beloved Husband, to find Lorne my son-in-law!

In the drawing-room I found Lord and Lady Dufferin (who are staying here), as well as Sir John and Lady Emma McNeill. She is the Duke's only sister, and he a very fine old man (now eighty), who was formerly my miniŝter in *Persia.* Went up stairs to rest and sketch the splendid *Ardkinglass Hills* from the window of the little turret which forms my dressing-room. Then had tea, and at half-past five drove out with Louise and Beatrice by the lodge called *Creitabhille,* through part of the wood or forest where the beeches are splendid, as also the spruces, on past *Ballachanooran,* by the upper road, green hills, trees, oaks, ferns, and broken ground all along, like at *Loch Eil,* past *Achnagoul,* a little village lying close under the hill, to the *Douglas Water,* a small rapid stream. Here we turned back and went along this pretty little mountain stream, past some cottages and a small farm, and then came upon the shore of *Loch Fyne,* the drive along which is lovely. As we drove, the setting sun bathed the hills in crimson,—they had been golden just before,—the effect was exquisite. Looking up and down the shores, the view was lovely, and the reflections on the calm surface of the lake most beautiful.

We drove back through the small town of *Inveraray,* which is close to the gates of the Castle, and looks pretty from my window with its small pier, where we landed in 1847, and near to which there is a curious old Celtic cross. There are two inns, three churches, and a jail, for it is a county town. On coming home we walked a little in the garden close to the house, and came in at ten minutes past seven. Resting. Writing. Dinner at half-past eight in the room in which we lunched. The Duke and Duchess, Louise, Beatrice, and Lady Churchill dined with me. Then went for a short while into the drawing-room, where, besides the family, which included Lord Colin, were Dr. MacGregor, Mr. Donald Macleod, and Mr. Storey (all clergymen staying in the house), and the following gentlemen: Lord Ardmillan (who was there for the assizes), Mr. Campbell, of *Stonefield* (Convener of the county of *Argyll*), Mr. and Mrs. Hector Macneal, of *Ugadale,* etc. Mr. Macneal showed me a brooch which had some resemblance to the *Brooch of Lorne,* and had been given by King Robert Bruce to one of his ancestors.

Thursday, September 23.

This sad anniversary, when my beloved sister was taken from me, whom I miss so continually, returns for the third time.

A fine morning. Breakfasted in my sitting-room at a quarter to ten with Louise and Beatrice. My sitting-room is generally Louise's bedroom, which had been specially arranged by her for me, and in the recess the Duchess had placed a picture of *Balmoral*, copied from A. Becker's picture. This opens into a small apartment, generally used as Lorne's dressing-room, in which my maid Annie sleeps and the two maids sit, next to which comes the bedroom, at the end of which is the nice cozy little turret-room with two windows, one of which looks on the loch with the very fine *Ardkinglass Range* in front, and the other on the front door, the bridge, and splendid trees. My dresser, Emilie Dittweiler, is next door to my bedroom, and Beatrice next to her in Louise's sitting-room.

At a little after eleven I walked out with Louise and Beatrice along the approach, and then turned up through the wood and up the lower walk of *Dunaquoich*, the hill opposite the house, which is wooded nearly to the top, on which is a tower, and walked along under magnificent trees, chiefly beeches and some very fine spruces, that reminded me of *Windsor Park* and *Reinhardtsbrunn*. We walked on some way, passed a well and a small cottage, where the poultry is kept, where there is a funny good-natured woman called Mrs. McNicholl, who kissed Louise's hand and knelt down when I came up, and said to Louise, when she heard I was coming, " How shall I speak to her ?" We went into the little cottage, where another old woman of eighty lives. She looked so nice and tidy with a clean white mutch. We then walked down and came back along the river, which flows quite close to the house into the sea, and is full of fish. We were in at twenty minutes to one. Luncheon at two, just like yesterday. The day was dull, but quite fair and clear. Drawing and painting.

At a quarter-past four drove out with Louise, Beatrice, and the Duchess, in my wagonette, driven by Bourner. After going for some distance the same way as yesterday afternoon, we turned into a wooded drive, leading to the *Glen of Essachosan*, where there are the most beautiful spruces, and some silver firs which reminded me in height and size of those on the road to *Eberstein*, near *Baden*, and on by what they call the *Queen's drive*, made for me in 1871, past *Lechkenvohr*, whence there is a fine view of the loch and surrounding hills, *Ben Een*, *Ben Buie*, etc. The road is very steep going down to the *Curling Pond* and *Black Bull Cottage*; then over *Car lonnan Bridge* down to some falls, and back along the approach to the *Dhu Loch*, under the avenue of fine old beeches which, joining as they do, almost form an aisle. Eleven, alas! were blown down two years ago : they were planted by the Marquis of Argyll two hundred years ago. You come rapidly upon the *Dhu Loch*, a small but very pretty loch—a complete contrast to our *Dhu Loch*, for this is surrounded by green and very wooded hills, with the extremely pretty and picturesque *Glen Shira* in the background, which is richly wooded. We drove along the right bank of the *Shira River*, up as far as the small farm of *Drum Lee*, most prettily situated on the hillside some way up, passing one or two other farms—one especially, a very strange old building. We took our (made) tea, and Elizabeth (the Duchess) greatly admired the convenient arrangement (viz. the bag into which cups, etc., are fitted), and then drove back the same way and along the shore road. Home at ten minutes to seven. A charming drive, but there was a very high and cold wind.

Louise, Beatrice, the Duchess of Argyll, Lord and Lady Dufferin, and Sir John and Lady Emma McNeill dined with me, as yesterday. Went again for a short while into the drawing-room, where the Duke presented some other people—the sheriff, Mr. T. Irvine of *Drum* (in *Aberdeenshire*), Mr. J. Malcolm of *Poltalloch* (a fine-looking man, whose son, a tall large man, dined here yesterday, and whose daughter has just married Mr. Gathorne Hardy's son), and Sir G. and Lady Home, who live just outside the town : he is sheriff-depute, and she a niece of Sir F. Grant. Went up stairs with Beatrice and Jane Churchill, Louise always remaining below.

Friday, September 24.

Raining and blowing. Breakfasted with my two dear daughters. The rain ceased, and at a little past twelve I walked with Louise and Beatrice up by the lodge at the stables, which are in the " *Cherry Park*," and looked at our horses and Louise's, and saw a little dog, the daughter of Louise's, poor old Frisky ; and then walked along at the back of the stables, where the trees are very fine—most splendid silver firs—and then back by the kitchen-garden and the straightest path, past a magnificent Scotch fir of great height and circumference. In at twenty minutes past one. It was dull and dark.

At a quarter-past five, after tea, started with Louise, Beatrice, and Jane Churchill in the rain, which turned to a heavy downpour. We drove up the way we had previously walked, by the private road, under trees the whole way, to *Lynn a*

Gluthen, the highest fall of the *Aray,* which is very pretty.
There we had to get out to walk over a wooden bridge, which
Louise said they did not like to drive over, and came back
by the high road.   By this time the weather had quite cleared,
and so we drove on past the inn of *Inveraray,* through a gate
which is always left open, and up what is called the " *Town
Avenue,*" consisting entirely of very old beeches joining over-
head and nearly a mile long, at the back of the town.   We
came back by the lime avenue in the deer park, and in by a
gate close to the pleasure-ground at half-past six.   The halberdiers, all tenants of the Duke, kept guard the whole day.
   We dined at a quarter-past eight on account of the ball—
only Louise, Beatrice, Jane Churchill, and I.   Went into the
drawing-room for a moment, where the Duke presented Sir
Donald Campbell of *Dunstaffnage* and his wife, and J. A.
Campbell of *New Inverawe (Loch Awe).* Sir Donald Campbell
is deputy-keeper of *Dunstaffnage Castle,* and wears a key in
consequence.   He is between forty and fifty, and wore a kilt,
as did also Malcolm of *Poltalloch* and the other gentlemen.
At a quarter-past ten we drove across to the temporary pa-
vilion, where the ball to the tenants was to take place.
Louise, Beatrice, and Jane Churchill went with me in the
Duke's coach.   The Duke, Lorne, and Colin received us,
and the Duchess and all the girls and the other ladies were
inside at the upper end on a raised platform, where we all
sat.   It is a very long and handsome room, I believe a hundred and thirty feet long, and was built at the time of Louise's
marriage.   It was handsomely decorated with flags, and
there were present between seven and eight hundred people
—tenants with their wives and families, and many people
from the town; but it was not like the Highland balls I have
been accustomed to, as there were many other dances besides
reels.   The band could not play reels (which were played by
the piper), and yet came from *Glasgow!* The ball began,
however, with a reel; then came a country dance, then another reel.   Louise danced a reel with Brown, and Beatrice
with one of the Duke's foresters; but the band could only
play a country dance tune for it.   Another reel with pipes,
in which Jane Churchill danced with Brown, and Francie
Clark with Annie (Mrs Macdonald, my wardrobe maid),
Louise and Beatrice dancing in another reel with one of the
other people and Mr. John Campbell.   Then came a " *schot-
tische,*" which seemed to be much liked there, and more reels,
and lastly a " *tempête,*" in which Louise and Beatrice danced.

In the early part a Gaelic song was sung by some of the people, including Mr. John Campbell. I remember some which were sung by the boatmen on *Loch Tay* in 1842. After the "*tempête*" we came away at nearly half-past twelve.

Saturday, September 25.

A pouring morning. Breakfast as usual with my two dear children—dear Louise so kind and attentive, so anxious I and all my people should be comfortable, thinking of everything. It cleared, and at half-past eleven I walked out with Louise (Beatrice walked with Jane Churchill and the girls) to the kennel, along the *River Aray*, which had risen a great deal since Thursday, when it was as low as possible. We went to the kennel and saw the dogs and the eagle; from here we went to the kitchen-garden, which is large. There are very fine peaches and a wonderful old laurel and thuja, which have spread to an immense size. Home at twenty minutes to one. Luncheon as before.

Louise introduced me to a good old lady, a Miss McGibbon, who was too ill to come out and see me; she patted Louise on the shoulder and said, " We are all so fond of the Princess; she is a great pet." Louise said, " Lorne was her great pet;" and she answered, "Yes; he is, and so you are a double pet." *

At ten minutes past four drove out with Louise, Beatrice, and the Duke in the wagonette, and took a charming drive, the afternoon being very fine and bright. We went out the same way we had been on Wednesday, and once or twice besides, along the avenue called *Ballachanovran,* by the deer park (a great many gates having to be opened, as they must be kept locked to prevent the deer getting out), and struck into the *Lochgilphead Road* beyond *Cromalt.* We then passed. as on the first day, *Dalchenna* and *Killean, Achnagoul* and *Achindrain.* The last two places are old Highland villages. where a common old practice, now fallen into disuse, continues, of which the Duke gave me the following account :—

In the *Highlands* of *Scotland* up to a comparatively recent date the old system of *village communities* prevailed as the common system of land tenure. Under this system the cultivators were collected into groups or villages, the cottages being all built close together on some one spot of the farm. The farm itself was divided into *pasture land* and *arable land.* The pasture land was held in *common* by all the families, and the

* She died soon after.

arable land was divided *by lot* every year, so that each family might get its turn or its chance of the better and the worse qualities of soil. This very rude system is quite incompatible with any improved culture, but is an extremely ancient one. Sir Henry Maine has lately published a very interesting little book on the subject, showing that it once prevailed all over *Europe*, and does still actually prevail over the greater part of *India*. It has now almost entirely disappeared in the *Highlands*, where such *crofters* or very small cultivators as remain are generally separate from each other—each living on his own *croft*—although there are still remaining many cases of pasture or hill land held in common among several crofters.

Achnagoul near *Inveraray*, is one of the old *primitive villages*, where all the houses are built close together, and where, as late as the year 1847, the old rude practice still held—that of an *annual casting of lots* for the patches of arable land into which the farm was divided. At that time there were sixteen families, and each of them cultivated perhaps twenty different patches of arable land separated from each other. About that year the families were persuaded with much difficulty to give up this old semi-barbarous system and to divide the arable land into fixed divisions, one being assigned to each tenant, so that he could cultivate on an improved system. But the village remains as it was, and is one of the comparatively few of that class which now remain in the *Highlands*.

They are said to be the only two villages of the kind in existence in the *Highlands*. The inhabitants are very exclusive, and hardly ever marry out of their own villages.

We went on between curious, rather low, grass hills on either side, some higher than others, and several of which have small lochs at the tops with excellent trout, as the Duke told us. He showed us some farms and other glens, and had something to say about each place. We next turned to the left, where we got into oak woods, passing some powder mills belonging to Sir G. Campbell, and a small village called *Cumlodden*, or rather a row of huts in which the people employed at the mills live, and from here turned to the village of *Furnace*, inhabited by the men who work the Duke's great quarries close to the sea, and which is so called from a number of furnaces which were used in the last century for smelting down lead brought from *England*. The Duke showed us one remaining, though in ruins, and we passed a quarry. The drive went by the shore of *Loch Fyne*. much reminding me of the drive along *Loch Eil* beyond *Banavie*, between trees on either side, oak, ash, beech, etc., with much underwood, hazel, bramble, etc., and we stopped at a point called *Pennymore*, where there is a small battery where Lorne's volunteers practise; and here the view, looking down the loch towards the sea and the *Kyles of Bute* with finely-shaped hills, was very beautiful. The more distant hills were those above *Ardrishaig.* I tried to sketch here after we had taken our tea. We went along by *Kenmore, Kilbryde,* and *Dalchenna* (again), and it was a lovely evening, with such soft tints on the distant hills, and the town in front backed by trees. I took another sketch (only very slight, in pencil) of this view from the Duchess's new school-house, called *Creggan's School.* We got home by half-past six. Besides our two daughters and the Duke and Duchess, Lady Dufferin and Colin Campbell dined with me. Went as usual into the drawing-room for a little while, and then up stairs to my room. Beatrice remained with Jane and me.

Sunday, September 26.

The morning was very wet, so decided after our usual nice breakfast not to go out, but wrote, etc. At a quarter to twelve we attended divine service in the house in the large dining-room, which is a long room. Dr. MacGregor performed the service. Went afterwards into the drawing-room and the two libraries, the newer of which had been arranged by Louise and Lorne. There are some fine pictures in the drawing-room—one of the Marquis of Argyll who was beheaded, of Field-Marshal Conway by Gainsborough, of Duke Archibald, who built the house, etc., also of the present Duke's handsome grandmother, who married first a Duke of Hamilton. secondly a Duke of Argyll.

Luncheon as usual. Then up stairs, and at twenty minutes to four walked out with Louise, Beatrice, and Jane Churchill, and went along by the river, which had been over the road in the night, on to the "*Miller's Lynn,*" the first falls, which are very pretty and were very full, but are not near as high as the Garbhalt. We met some of the party coming back, and then some way farther up the river got into the carriage and drove to the "middle fall" or *Essach-lay,* where we got out and walked to look at the fall; then drove to *Lynn a Gluthen* and saw the third fall, after which we drove some distance up *Glen Aray,* beyond *Stronmagachan* to *Tullich Hill,* then back again past the stables, and on through the *Town Avenue* back, and in by ten minutes past six.

Took tea with Beatrice and Louise, who came in rather late, afterwards read and wrote. Besides Louise and Beatrice, Lorne, Elizabeth Campbell, Jane Churchill. and General Ponsonby dined with me. We went into the drawing-room for a short while as usual.

Monday, September 27.

It was a dreadfully rough night, pouring and blowing fearfully, and we heard it had thundered and lightened. After our nice little breakfast and writing, I went out at eleven with Louise, and met the Duke and the rest in the pleasure-grounds, where I planted a small cedar of Lebanon, the seed of which Lady Emma McNeill had brought back from the East. Then went on a little farther to where the road turns near the river, and planted a small silver fir, opposite to a magnificent one which my beloved Albert had admired in 1847. Beatrice walked up mean while with Jane Churchill, Evelyn, and Frances Campbell, to the top of the fine hill of *Dunaquoich*, opposite the Castle, after seeing the trees planted, and was to plant one herself when she came down. I drove off with Louise past the *Creitabhille* Lodge, the granite quarry (not, of course, the large ones which we saw on Saturday in the deer forest), and then got out and walked up a long steep path in the wood to obtain a view, of which, however, we did not see much. I am sure we walked a mile and a half up to the top, and it was a long pull, but I walked well. However, in going down, the wet grass and moss made me slip very much, having no nails to my boots, and twice I came down completely.

We drove back by *Essachosan* as quickly as we could at a quarter to one. The trees are wonderfully thick, and the tangled undergrowth of fern etc., is almost like a jungle. We had hardly any rain. Luncheon as usual. Drawing. The views from my room were so fine. While I was dressing to go out, Louise brought in Archibald Campbell's two lovely little children, little Neil, a dear pretty fair boy of three, very like Archie as a child, and the baby, Elspeth, who is beautiful : brown curly hair, enormous dark blue eyes fringed with very long dark eyelashes, and a small mouth and nose.

At ten minutes to four drove off in the wagonette with Louise, Beatrice, and Lorne, out by the approach along the foot of *Dunaquoich*, past the yew and chestnut avenue over the *Garonne Bridge*, along the lochside, an excellent road, much wooded, and commanding a beautiful view of the opposite shore and hills of *Ardkinglass*, past the *Strone Point, Achnatra*, and the ruins of the old castle or tower of *Dunderave*, which formerly belonged to the McNaghtons, who subsequently settled in Ireland, on to the head of *Loch Fyne*. There we turned up to the left and drove up *Glen*

Fyne, a very wild narrow glen with hardly any trees, and the water of the *Fyne* running through it. The high green hills with rugged gray rocks reminded me of the *Spital of Glenshie* and of *Altanour* (Lord Fife's). We drove up to a very small shooting-lodge, the property of Mr. Callander, brother-in-law to Lord Archibald, where a keeper with a nice wife lives. As it was beginning to rain, we went into the house and took our (made) tea, and I sketched. Janie Campbell (Lady Archibald) and her two sisters lived here for some time. The Duke was their guardian. We drove back the same way, and encountered a tremendous shower, which only ceased as we were quite near home. We were home at twenty minutes to seven. Besides Louise and Beatrice, the Duke and Duchess and Sir John and Lady Emma McNeill dined with me Mr. D. Macleod gone; the others remain.

Tuesday, September 28.

Bright and then showery. At a little past eleven drove with Louise and Beatrice along the sea-shore as far as *Douglass Water Point*, where we stopped to sketch between the frequent showers, the view being lovely and the lights so effective.

Home through the town by a quarter to one.

Painting. Luncheon as each day, after which again painting. At a quarter to four started off in a shower in the wagonette, with Louise, Beatrice, and Jane Churchill, for *Glen Shira.* We drove by the approach through the fine old avenue of beeches which suffered so much two years ago. This time along the right side of the *Dhu Loch*, which is three-quarters of a mile long, up to the head of *Glen Shira*, which is seven miles distant from the upper end of the loch, and is lovely. We had driven up a good way last Thursday as far as *Drumlee*. It is a lovely glen, wilder and much shut in as you advance, with fine rocks appearing through the grassy hills, and thickly wooded at the bottom. We passed two farms, and then went up to where the glen closes, and on the brae there is a keeper's cottage, just above which are the remains of a house where Rob Roy lived for some time concealed, but on sufferance. His army or followers were hidden in Glen Shira.

We got out here to look at some fine falls of the river *Shira*, a linn falling from a height to which footpaths had been made. Then drove on a little farther, and stopped to take our tea. We stopped twice afterwards to make a slight sketch of this lovely green glen, so picturesque and peaceful-looking, and then to take another view from the lower end of the *Dhu Loch*, in which Louise helped me. She also sketched the glen, and had done a sketch this morning. She has such talent, dear good child, and I felt so sad to leave her. The evening was quite fine, it having cleared up and all the heavy clouds vanished when we arrived at the head of the glen. In at twenty minutes past six. Busy arranging papers, painting, etc. Besides Louise and Beatrice, the Duke and Duchess, Lady Dufferin and Mr. J. Campbell dined with me. Went again into the drawing-room and took leave of the Dufferins, who were to go next day. He starts on the 8th for *Canada*. Dear Louise came up with me to my room, and stayed a little while talking with me.

Wednesday, September 29.

Vicky's and Fritz's engagement day—already twenty years ago! God bless them!

Got up before eight, and at half-past eight breakfasted for the last time with dear Louise and Beatrice. Then dressed before half-past nine and went down stairs. The early morning was fair, though misty, but unfortunately by half-past eight the mist had come down and it rained. It was decided that the horses should go back overland (having had such a terrible journey from the difficult embarkation and landing) by *Dalmally*, stopping all night at *Tyndrum* and coming on next day. The van was to go by sea. Some of the things belonging to our toilettes (which were in far too cumbrous boxes) we kept with us. I took leave of the whole family,* including the McNeills, and, with a heavy heart, of my darling Louise. It rained very much as we drove off, and for some time afterwards, to make it more melancholy.

We left *Inveraray* at half-past nine, and drove out by the same gateway as on our arrival, but afterwards went along the sea-shore to the head of the loch. We then turned to the right, still along the lochside, and changed horses at twenty minutes to eleven at a small inn called *Cairndow*, where the dear little Campbell children are staying, and who were at the window—such lovely children! There were a few people collected, and the harness as well as the horses had to be changed, and a pair of leaders put on to pull us up the long steep ascent in *Glenkinglass*. This caused a delay of ten minutes or a quarter of an hour. It rained rather heavily, the

* Elizabeth, Duchess of Argyll, died May 25, 1878.

mist hanging over the hills most provokingly. We passed *Ardkinglass* (Mr. Callander's), and then turned up to the left through the very wild and desolate *Glenkinglass.* The high green hills with hardly any habitations reminded me of the *Spital of Glenshee.* The mist lifted just enough to let one see the tops of the hills below which we were passing. The road was steep, and, just as we were getting near the top, the leaders, which had repeatedly stopped, refused to pull any farther, reared and kicked and jibbed, so that we really thought we should never get on, and should perhaps have to sleep at some wayside inn. But we stopped, and Brown had the leaders taken off near a small tarn, called *Loch Restel,* and he and Francie walked. We then got on much better. A little farther on we passed a few scattered huts, and at last we reached the top of this long ascent. The rain, which had been very heavy just when our plight was at its worst, stopped, and the day cleared.

At the summit of the pass is the spot called *Rest and be thankful,* from an inscription cut upon a stone by the regiment that made the road, which was one of the military roads to open up the *Highlands* constructed by Government under the superintendence of Marshal Wade. The stone still remains, but the words are much defaced. Here we came upon the splendid steep wild pass of *Glen Croe,* something like *Glencoe,* but not so fine and the road much steeper. It reminds me of the *Devil's Elbow,* and even of the *Devil's Bridge,* in the *Göschenen Pass* on the *St. Gothard.* We got out and walked down the road, which goes in a zigzag. A few people who had walked up from the coach were standing there. As at *Glencoe* the stream flows in the hollow of the pass, and there were some cattle and a house or two. The sun even came out all at once and lit up the wild grand scene. We got into the carriage near the bottom, and drank Fritz and Vicky's healths.

There was no more heavy rain, though there were frequent showers succeeded by most brilliant sunshine. We drove on under and by trees, and saw high hill-tops, including the peak of *Ben Lomond,* and then came upon *Loch Long,* a sea loch, which we sailed up in 1847, and drove part of the way along the shore, on the opposite side of which lie *Arrochar* and several pretty villas. We went round the head of the loch, where stood Lady Welby (formerly Victoria Wortley) and her children, and drove along under an arch near the bridge, passing through the village of *Arrochar,* which is in *Dumbar-*

tonshire, and here had a very good view of the celebrated
Cobbler, or *Ben Arthur.* We next changed horses at *Tarbet,*
quite a small village, where there was a sort of arch, composed of laurels and flowers stretched across the road. There
were a good many people here, who pressed in upon us a
good deal. Here General Ponsonby presented Mr. H. E.
Crum Ewing, Lord Lieutenant of *Dumbartonshire.* He preceded us a little way in his carriage, and then followed us.

The drive along *Loch Lomond,* which we came upon almost
immediately after *Tarbet,* was perfectly beautiful. We wound
along under trees on both sides, with the most lovely glimpses
of the head of the loch, and ever and anon of *Loch Lomond*
itself below the road; the hills which rose upon our right reminding me of *Aberfoyle,* near *Loch Ard,* and of the lower
part of the *Pilatus.* Such fine trees, numbers of hollies growing down almost into the water, and such beautiful capes and
little bays and promontories! The loch was extremely rough,
and so fierce was the wind, that the foam was blown like
smoke along the deep blue of the water. The gale had
broken some trees. The sun lit up the whole scene beautifully, but we had a few slight showers. It reminded me of
Switzerland. I thought we saw everything so much better
than we had formerly done from the steamer. As we proceeded, the hills became lower, the loch widened, and the
many wooded islands appeared. We next changed horses at
Luss, quite a small village—indeed the little inn stands almost alone, and they drove us close up to it, but there was a
great crowding and squeezing, and some children screamed
with fright; two presented nosegays to Beatrice and me, and
a poor woman offered me a bag of "*sweeties.*"

From here we drove along past the openings of *Glen Luss*
and *Glen Finlas,* which run up amongst the fine hills to the
right, the loch being on our left, and the road much wooded.
There are slate quarries close to *Luss.* About two miles
from *Luss* we drove through Sir J. Colquhoun's place, *Rossdhu,*
which commands a beautiful view of *Ben Lomond* and the loch,
and drove up to the house, where Highland volunteers were
drawn up, and where we stopped without getting out of the
carriage, and I received a nosegay from Sir J. Colquhoun's
little girl and a basket of fruit. His uncle was drowned two
years ago in the loch, crossing over from an island where he
had been shooting, and the body was not found for a fortnight; the keepers with him were also drowned. We drove
on, passing several other places, and everywhere were arches

of flowers, flags, etc., and the poorest people had hung out handkerchiefs for flags. We were followed by endless " machines" full of people, and many on foot running, and our horses were bad and went very slowly. However, as we approached *Balloch*, through which we did not pass, but only went up to the station, though the crowds were very great, perfect order was kept. The militia was out, and we got quite easily into the train at a quarter-past three.

Here again a nosegay was presented, and Mr. A. Orr Ewing, member for the county, and Mr. Smollett, the Convener, whom we had seen on board the steamer six years ago, were presented. *Balloch* is a manufacturing place for dyeing, and is connected with the trade in *Glasgow*. We had some cold luncheon as soon as we got into the train.

Our next stoppage was at *Stirling*, where there was an immense concourse of people, and the station prettily decorated. The evening was very fine, the pretty scenery appearing to great advantage, and the sky lovely. After this it got rapidly dark. We stopped at *Perth* and at the *Bridge of Dun*, where Jane Churchill got into our carriage and we had some tea; and then at *Aberdeen*, where it poured. At twenty minutes of ten we arrived at *Ballater*, and at once got into our carriage, and reached *Balmoral* at twenty-five minutes to eleven.

HIGHLAND FUNERAL, OCTOBER, 1875.

Thursday, October 21. 1875.

MUCH grieved at its being a worse day than ever for the funeral of Brown's father,* which sad ceremony was to take place to-day. The rain is hopeless—the ninth day! Quite unheard of! I saw good Brown a moment before breakfast; he was low and sad, and then going off to *Micras*. At twenty minutes to twelve drove with Beatrice and Janie Ely to *Micras*. As we drove up (unfortunately raining much) we met Dr. Robertson, and all along near the house were numbers of people—Brown told me afterwards he thought above a hundred. All my keepers, Mitchell the blacksmith (from *Clachanturn*), Symon, Grant, Brown's five uncles, Leys, Thomson (postmaster), and the forester, people below *Micras* and in *Aberarder*, and my people; Heale, Löhlein (returned

---

* He had died on the 18th, aged 86, at Micras, opposite Abergeldie, on the other side of the river.

this day from a week's leave), Cowley Jarrett, Ross and
Collins (sergeant footman), Brown and his four brothers,[*]
including Donald (who only arrived last night, and went to
the *Bush*, his brother William's farm), took us to the kitchen,
where was poor dear old Mrs. Brown sitting near the fire and
much upset, but still calm and dignified; Mrs. William Brown
was most kind and helpful, and the old sister-in-law and her
daughter; also the Hon. M. West, Mr. Sahl, Drs. Marshall
and Profeit, Mr. Begg, and Dr. Robertson, who came in later.
The sons, and a few whom Brown sent out of the kitchen,
were in the other small room, where was the coffin. A small
passage always divides the kitchen and the sitting-room in
this old sort of farmhouse, in front of which is the door—the
only door. Mr. Campbell, the minister of *Crathie*, stood in
the passage at the door, every one else standing close outside. As soon as he began his prayer, poor dear old Mrs.
Brown got up and came and stood near me—able to hear,
though, alas! not to see—and leant on a chair during the
very impressive prayers, which Mr. Campbell gave admirably.
When it was over, Brown came and begged her to go and sit
down while they took the coffin away, the brothers bearing
it. Every one went out and followed, and we also hurried
out and just saw them place the coffin in the hearse, and then
we moved on to a hillock, whence we saw the sad procession
wending its way sadly down. The sons were there, whom I
distinguished easily from their being near good Brown, who
wore his kilt walking near the hearse. All walked, except
our gentlemen, who drove. It fortunately ceased raining
just then. I went back to the house, and tried to soothe and
comfort dear old Mrs. Brown, and gave her a mourning
brooch with a little bit of her husband's hair which had been
cut off yesterday, and I shall give a locket to each of the
sons.

When the coffin was being taken away, she sobbed bitterly.
We took some whiskey and water and cheese, according to
the universal Highland custom, and then left, begging the
dear old lady to bear up. I told her the parting was but for
a time. We drove quickly on, and saw them go into the kirkyard, and through my glasses I could see them carry the
coffin in. I was grieved I could not be in the kirkyard.

Saw my good Brown at a little before two. He said all
had gone off well, but he seemed very sad; he had to go

---

[*] The fifth, Hugh (who, since May, 1883, has been my Highland attendant), was
then in New Zealand.

back to *Micras* to meet all the family at tea. All this was terribly trying for the poor dear old widow, but could not be avoided. Already yesterday morning, she had several of the wives and neighbors to tea. Every one was very kind and full of sympathy, and Brown was greatly gratified by the respect shown to him and his family to-day.

UNVEILING OF THE STATUE OF THE PRINCE CONSORT AT
EDINBURGH, 1876.

HOLYROOD, *August* 17, 1876.

BELOVED Mama's birthday.

How often she came to *Edinburgh* for a few days on her way to and from *Abergeldie*, and how much she always liked it !

We arrived yesterday morning at *Edinburgh* at eight o'clock. Had had a good night. Unfortunately the weather was misty, and even a little rain fell. No distance could well be seen. Dear Arthur came to breakfast (always in uniform).* At eleven o'clock went and sat out till half-past twelve, under an umbrella and with screens, on the side of the Abbey facing *Arthur's Seat.* Wrote and signed, Brown always helping to dry the signatures.

Read also in the papers a very nice account given in the " Courant " of what passed yesterday. Many interruptions. The day improving. Crowds flocking into the town, troops marching, bands playing—just as when any great event takes place in *London.*

The last time that my dearest Albert ever appeared in public was in *Edinburgh* on October 23 [1861], only six weeks before the end of all, when he laid the first stone of the new Post Office, and I looked out of the window to see him drive off in state, or rather in dress, London carriages, and the children went to see the ceremony. It was in *Edinburgh*, too, that dearest Mama appeared for the last time in public—being with me at the Volunteer Review in 1860, which was the first time she had driven with me in public for twenty years !

Dear Arthur could not come to luncheon, as he was on duty. At half-past three we started in three carriages :

* He was then Major in the 7th Hussars, and living at the Piers Hill Barracks, near Edinburgh. where his regiment was quartered.

Beatrice, Leopold, and I in the third ; Brown (in full dress) and Collins behind ; Leopold in the Highland dress ; dear Arthur, commanding the full Sovereign's escort of the 7th Hussars, riding next to me.

We drove out to the right—by *Abbey Hill*, the *Regent Road*, *Princes Street*, then turning into *St. Andrew Square*, along *George Street* to *Charlotte Square.* Enormous crowds everywhere clustering upon the *Calton Hill* and round and upon all the high monuments. The decorations were beautiful along the streets and on the houses, Venetian masts with festoons of flags on either side of *Princes Street* and *St. Andrew Street. St. Andrew Square* also was beautifully decorated, and the few inscriptions were very touching and appropriate. The day was quite fair, though dull (which, however, under the circumstances, was better than a very scorching sun like yesterday) and heavy, and not clear as to distance. The crowd, which was all along most hearty and enthusiastic, was densest at *Charlotte Square.* The Duke of Buccleuch received us, and the Royal Archers kept the ground.

We walked up to a daïs handsomely arranged, where I stood between Beatrice and Leopold (who were a little behind me). Dear Arthur's sense of duty was so great, that he would not dismount and stand near me, but remained with the escort which he commanded, and which waited near our carriage. The ladies and gentlemen, Mr. Cross (Home Secretary), etc., standing behind them ; the Committee, with the Duke of Buccleuch at their head, below. A large enclosure railed off was full of spectators, including all the highest and principal people, the Duchesses of Athole and Roxburghe, the Dowager Lady Ruthven, Sir Thomas Biddulph, etc. ; and our maids also were there, but I saw none of them.

The ceremony began by a short prayer (which was somewhat disturbed by a great noise made by the crowd) offered up by Dr. Milligan, one of the Deans of the Chapel Royal. Then my dearest Albert's Chorale, with words like a National Anthem, was beautifully sung by a choir, accompanied by the band of the 79th, led by Professor H. Oakeley, Mus. Doc. and Professor of Music in the University of Edinburgh. The Duke of Buccleuch then presented the Executive Committee, of which he himself is Chairman, and which consisted of Sir J. McNeill, G.C.B., Sir William Gibson Craig, Sir Daniel McNee. Dr. Lyon Playfair, and Mr. William Walker.

After this, the Duke of Buccleuch read a very pretty address, in which, besides my beloved Husband, dear Mama was alluded to, and I read a reply.

Mr. Cross then declared that I wished the Statue (an equestrian one) to be unveiled, which was done most successfully, without a hitch. The effect of the monument as a whole, with the groups at the angles of the pedestal, is very good. The Coburg March was played, and its well-known strains * ever bring back dear and sweet memories.

Mr. Steell, the sculptor, was presented, and this was followed by the singing of another beautiful chorale, with touching words and music, the latter composed by Professor Oakeley, who is a wonderful musician, and plays beautifully on the organ. We then, followed by our own suite, the Committee, and Mr. Steell, walked round the Statue and examined the groups of bas-reliefs. The three sculptors who had executed the groups were also presented. Brown followed us round, having stood behind us the whole time. He was delighted with the reception.

We drove back by *South Charlotte Street* and *Princes Street.* The horses of the Yeomanry and even some of the Hussars were very restive, and kept plunging and whirling round upon our horses. One of the Hussars, in particular, got in between our horses, and nearly caused an accident. We got back by ten minutes to five o'clock.

We looked out of the window to see Arthur ride off, and then I knighted Mr. Steell, who looked very happy. He has now long white hair—such a kind, good man ! I also knighted Professor Oakeley, who is still very lame, having met with a dreadful accident in *Switzerland* some years ago. His mother was a Murray (daughter of Lord Charles Murray Aynsley) and sister to the mother of Mrs. Drummond of *Megginch*, and his sister married an uncle of Fanny Drummond. Dear Augusta Stanley took much interest in him.

I had a large dinner in the old dining-room below, where I had not dined since my darling Albert's time in 1861. I sat in the middle, opposite to where I used to sit. The party consisted of Arthur, who led me in and sat near me, and Leopold and Beatrice, all our people, the Duke of Buccleuch (who sat near me) and Lady Mary Scott, Lord Lothian (the Duke's son-in-law), Lord Dalkeith, young Lord Elgin, Lord Rosebery, the Dowager Lady Dunmore and Lady Adine

* This March was always played for dear Albert, and was originally composed for our granduncle, Field-Marshal Prince Francis Josias of Saxe-Coburg-Saalfeld.

Murray, Lord and Lady Elphinstone, Sir John and Lady Emma McNeill, Mr. Cross, the Honorable B. Primrose, Major-General J. N. Stuart, and Colonel Hale of the 7th Hussars (Colonel of dear Arthur's regiment). The band of the 7th Hussars played during dinner, and Ross played during dessert. Brown * waited on me.

Every one seemed pleased, and talked of the great success of the day. Mr. Cross was delighted. I remained talking some little time in the drawing-room, and then went up stairs and looked with Beatrice out of the window at the rockets. Such a noise in the streets and from the trains!

PRESENTATION OF COLORS TO "THE ROYAL SCOTS," SEPTEMBER, 1876.

BALMORAL, *September* 26, 1876.

An earlier lunch. It had appeared to clear, and the rain was far less heavy. We started at three. The ladies and gentlemen had all gone on before in carriages, and many of our people went to *Ballater*, as it was a great novelty for the people here—William Brown and his wife, who had said yesterday she had never seen so many soldiers together and would therefore like to go; Hugh Brown and his wife. Mrs. Profeit † with her children was there also. Alice, Beatrice, and Arthur were with me. The weather held up while we were going to *Ballater*, which we did in a closed landau (Brown and Collins on the rumble). Just outside the village we opened the carriage. We drove to the left of the railway through a wood, avoiding the town, preceded by Captain Charles Phipps, as Assistant Adjutant Quartermaster-General, on to the open space—a beautiful position, with the noble rocky high hill of *Craig an Darrach*, at the foot of which lie the *Pass of Ballater* and the park of *Ballater House* with the hills opposite. Nothing could be finer. A great many people were there, it is said between two and three thousand; but none of the spectators were in uniform. Alix was in a carriage, Bertie and the boys (in Highland dress) and Prince John of Glücksburg ‡ on foot. They stood near me, so did

----

* It was hard for him to have to appear on such a festive occasion, having lost his much-loved mother only a fortnight before; but his sense of duty ever went before every feeling of self.
† Wife of my Commissioner at Balmoral.
‡ Uncle of the Princess of Wales.

Arthur (also in his kilt), who had got out of the carriage. Then followed, after the Royal salute, the trooping of the colors, with all its peculiar and interesting customs, marching and counter-marching, the band playing the fine old marches of the "Garb of old Gaul" and "Dumbarton Drums," also the march from the "Fille du Régiment," which was evidently played as a compliment to me, whom they considered as "born in the regiment," my father having commanded it at the time I was born. Then came the piling of the drums and the prayer by Mr. Middleton, minister of *Ballater*, after which the new colors were given to me. I handed them to the two sub-lieutenants who were kneeling, and then I said the following words :—

"In entrusting these colors to your charge, it gives me much pleasure to remind you that I have been associated with your regiment from my earliest infancy, as my dear father was your Colonel. He was proud of his profession, and I was always told to consider myself a soldier's child. I rejoice in having a son who has devoted his life to the army, and who, I am confident, will ever prove worthy of the name of a British soldier. I now present these colors to you, convinced that you will always uphold the glory and reputation of my first Regiment of Foot—the Royal Scots."

Colonel M'Guire then spoke a few words in reply, and brought the old colors to me, and begged me to accept them. In doing so, I said I should take them to *Windsor*, and place them there in recollection of the regiment and their Colonel. Then they marched past well (they were fine men), and after the Royal salute gave three cheers for me. The 79th kept the ground and took charge of the old colors. We left at once.

The rain continued persistently, having got worse just as the prayer began ; but we kept the carriage open, and were back by half-past five.

I was terribly nervous while speaking.

EXPEDITION TO LOCH MAREE, SEPTEMBER 12–18, 1877.

Wednesday, September 12, 1877.

A DULL morning, very mild. Had not a good night. Up at a quarter-past eight, breakfasting at a quarter to nine (I had packed my large boxes with papers etc., with Brown, be-

fore breakfast on Monday, as all the heavier luggage had to
be sent on in advance), and at a quarter-past nine left *Balmoral* with Beatrice and the Duchess of Roxburghe, leaving
Leopold, who was himself to start at ten A.M. for Dunkeld.
Brown on the rumble of the landau, his leg now really fairly
well, but he looks pulled.* It began to rain very soon, and
went on till we almost reached *Ballater*, when we got into
the railway. Here General Ponsonby and Sir William Jenner
met us. Wilmore, Morgan, Cannon, Francie Clark (with
darling Noble), and Heir went with us. Annie Macdonald,
Hollis the cook, Lockwood, Seymour, (who replaced poor
Goddard), and Lizzie Stewart (the housemaid) went on before
us on Monday.

The day cleared and gradually became very fine. Passed
through *Aberdeen*, which looked very handsome, and where
we much admired a new tower added to a college. Stopped
at *Dyce Junction* at nineteen minutes to twelve. Near *Aberdeen* we saw the corn already cut, which is unusually early.
Passed close under *Benachie*, the heather beautiful everywhere. At one o'clock we had our luncheon, and dear Noble
came in and was so good and quiet. At twenty-five minutes
past one stopped at *Keith*, where we had stopped in 1872, and
where we had then been obliged to take two people into the
carriage to open a door through which the maids passed, and
which had got fixed.† The volunteers and a number of people were waiting for us here. About *Beith* the corn was
sadly destroyed, but around *Elgin* it was better. Soon after
this appeared the lovely hills of the *Moray Frith*—really
beautiful: the land-locked sea so blue, with heavy fields of
yellow corn (harvesting going on) in the undulating ground,
with trees and woods here and there, formed a lovely picture.
An old ruined church (*Kinloss Abbey*) we passed to the right,
and *Forres* at eighteen minutes past two. Then *Nairn*, lying
low on the *Frith*, but very picturesque with the hills rising
around. Near here poor Jane Churchill's sister, Cecilia
Brinckman, died on August 16, which is the cause that dear
Jane is not with us now. The heather was so brilliant, and
the sea, though very rough, was blue, which had a lovely effect; but the bracken, and even the trees, have begun to

* When we went on board the " Thunderer," August 12, at Osborne, Brown had
fallen through an open place inside the turret, and got a severe hurt on the shin.
He afterwards damaged it again, when it was nearly healed, by jumping off the
box of the carriage, so that when he came to Balmoral about a fortnight afterwards, it was very bad, and he was obliged to take care of it for some days previous
to the fresh journey.
† *Vide* Expedition to Dunrobin, p. 178.

turn here, as well as with us. Good crops about here. We passed near *Fort George*, which lies very prettily on the shore of the *Frith*, but where we did not stop, and *Culloden*. At three minutes past three passed through *Inverness*, where many people were out, and went quickly past *Beauly*. As far as *Dingwall* we had travelled precisely the same way in going to *Dunrobin* in 1872. At twenty minutes to four reached *Dingwall*, charmingly situated in a glen, where we stopped, and where there were a good many people waiting for us.

Here Sir Kenneth and Lady Mackenzie of *Gairloch* met us with their three children, two boys and a girl. He is a pleasing courteous person, and wore the kilt. He has an immense property about here, and all round is the *Mackenzie country*. Lady Mackenzie is the elder sister of Lady Granville, and excessively like her. Soon after this we took tea, which was pleasant and refreshing. From *Dingwall* we turned to the left, and, instead of going on by the main line to *Tain*, went through the celebrated *Strathpeffer*, which is extremely pretty—a wooded glen with houses and cottages dotted about; then on through a wild glen, with hills, partly rocky, but with grass, heather, and bracken, and some trees running up amidst them. The railway goes along above and at some distance from the village, proceeding by way of *Strath Bran* and *Loch Luichart.* There were occasional showers, with gleams of sunshine always between.

We left the railway at *Achnasheen*, where we arrived at a quarter to five, and where there are only a small station and two or three little cottages. We three ladies got into the sociable (Brown and Cannon on the box), the two gentlemen and three maids following in the wagonette, and the other servants in "traps." Sir Kenneth Mackenzie came as far as this small station, where there were a Gaelic inscription and some plaids arranged in festoons. The twenty miles drive from here, through a desolate, wild, and perfectly uninhabited country, was beautiful, though unfortunately we had heavy showers. The first part winds along *Loch Rusque* (Gaelic *Chroisg*), a long narrow loch, with hills very like those at the *Spital* and at *Glen Muich* rising on either side. Looking back you see the three high peaks of *Scour-na-Vuillin.* The road continues along another small loch; and then from the top of the hill you go down a very grand pass called *Glen Dochart.* Here *Loch Maree* came in view most beautifully. Very shortly after this you come upon the loch, which is grand and romantic. We changed horses at *Kin-lochewe*, a small inn, near to which is a shooting-lodge, which was for some time rented by Lady Waterpark's son-in-law, Mr. Clowes, and he and his wife used to live there a good deal. They are now living near *Gairloch*, at *Flowerdale*, another shooting-lodge of Sir Kenneth Mackenzie.

The drive along the lochside, for ten miles to the hotel of *Loch Maree*, is beautiful in the extreme. The hills to the right, as you go from *Kinlochewe*, are splendid—very high and serrated, with wood at the base of some of them. One magnificent hill towers above the rest, and is not unlike the *Pilatus* in shape, seen as it is from our hotel, just as the *Pilatus* is seen from the *Pension Wallis*. The windings of the road are beautiful, and afford charming glimpses of the lake, which is quite locked in by the overlapping mountains. There are trees, above and below it, of all kinds, but chiefly birch, pine, larch, and alder, with quantities of high and most beautiful heather and bracken growing luxuriantly, high rocks surmounting the whole. Here and there a fine Scotch fir, twisted, and with a stem and head like a stone-pine, stands out on a rocky projection into the loch, relieved against the blue hills as in some Italian view. Part of the way the road emerges altogether from the trees, and passes by a mass of huge piled-up and tumbled-about stones, which everywhere here are curiously marked, almost as though they were portions of a building, and have the appearance of having been thrown about by some upheaving of the earth. We had several heavy showers, which produced a most brilliant rainbow, with the reflection of a second quite perfect. Then it quite cleared up, and the sky was radiant with the setting sun, which gave a crimson hue to all the hills, and lit up *Ben Sleach* just as I remember having seen it light up *Ben Nevis* and the surrounding hills at *Inverlochy*.

It was a little after seven when *Loch Maree Hotel*, which stands close to the loch and to the road and is surrounded by trees was reached. At the entrance there is no gate, merely a low wall open at either side to admit carriages etc. It is a very nice little house, neatly furnished. To the left, as you enter, are two good rooms—a large one called the coffee-room, in which we take our meals, and the other, smaller, next to it, in which the gentlemen dine. Up the small but easy short winding staircase to the right come small though comfortable, rooms. To the left Beatrice's, and Brown's just opposite to the right. Then up three steps is a small passage; at the

end, to the left, is my dear little sitting-room, looking on to
the loch, and to *Ben Sleach* and the road ; it is very full with
my things. At the other end is my bedroom, with two small
rooms between for Wilmore and Annie.

On arriving heard that the Russians had bombarded *Plevna*
on the 9th, and had repulsed a sortie of the Turks with heavy
loss. The bombardment continued again the following day,
and General Skobeleff occupied the heights. We two and
the Duchess dined together. The Duchess read to me a
sketch of Thiers' life. Good Brown waited, and brought in
my usual glass of water. Felt rather tired.

Dear Louis of Hesse's birthday—God bless him !

Thursday, September 13.

It had rained a great deal through the night, and the
morning was dull. Had slept well. Beatrice and I breakfasted together down stairs, where we also lunched. Began
to sketch, though there was no light and shade ; but the
splendid mountain was clear. At eleven walked out with
Beatrice on the road to *Kinlochewe,* about a mile, and back,
greatly admiring the magnificent hills. There is a bridge
over a stream called *Talladale,* and near it was a cottage,
a miserable hovel, in which an old man lived ; he wore a
coat and a high hat, and was much pleased to see me, but
said he " had very little English," which is the case with most
people here. We gave him something, and when Brown took
it to him he asked the old man the names of some of the
hills.

The atmosphere was very close. In at half-past twelve,
and then I drew and painted. So hot ! It turned to rain.
Painted, read, wrote, etc., and then we took tea, and at half-
past five started with Beatrice and the Duchess of Roxburghe
(Brown and Francie on the box), and drove on down the loch
(the contrary way to that by which we had come), under trees,
through a larch wood, winding above the loch for two miles,
till we reached a bridge, which goes over the stream of *Gar-
vaig,* where there is a descent to above *Slatterdale,* and
thence drove up a mountain pass to the left. There the hills
are much lower and curiously tumbled about, grass, fern, and
heather growing up their sides, with rocks at the tops—curious serrated, knobbed hills.

Passed a small loch called *Padnascally,* out of which runs
the *Kerrie Water* into another little loch. Here the road
winds along almost like the roads in *Switzerland,* and is

ery precipitous on one side, passing above the fine falls of
the *Kerrie*, of which there are two or three successions,
with fine rocks and wooded banks, through which the river
seems to force its way.   As Brown truly observed, it was
like *Glenfeshie*, only *Glenfeshie* has no road, but a very
narrow path, where one has to ford.   Looking back before
you come to the falls there is a fine view of *Ben Evy*.   We
drove quite down this pass to *Kerriesdale*, at the bridge of
which is a very pretty spot with wooded hills leading on to
Gairloch.   We turned, as it was late, and drove back the
same way, getting home by half-past seven.   It was dull, and
gray, and dark, but did not rain till we came back.   The
Duchess finished reading Thiers' life.

Friday, September 14.

An awful storm of rain, with wind, all night and a good
part of the morning.   Breakfasted as yesterday.   At length
we two went out, and walked for more than a mile on the
road by which we drove yesterday.   The rocky hills, rising
above the road, with the fine trees and undergrowth beneath
them, remind me of the *Lion's Face*, and of the *Trossachs*
and *Loch Eil*.   It cleared, the rain ceased, and the day became fine, but very hot and oppressive.   In at twenty minutes to one.   The view from my little sitting-room is quite
beautiful, *Ben Sloach* on one side, and the splendid loch,
with the other fine rocky mountains and green island, on the
other.   One would like to sketch all day.   More telegrams.

At half past three we started in two carriages, we three
ladies in one, and the two gentlemen in the wagonette (Brown
with us, and Francie with the next).   We went just the same
way as yesterday, but changed horses at *Kerrie's Bridge*, and
turning to the left went a short way down a bad road, through
a small wood of oaks, to *Shieldaig*, where there is a small
cottage on the sea with a pretty garden, where Lord Bristol
and Mr. Bateson live.   But there is no road beyond, and we
had to turn and go back again.   We then drove over the
bridge by a lovely wood of larch and other trees, through
which flows a small river, and ascended a hill, passing by
Flowerdale to *Gairloch*, which is on the sea.   It consists of
only a very few houses dotted about—the kirk, manse, bank,
and on the highest point the hotel.   The hills immediately
to the right and left of the fine bay are not very high.   But high
wooded hills are at the back of the *Gairloch*, which is open to
the *Atlantic*.   Here we turned round and drove straight back

again the same way, the few inhabitants having come out to
greet us. After passing *Kerric's Bridge*, we stopped to take
our (made) tea. The afternoon and evening were beautiful.
We got home at a quarter to seven. The post comes in at a
quarter to four and at half-past nine. The climate is very
warm and muggy. Dinner as usual. After dinner played
with Beatrice on the piano.

Saturday. September 15.

A fair morning. Up early after a very good night. There
is a perfect plague of wasps, and we are obliged to have
gauze nailed down to keep these insects out when the windows are open, which, as the climate is so hot, they have to
be constantly. I had to put on quite thin things again. Decided, after some little doubt, to make an expedition for the
day to *Torridon*, described as fine and wild. There was a
heavy shower before we started. Had been sketching and
painting.

At half-past twelve we started in the wagonette, with Beatrice, the Duchess (who is delighted with everything), and
General Ponsonby and Brown on the box. The day was
very fine ; we had only two or three showers, which lasted
a few minutes. We drove on to *Kinlochewe*, where we took
fresh horses, and a capital pair of bay ones we had. The
sun was brilliant, and lit up the magnificent scenery beautifully. Halfway we crossed the bridge of Grudie (from which
Ben Sleach is seen to advantage), a very pretty rapid burn,
with fine fir trees, and a glen running up to the right—*i.e.*, to
the south. At *Kinlochewe* we turned up to the right by the
stream of *Garry*, mountains towering up, as we advanced,
like mighty giants, and coming one by one and unexpectedly
into view. To the left we passed a pretty, small loch, called
Loch Clare, which runs back into a wooded glen at the foot
of high hills. Sir Ivor Guest has a shooting-lodge near, and
you can just see a small house amongst the trees.

Soon after this the grand, wild, savage-looking, but most
beautiful and picturesque *Glen of Torridon* opened upon us,
with the dark mural precipices of that most extraordinary
mountain *Ben Liughach*, which the people pronounce *Liarach*.
We were quite amazed as we drove below it. The mountains
here rise so abruptly from their base that they seem much
higher than our *Aberdeenshire* mountains, although, excepting
Ben Sleach (3216 feet) and a few others, the hills are not of
any remarkable height, and the level of the country or land

itself is barely a hundred feet above the sea, whereas *Balmoral* is eight hundred feet to begin with.   All the hills about *Loch Maree* and this glen, and elsewhere in this neighborhood, are very serrated and rocky.   *Ben Liarach* is most peculiar from its being so dark, and the rocks like terraces one above the other, or like fortifications and pillars—most curious; the glen itself is very flat, and the mountains rise very abruptly on either side.   There were two cottages (in one of which lived a keeper), a few cattle, and a great many cut peats.

We came to the *Upper Loch Torridon*, which is almost land-locked and very pretty.   In the distance the hills of *Skye* were seen.   Village there really is none, and the inn is merely a small, one-storied, "harled" house, with small windows. We drove beyond the habitations to a turn where we could not be overlooked, and scrambled up a bank, where we seated ourselves, and at twenty minutes to three took our luncheon with good appetite.   The air of the mountains and the sea was delicious, and not muggy.   We two remained sketching, for the view was beautiful.   To the right were the hills of *Skye*, rising above the lower purple ones which closed in the loch.   To the south, nearly opposite to where I sat, was *Applecross* (formerly Mackenzie property), which now belongs to Lord Middleton, and the high mountains of *Ben Hecklish* and *Ben Damph*, with, in the distance northwards, the white peaks of *Ben Liarach*.   We were nearly an hour sitting there, and we got down unwillingly, as it was so fine and such a wild uncivilized spot, like the end of the world.   There was a school, standing detached by itself, which had been lately built.   The property here belongs to a Mr. Darroch, whose two little boys rode past us twice with a groom   An old man, very tottery, passed where I was sketching, and I asked the Duchess of Roxburghe to speak to him; he seemed strange, said he had come from *America*, and was going to *England*, and thought *Torridon* very ugly!

We walked along, the people came out to see us, and we went into a little merchant's shop, where we all bought some trifles—just such a "shoppie" as old Edmonston's, and the poor man was so nervous he threw almost everything down. I got some very good comforters, two little woven woollen shawls, and a very nice cloak.   We had spoken to a woman before, but she could not understand us, only knowing Gaelic, and had to ask another younger woman to help.

A little farther off the road, and more on the slope of the

hill, was a row of five or six wretched hovels, before which stood barelegged and very ill-clad children, and poor women literally squatting on the ground. The people cheered us and seemed very much pleased. Hardly any one ever comes here. We had now to get into the carriage, and one of the horses was a little restive; but we soon started off all right, much interested by our adventures. We admired the splendid mountain again on our way back, and enjoyed our expedition very much. One very short shower we had, before coming to *Kinlochewe*, where we again changed horses, and were home at our nice little house by nearly seven, when Beatrice and I had some welcome tea. Later our usual dinner; then Beatrice played, and we afterwards played together.

Sunday, September 16.

A most beautiful bright morning, with a slight cloud overhanging *Ben Sleach*, which is very often not clear at the top. There was a heavy shower, which came on quite unexpectedly. We walked out at half-past eleven, and after some three hundred yards turned up a path to the right, off the road to *Kinlochewe*, under oak and rowan trees, through very wet grass and fern, to where stood two very poor-looking low cottages. We looked into one, out of which came a tidy-looking woman, but who could hardly understand or speak a word of English. We then looked into the second, where Baldry lodged; it was wet and muddy, almost to the door, and the inside very low and close, but tidy. The " gudewife " came up and spoke to us, also like a foreigner, with difficulty. She was a nice, tidy-looking woman, and gave her name as Mrs. McRae, and the place is called " *Sliorach*." She knew us—at least Brown told her it was the " Bhan Righ " with her daughter, and gave her some money.

We returned as we had come, and went on some way in the other direction, coming in at twenty minutes to one. Read prayers, etc. There is no kirk nearer than *Kinlochewe* and *Gairloch*, and people had been seen passing on foot as early as half-past seven to *Gairloch*. At half-past four Beatrice, the Duchess of Roxburghe, and I started in a four-oared gig, steered by Hormsby the landlord, a very nice, quiet, youngish man, and rowed to the *Isle of Maree* (" *Eilan Maree* "), which is not visible from the house, being concealed by some of the larger islands. Contrary to what is stated in the *Guide*, it is the smallest of them. It was delightful rowing through these wooded and rocky islands, with the blue, calm loch—not another sound but the oars—the lovely blue and purple distant hills on the one side, and the splendid peaks of *Ben Sleach* and its surrounding mountains on the other.

The boat was pushed on shore, and we scrambled out and walked through the tangled underwood and thicket of oak, holly, birch, ash, beech, etc., which covers the islet, to the well, now nearly dry, which is said to be celebrated for the cure of insanity. An old tree stands close to it, and into the bark of this it is the custom, from time immemorial, for every one who goes there to insert with a hammer a copper coin, as a sort of offering to the saint who lived there in the eighth century, called Saint Maolruabh or Mulroy. The saint died near *Applecross* in 722, and is said to have rested under a rock, which is still shown, close to *Torridon*. Some say that the name of *Maree* was derived from " *Mulroy*," others from " *Mary*." We hammered some pennies into the tree, to the branches of which there are also rags and ribbons tied. We then went on to where there are some old grave-stones : two belonged to the tomb of a Norwegian or Danish princess, about whose untimely death there is a romantic story. There are also modern graves, and only eight years ago one of the family of the McLeans was buried there, the island being their burying-place. The remains of the old wall of the monastery are still to be seen. The island is barely a quarter of a mile across at the widest part, and not above half a mile in circumference. Some of the larger islands have red deer on them. We walked along the beach and picked up stones, then rowed back as we had come. It took about twenty minutes. Four very respectable-looking men (one a very good-looking young farmer) rowed the boat. After landing, we got into the wagonette and drove to a bridge just beyond where the trees cease on the *Gairloch Road*, about two miles from the hotel. Here we first took our tea, and then got out and scrambled up a steep bank to look at a waterfall, a pretty one, but very inferior to those in our neighborhood at *Balmoral;* walked down again and drove home by a quarter-past seven.

Reading; writing. Beatrice's room is a very pretty one, but very hot, being over the kitchen. Brown's, just opposite, also very nice and not hot, but smaller. After dinner the Duchess of Roxburghe read a little out of the newspapers. Saw Sir William Jenner.

Monday, September 17.

A splendid bright morning, like July! Have had such good nights since we came, and my own comfortable bed. Sketched and painted after breakfast. At ten minutes past eleven walked out with Beatrice the same way as yesterday, and turned up to the right and looked at the farm, where the horses for the coach are kept. This coach is like a great break, and is generally full of people; we met it each morning when out walking. We then went on past *Talladale*, where lives the old man to whom we spoke on Thursday, and whom we saw get off the coach this morning, having been to *Gairloch* for church, of which he is an elder. Here three or four very poorly dressed bairns were standing and sitting about, and we gave them biscuits and sandwiches out of the luncheon-box. The midges are dreadful, and you cannot stand for a moment without being stung. In at twenty minutes to one. I remained sketching the lovely views from the windows in the dining-room, and then sketched the beautiful mountain also.

After luncheon some doubt as to what should be done, but decided not to go to *Pool Ewe*, beyond *Gairloch*, but on to *Kerrie's Bridge* to meet the good people who had asked permission to come over from *Stornoway*, in the *Isle of Lewis*, to see "their beloved Queen." Drew again. At ten minutes past four we two and the Duchess of Roxburghe started in the wagonette, General Ponsonby and Brown on the box. We went by the same pretty winding road; but the *Kerrie Falls* were not nearly so full as on Friday after the heavy rain.

As we approached *Kerrie's Bridge*, we saw a number of people standing on the road, and we drew up to where they were and stopped the carriage. General Ponsonby presented the minister, Mr. Greenfield, who had come over with them. They sang "God save the Queen" with most loyal warmth; and their friendly faces and ringing cheers, when we arrived and when we left, were very gratifying. It took them three hours to come over, and they were going straight back. There were two hundred and fifty of them of all classes, from the very well dressed down to the poorest, and many fishermen amongst them. We met many of these on Saturday coming back from having sold their fish, and also on the coaches. As we returned, we met the coach where there was only just room to pass.

We stopped after we had got up to the top of the hill, over-looking the falls, and took our tea (already made, and brought with us), but were much molested by midges. We drove to above *Slatterdale,* where there is such a splendid view of the loch and of *Ben Sleach ;* and the hills looked so beauti-fully pink. We walked on down to the small waterfall which we visited yesterday, and then drove home (General Ponsonby having walked back) by half-past seven. Reading and writ-ing. Continued telegrams. General Ponsonby and Sir William Jenner dined also with us.

Got a few trifles from *Gairloch,* though very few were to be had, to give as souvenirs to my good people. Brown's leg, though he had to stand so much, did not hurt him, which I was thankful for, and he has waited at all our meals, made my coffee in the morning, etc. I was sorry it was our last night here, and would have liked to stay two or three days longer ; but dear Arthur has been, since Saturday, at *Bal-moral,* and he must leave again on the 29th. Have en-joyed this beautiful spot and glorious scenery very much. The little house was cozy and very quiet, and there were no constant interruptions as at home. Only dear Beatrice suf-fered much from rheumatism, which was very vexatious. Nearly opposite is a Mr. Banks's place, called *Letter Ewe,* which he lets.

Tuesday, September 18.

A wet, misty morning, no hills whatever to be seen. Got up early and breakfasted at half-past eight, and at a quarter to nine we left with regret our nice cozy little hotel at *Loch Maree,* which I hope I may some day see again. Changed horses at *Kinlochewe.* The beautiful scenery was much obscured, but it got better as we went on, though it was not a really fine day. At a little before half-past eleven we reached *Achnasheen,* where Mr. (now Sir Alexander) Mathe-son, M.P. (who is chairman of the railway company, and has property farther north), met us. Here we got into the train, and went on without stopping to *Dingwall. Strathpef-fer,* and *Castle Leod,* which belongs to the Duchess of Sutherland, partly hidden among trees, looked very pretty. The lochs of *Luichart* and *Garve* are most picturesque. We stopped at *Dingwall,* and *Keith,* and *Dyce Junction* as before. We had our luncheon at one o'clock, before com-ing to *Keith,* and tea after the *Dyce Junction.* Dear Noble was so good on the railway, and also at *Loch Maree,* where

he came to our meals ; but he was lost without his companions.
We reached *Ballater* at six. A very threatening evening.
Such dark. heavy clouds. and the air much lighter than at
Loch Maree. We reached *Balmoral* at a quarter to seven.
Dear Arthur received us down stairs, and came up with us and
stayed a little while with me. He had been out deer-stalk-
ing these two days, but got nothing.

VISIT TO BROXMOUTH.

Friday, August 23, 1878.

HAD to dine at half-past five. At six o'clock, with much
regret, left dear *Osborne*, with Beatrice and Leopold, and embarked on board the " Alberta " at *Trinity Pier.* We had a
delightful passage, but the weather looked very threatening
behind us. Passing close to the " Osborne," we saw Bertie,
Alix, the boys, and the King of Denmark standing on the
paddle-box. As we steamed across we saw the poor " Eury-
dice " lying close off what is called " *No Man's Land* " as we
had seen her the day of the Review, in fearful contrast to the
beautiful fleet ! We at once entered the railway train ; poor
Sir J. Garvock (who has resigned) was too ill to appear.
We stopped at *Banbury* for refreshments, and I lay down
after eleven o'clock. At *Carlisle* (at five or six in the morning) Lord Bridport, Harriet Phipps, and Mary Lascelles (who
had joined at *Banbury*), Fräulein Bauer, and two of my maids
left us to go to *Balmoral,* while Janie Ely, General Ponsonby,
Sir W. Jenner, Mr. Yorke, Brown, Emilie, Annie, and three
footmen went on with us to *Broxmouth.*

Saturday, August 23.

Had not a very good night, and was suffering from a rather
stiff shoulder. It was a very wet morning. At *Dunbar,*
which we reached at a quarter to nine (where the station was
very prettily decorated), where the Duke and Duchess of
Roxburghe, the *Grant-Sutties*, the Provost, and Lord Haddington, Lord-Lieutenant of the county. We got into one
of my closed landaus—Beatrice, Leopold, the Duchess of Roxburghe, and I—the others following, and drove through a
small portion of *Dunbar*, Lord Haddington riding to *Broxmouth*, about a mile and a quarter from *Dunbar.* People all

along the road, arches and decorations on the few cottages, and very loyal greetings.

The park is fine, with noble trees and avenues. It is only a quarter of a mile from the sea, which we could see dimly as we drove from *Dunbar*. The house is an unpretending one, the exterior something like *Claremont,* only not so handsome, and without any steps leading up to the entrance. It has been added to at different times, and was much improved and furnished by the Duke's mother, who lived there. It is built on a slope; consequently on one side there is a story more than on the other. The house is entered by a small hall, beyond which is a narrow corridor with windows on one side and doors on the other. Turning to the left and going straight on, we came to my sitting-room (the Duchess's own sitting-room), with bow-windows down to the ground, and very comfortably arranged. Next to it, but not opening into it, was Beatrice's sitting-room, a very handsomely furnished room—in fact, the drawing-room. On the other side of the hall is the dining-room—very nice and well furnished, but not large. Just opposite Beatrice's room is the staircase, also not large, and below it you turn to where Leopold had a room. The staircase lands on a corridor like the lower one. My bedroom is just over the sitting-room, with a nice little dressing-room to the right next to it (the Duchess's room). Next to the bedroom on the other side my two maids' rooms, then Janie Ely's, and beyond Beatrice's and the maids, at the end; just outside the corridor, Brown's. All most comfortable. We came down almost directly again, and had (we three) an excellent breakfast in the dining-room. Brown waited on us with a footman, Cannon, who had gone on before. Charlie Thomson, Lockwood, and Shorter (a new footman) came with us.

As it was raining I did not go out, but soon afterwards went up stairs. After dressing, came down and rested, and read and wrote. Saw Lady Susan Suttie and her two very pretty daughters, Harriet (Haddie), like Susan Dalrymple, only much darker. Rested on the sofa, and while there received the very startling and distressing account of dear Madame Van de Weyer's death, which affected me much. It came direct and was given me straight, there being no telegraph in the house. At home this would not have happened. Sent to tell Brown, who was very much shocked.

She was not, of course, the friend her beloved and honored husband was; but we saw so much of her with him ever since

1840, and so much of them both when they were at *Abergel-die* in 1867, 1868, and 1870. They were always most kind to us and to our children, who grew up with theirs ; and when my great sorrow came, who was kinder and more ready to help than dear M. Van de Weyer? Then, after his and his poor son Albert's death, she talked so openly to me, and I tried to comfort her. Dear pretty *New Lodge,** kept just as he left it, was ever a pleasure for us to go to, as there was still a sort of reflected light from former times, when he charmed every one. To feel that for us it is gone forever is dreadful, and upset me very much. Another link with the past gone !— with my beloved one, with dearest Uncle Leopold, and with *Belgium !* I feel ever more and more alone ! Poor Louise Van de Weyer, who has been everything to her mother since Albert's death, and Nellie, how *I* feel for them ! It was only on the 16th that their sister Alice was married to the youngest brother of poor Victoria's husband, Mr. Brand.

I had tea with Beatrice, and at a quarter-past five, the weather having cleared, drove out with her, the Duke of Roxburghe, and Leopold ; Lady Ely, the Duke, General Ponsonby, and Mr. Yorke in the second carriage, and Lord Haddington on horseback in his uniform. We drove to and through *Dunbar*, escorted by the *East Rothian* Yeomanry. The town was beautifully decorated and admirably kept. There were triumphal arches, and many very kind inscriptions. We turned into the park in front of the house, formerly occupied by the Lord Lauderdale of that day, facing the old *Castle of Dunbar* (of which very little remains) to which Queen Mary was carried as a prisoner by Bothwell after the murder of Darnley, and where lies the harbor—a very small one. Thence past the old watch-tower hill, called *Knock-enhair*, where some gypsies—in fact, the "gypsy queen" —from *Norwood* had encamped ; and where we saw several women, very dark and rather handsome and well dressed, standing close to the wall.

On through the small villages of *Belhaven* and *West Barns* by the paper mills, a large and rather handsome building, turning from the high road to the west lodge of *Biel*, Lady Mary Nisbet Hamilton's (dear Lady Augusta Stanley's elder sister), and pass the house (a dull-looking stone one, but the park is fine), and by *Belton*, Mr. Baird Hay's, to *Broxburn.* Home by seven. There was a thick fog (or "haar," as they call it in *Scotland*) from the sea, which obscured all the

* It is close to Windsor.

distance, with occasionally some rain, but nothing to
signify.

Only ourselves, the Duke and Duchess, and Janie Ely to
dinner in the same dining-room. One of the Duke's people
attended, besides Brown and one of our footmen. Went to
my room soon after. Wrote a letter, but went early to bed
—by twelve o'clock.

Sunday, August 25.

A fine hot morning. After breakfast, walked with Beatrice down under the trees to the left, along a broad walk
next to the *Broxburn*, on to the end of the walk which led to
the garden wall, on which roses were growing, and which is
quite on the sea, which was of a deep blue. The rocks are
very bad for boats. There is a walk along the top of the
rocks that overhang the sea—the *Links*. This road goes on
to *Dunbar*, which, with its fine church that stands so high as
to be a landmark, is well seen from here. We walked back
again, and I sat out near the house on the grass, under one
of the small canopies which we had brought with us, and
signed papers and wrote. At twelve there was service in the
dining-room, performed by Mr. Buchanan of *Dunbar*, who
had been for some little time tutor to Lord Charles Ker.
Beatrice, Janie Ely, the Duke and Duchess, General Ponsonby
Mr. Yorke, and the Duke's upper servants were present.
It was very well performed. Afterwards wrote and rested.
Selected presents for the servants in the house, and things
from *Dunbar* for my people.

At a quarter-past five, after tea, drove out with Beatrice,
the Duchess, and Janie Ely, in the landau and four. The
afternoon very bright and fine. We drove on towards *Eng
land*, in the opposite direction from yesterday's drive and
parallel to the sea, though well inland. The sea of a deep
blue, but a haze so dense that the distance could hardly be
seen. We drove past *Baring Hill* (Sir William Miller's) to
Dunglass (Sir Basil Hall's), a most beautiful place with
splendid trees, firs like those near the *Belvidere* in *Windsor
Park*, sycamores, beech, oak, etc. The road passes above a
deep ravine, at the bottom of which flows the *Brox*, and past
the ruins of an old abbey or castle. The house itself (at the
door of which we stopped for a few minutes to speak to Sir
Basil and Lady Hall) is a large, rather dreary-looking stone
house with columns. It must formerly have belonged to the
Home family. The distance was so hazy that as we drove
there, we could with great difficulty faintly discern *St. Abb's*

Head,* and the point on the *Wolf's Craig* mentioned in the
" Bride of Lammermoor."   Coming back we took a long
round inland, down steepish hills, through the very picturesque villages of *Brankeston* and *Innerwick.*

Home at half-past seven.   Dinner as yesterday with the
Duke and Duchess of Roxburghe, with the addition of Lord
Haddington and General Ponsonby.   Lord Haddington's
father (who was for a short time one of my lords in waiting,
but never took a waiting) was brother to the late beautiful
Marchioness of Breadalbane (wife of my dear old lord
Breadalbane), to the present Dowager Lady Aberdeen, to
the late Lady Polwarth, and the present Dowager Lady Ash-
burnham.

After dinner the other gentlemen were presented, including Mr. Buchanan, who seems a very nice person.   Then
went to my room, and Janie Ely stayed with me a short
while.

Monday, August 26.

Again this dear and blessed anniversary returns, and
again without my beloved blessed One !   But he is ever with
me in spirit.

When I came down to breakfast. I gave Beatrice a mounted
enamelled photograph of our dear Mausoleum, and a silver
belt of Montenegrin workmanship.   After breakfast I gave
my faithful Brown an oxidized silver biscuit-box, and some
onyx studs.   He was greatly pleased with the former, and
the tears came to his eyes, and he said " It is too much."
God knows, it is not, for one so devoted and faithful.   I
gave my maids also trifles from *Dunbar;* and to Janie Ely,
the gentlemen, and the servants a trifle each. in remembrance
of the dear day and of the place.

Walked out at half-past ten with Beatrice and the Duchess to the very fine kitchen-garden, and into the splendid
hothouse where they have magnificent grapes.   The peaches
are also beautiful.   From here we walked again along the
burnside to the sea, the Duchess's pretty and very amiable
collie (smaller than Noble, but with a very handsome head),
Rex, going with us.   We looked at the " Lord Warden "
(Captain Freemantle) which arrived yesterday from *Spithead,*
where we saw her in the Fleet.   She had been guardship
last year.

There is a pretty view from this walk to the sea over a

* Belonging to Mr. Home Drummond Moray of Blair Drummond and Aber-
cairny.

small lake, with trees, beyond which *Dunbar* is seen in the distance. Then I sat out in the garden and wrote. After that, when Beatrice returned from a walk near the sea with the Duchess, I went to look at the gravestone of Sir William Douglas, which is quite concealed amongst the bushes near the lawn. The battle of *Dunbar* took place (September 3, 1650) close to *Broxmouth*, and Sir Walter Scott says Cromwell's camp was in the park ; but this is doubtful, as it is described as on the north of the *Broxburn*. Leslie's camp was on *Doune Hill*, conspicuous for miles around. When the Scottish army left their strong position on the hill, they came to the low ground near the park wall. Cromwell is said to have stood on the hillock where the tower in the grounds has been built, and the battle must have been fought close to the present park gate. I afterwards planted a deodara on the lawn, in the presence of the Duke and Duchess.

Indoors near one o'clock. Directly after our usual luncheon we saw Lady Susan Suttie with her two youngest children—Victoria, eleven years, and a boy of nine—and afterwards Lord and Lady Bowmont and their two fine children— the eldest, Margaret, three, and the youngest, Victoria, nine months. The boy did not come.

At half-past three started with Beatrice, Leopold, and the Duchess in the landau and four, the Duke, Lady Ely, General Ponsonby, and Mr. Yorke going in the second carriage, and Lord Haddington riding the whole way. We drove through the west part of *Dunbar*, which was very full, and where we were literally pelted with small nosegays, till the carriage was full of them, by a number of young ladies and girls ; then on for some distance past the village of *Belhaven, Knochindale Hill*, where were stationed, in their best attire, the queen of the gypsies, an oldish woman with a yellow handkerchief on her head, and a youngish, very dark, and truly gypsy-like woman in velvet and a red shawl, and another woman. The queen is a thorough gypsy, with a scarlet cloak and yellow handkerchief round her head. Men in red hunting-coats, all very dark, and all standing on a platform here, bowed and waved their handkerchiefs. It was the English queen of the gypsies from *Norwood*, and not the Scottish border one.

We next passed the paper mills, where there were many people, as indeed there were at every little village and in every direction. We turned to the right, leaving the *Traprain Law*, a prominent hill, to the left, crossed the *Tyne*, and entered the really beautiful park of *Tyningham*—Lord Haddington's. More splendid trees and avenues of beech and sycamore, and one very high holly hedge. The drive under the avenues is very fine, and at the end of them you see the sea (we could, however, see it but faintly because of the haze). We passed close to the house, a handsome one, half Elizabethan, with small Scotch towers, and a very pretty terrace garden, but did not get out. Driving on through the park, which reminded me of *Windsor* and *Windsor Forest*, we again came upon the high road and passed by *Whitekirk*, a very fine old church, where numbers of people were assembled, and very soon after we saw through the haze the high hill of *North Berwick Law*, looking as though it rose up out of the sea, and another turn or two brought us to *Tantallon*, which is close to and overhangs the sea. We drove along the grass to the old ruins, which are very extensive. Sir Hew Dalrymple, to whom it belongs, received us, and took us over the old remains of the moat, including the old gateway, on which the royal standard had been hoisted. Lady Dalrymple (a Miss Arkwright) received us. No one else was there but Sir David Baird, who had joined us on the way on horseback. Sir Hew Dalrymple showed me about the the ruins of this very ancient castle, the stronghold of the Douglases. It belonged once to the Earl of Angus, second husband to Queen Margaret (wife of James IV.), and was finally taken by the Covenanters.

It was unfortunately so hazy that we could not distinguish the *Bass Rock*, though usually it is quite distinctly seen, being so near; and all the fine surrounding coast was quite invisible. There was a telescope, but we could see nothing through it; it was, besides, placed too low. Seated on sofas near the ledge of the rock, we had some tea, and the scene was extremely wild. After this we left, being a good deal hurried to get back (as it was already past six), and returned partly the same way, by *Binning Wood*, also belonging to Lord Haddington (which reminds one of *Windsor Forest*), but which we could not drive through, through *Tyningham* village to *Bellowford*, where the cross-road turned off. This brought us soooner back, and we reached *Broxmouth* by twenty-five minutes to eight, Lord Haddington riding the whole way.

We dined at half-past eight, only the Duke and Duchess of Roxburghe with ourselves. At ten or eleven o'clock we left *Broxmouth* with regret, as we had spent a most pleasant time there. We went in the same carriage (a landau), the Duchess of Roxburghe with us, and were driven by the same horses which had been out each day, including this day's long drive, the postilion Thomson riding admirably. *Dunbar* was very prettily illuminated, and the paper mills also. We took leave of the kind Duke * and Duchess with real regret, having enjoyed our visit greatly. All had gone off so well.

DEATH OF SIR THOMAS BIDDULPH, AT ABERGELDIE MAINS, SEPTEMBER 28, 1878.

Wednesday, September 25, 1878.

AT twenty minutes to five drove in the wagonette with the Duchess of Roxburghe and Harriet Phipps to the *Glen Gelder Shiel,* and had tea there ; and then drove to *Abergeldie Mains,* where Sir Thomas Biddulph had been very ill for a week. We got out, and I went up stairs and saw Mary (Lady) Biddulph. Sir William Jenner came into the drawing-room, and said Sir Thomas would like to see me. I went to his room with Sir William, and found Sir Thomas in bed, much the same as when I saw him on Saturday, looking very ill, but able to speak quite loud. He said "I am very bad ! " I stood looking at him, and took his hand, and he said, "You are very kind to me," and I answered, pressing his hand, "You have always been very kind to *me.*" I said I would come again, and left the room.

Saturday, September 28, 1878.

At eleven o'clock started off with Beatrice for *Abergeldie Mains* to inquire after Sir Thomas. I went up stairs, and Blake, the former nurse, came in much distressed, saying how ill he was. Then she asked if I would like to look at him, which I did from the door. We (Beatrice and I) were both much upset. We left, intending to return in the afternoon, and got back to *Balmoral* by a quarter to twelve. Sat writing in the garden-cottage. While I was writing, at a quarter to one Brown came round with a note in his hand, crying, and said " It's all over ! " It was from Sir William, saying that dear " Sir Thomas passed away at twenty minutes past twelve. Lady Biddulph as well as the children were with him to the

* He died April 23, 1879.

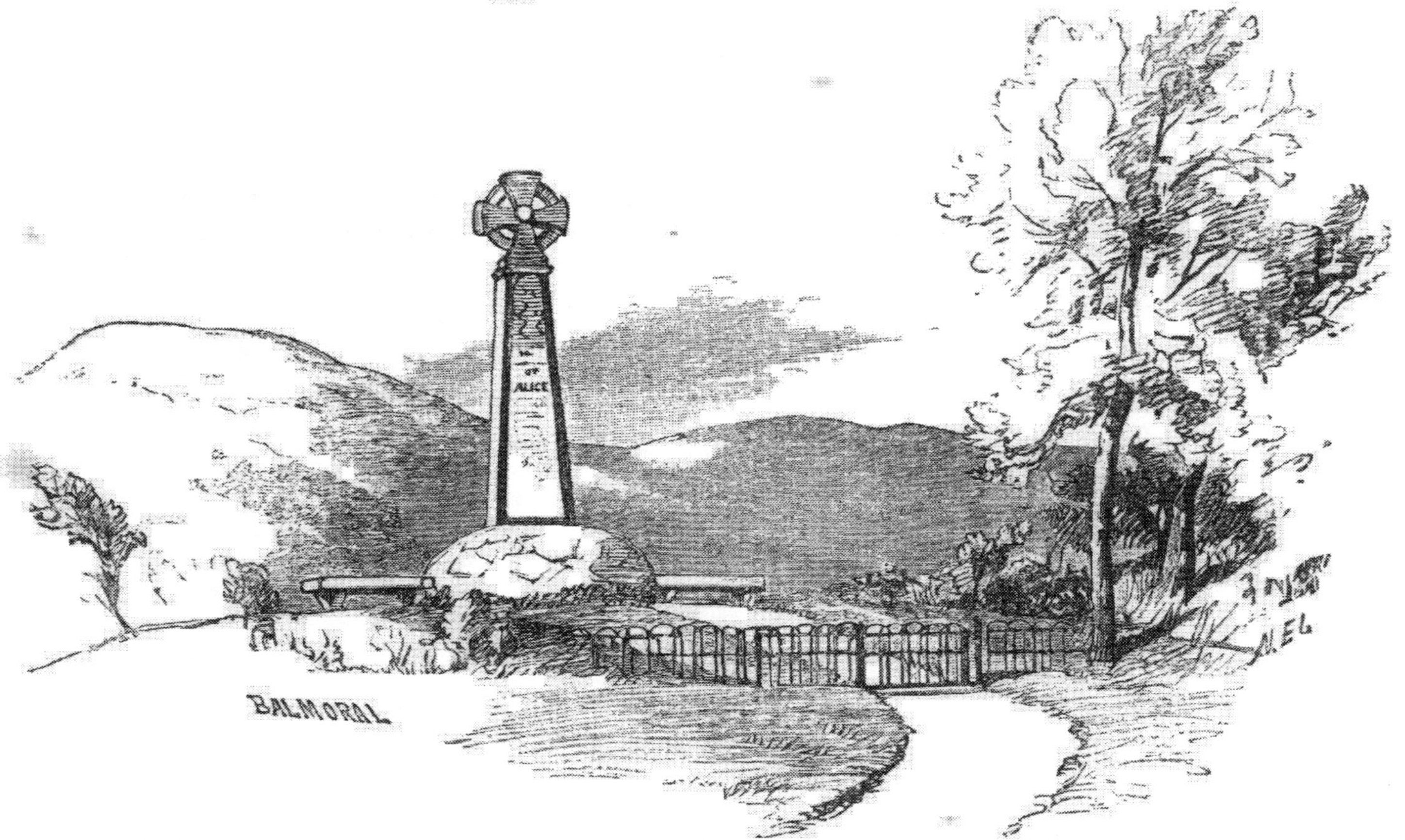
OF
ALICE
BALMORAL

last." We were so distressed that we had not remained at the house, and Brown so vexed and so kind and feeling. Dreadful! Such a loss! Dear Sir Thomas was such an excellent, honest, upright, wonderfully unselfish and disinterested man—so devoted to me and mine. Under a somewhat undemonstrative exterior, he was the kindest and most tender-hearted of men. How terrible is this loss for his poor, poor wife and the children who adored him!

Thursday, October 3, 1878.

A most lovely, almost summer day, and very warm. At a quarter-past ten drove with Beatrice, the Duchess of Roxburghe, and Lady Ely (Harriet Phipps, Fräulein Bauer, and the gentlemen having gone on before), to *Abergeldie Mains.* We got out and went into the dining-room, where the coffin was placed. Poor Mary Biddulph and her two children received us there. Her brother, Captain Conway Seymour, and the female servants, ourselves, and the ladies were present. No men came into the room; they remained in the hall, the door being left open. Mr. Campbell came in a few minutes afterwards, and performed a short but very impressive service, just reading a few verses from Scripture, and offering up a beautiful prayer. The coffin left the house directly after, followed by Captain Conway Seymour. Bertie and his three gentlemen, Lord Bridport, General Ponsonby, Sir William Jenner, and Dr. Profeit* followed in carriages to *Ballater*, as also did Lord Macduff and Colonel Farquharson.

We sat a little while with poor Mary, and then left. Lady Biddulph and her children went in the same train with the honored remains of her dear husband to *Windsor.*

MEMORIAL CROSS TO THE PRINCESS ALICE, GRAND
DUCHESS OF HESSE.

BALMORAL, *May* 22, 1879.

WE arrived at *Balmoral* at a quarter-past three. At a quarter to six walked with Beatrice to look at the Cross which I have now put up to my darling Alice. It is in *Aber-*

* My Commissioner since November, 1875: an excellent man, universally beloved.

deenshire granite, twelve feet three inches high. It is beautiful. The inscription is :—

> " TO THE DEAR MEMORY
> OF
> ALICE, GRAND DUCHESS OF HESSE,
> *Princess of Great Britain and Ireland,*
> BORN APRIL 25, 1843, DIED DEC. 14, 1878,
> THIS IS ERECTED
> BY HER SORROWING MOTHER
> QUEEN VICTORIA.
> "Her name shall live, though now she is no more."

We then walked on to Donald Stewart's, where we went
in ; thence down to Grant's. In both places they were quite
overcome to see us after darling Alice's loss, and poor Grant
began sobbing and could not come into the room where we
were.* The arrival at *Balmoral* to-day was most sad.
Everything came before me—the dreadful anxiety about
little Ernie,† the sorrow about dear little May,‡ and the
anxiety about the others. And, to crown all, the thought of
darling Alice gone, and, after her, dear little Waldie.§

DEATH OF THE PRINCE IMPERIAL, JUNE, 1879.

BALMORAL CASTLE, *Thursday, June* 19, 1879.

AT twenty minutes to eleven Brown knocked and came
in, and said there was bad news ; and when I, in alarm,
asked what, he replied, "The young French Prince is killed ;"
and when I could not take it in, and asked several times
what it meant, Beatrice, who then came in with the telegram
in her hand, said, "Oh! the Prince Imperial is killed!" I
feel a sort of thrill of horror now while I write the words.

* Grant died November 17, 1878, in his 70th year, at Robrec, close to Balmoral,
where he had lived since 1875, when he was pensioned, and where we went very
often to see him. I visited him almost daily during the last days of his life, and
was present at the funeral service at his house (November 21). He is buried in
the churchyard at Braemar.
† Alice's son, who, with four of his sisters and his father, was lying ill of diphtheria in November.
‡ Dear Alice's youngest child, who died of diphtheria November 16, 1878. We
received the news while we were at Balmoral.
§ Prince Waldemar, the Crown Princess of Germany's third and youngest son,
who died of diphtheria on March 27 of this year.

I put my hands to my head and cried out, " No, no! it cannot, cannot be true! It can't be!" And then dear Beatrice, who was crying very much, as I did too, gave me the annexed telegram from Lady Frere:—

GOVERNMENT HOUSE, CAPE TOWN, *June* 19, 1879.

To General Sir Henry Ponsonby, Balmoral Castle.—For the Information of Her Majesty the Queen.

The melancholy tidings have been telegraphed from Natal, that the Prince Imperial, when out on a reconnaissance from Colonel Wood's camp on the 1st of June, was killed by a number of Zulus concealed in a field in which the Prince Imperial and his party had dismounted to rest and feed their horses. No official particulars yet received by me. The Prince Imperial's body found and buried with full military honors at Camp Itelezi, and after being embalmed will be conveyed to England. This precedes the press telegrams by one hour. I have sent to Lord Sydney to beg him, if possible, to break the sad intelligence to the Empress before the press telegrams arrive.

To die in such an awful, horrible way! Poor, poor dear Empress! her only, only child—her all gone! And such a real misfortune! I was quite beside myself; and both of us have hardly had another thought since.

We sent for Janie Ely, who was in the house when he was born, and was so devoted to him; and he was so good! Oh! it is too, too awful! The more one thinks of it, the worse it is! I was in the greatest distress. Brown so distressed; every one quite stunned. Got to bed very late; it was dawning! and little sleep did I get.

Friday, June 20.

Had a bad, restless night, haunted by this awful event, seeing those horrid Zulus constantly before me, and thinking of the poor Empress, who did not yet know it. Was up in good time.

My accession day, forty-two years ago; but no thought of it in presence of this frightful event.

Had written many telegrams last night. One came from Lord Sydney, saying he was going down early this morning to break this dreadful news to the poor afflicted mother. How dreadful! Received distressed and horrified telegrams from some of my children. Heard by telegram also from Sir Stafford Northcote that the news arrived in the House of Commons: that much sympathy had been shown. It came to Colonel Stanley. Telegraphed to many.

Packed my boxes with Brown. Was so horrified. Always, at

12

Balmoral in May or June, dreadful news, or news of deaths of Royal persons, come, obliging the State parties to be put off.

At twenty minutes past eleven drove to Donald Stewart's and got out to say "Good-by," as well as to the Profeits, and stopped at the door of the shop to wish Mrs. Symon good-by, and also at Brown's house, to take leave of the Hugh Browns. Home at twenty minutes past twelve. Writing.

Received a telegram from Lord Sydney, saying that he had informed the poor dear Empress of the dreadful news. She could not believe it for some time, and was afterwards quite overwhelmed.

How dreadful! Took luncheon with Beatrice in my darling Albert's room. Beatrice was much upset, as indeed we all were. Even those who did not know them felt the deepest sympathy, and were in a state of consternation. He was so good and so much beloved. So strange that, as last time, our departure should be saddened, as, indeed, it has been every year, at least for three or four years, by the occurrence of deaths of great people or of relations.

We left *Balmoral* at half-past one. Janie Ely and Leila Erroll (full of feeling) going with Beatrice and me. It was a pity to leave when everything was in its greatest beauty. The lilacs just preparing to burst. Near *Ballater* there was a bush of white lilac already out. The dust dreadful. Very little whin, and far less of that beautiful broom, out, which was always such a pretty sight from the railway at this time of the year. We reached *Aberdeen* at twenty-eight minutes to four, and soon after had our tea.

At the *Bridge of Dun* we got newspapers with some of the sad details. Thence we turned off and passed again close to the sea by *Arbroath, East Haven, Carnoustie* (where poor Symon went and got so ill he had to be taken back), all lying low, with golf links near each, and the line passing over long grass strips with mounds and small indentations of the sea, such as are seen near sands, where there are no rocks and the coast is flat; but the ground rises as you approach *Dundee.*

We reached the *Tay Bridge* station at six. Immense crowds everywhere, flags waving in every direction, and the whole population out; but one's heart was too sad for anything. The Provost, splendidly attired, presented an address. Ladies presented beautiful bouquets to Beatrice and me. The last time I was at *Dundee* was in September, 1844, just after Affie's birth, when we landed there on our way to *Blair*, and Vicky, then not four years old, the only child with us, was carried through the crowd by old Renwick.* We embarked there also on our way back.

We stopped here about five minutes, and then began going over the marvellous *Tay Bridge*, which is rather more than a mile and a half long.† It was begun in 1871. Thére were great difficulties in laying the foundation, and some lives were lost. It was finished in 1878.

Mr. Bouch, who was presented at *Dundee*, was the engineer. It took us, I should say, about eight minutes going over. The view was very fine.

The boys of the training-ship, with their band, looked very well. The line through the beautifully wooded county of *Fife* was extremely pretty, especially after *Ladybank Junction*, where we stopped for a few minutes, and where Mr. Balfour of *Balbirnie* brought a basket of flowers. We met him and his wife, Lady Georgiana, in *Scotland* in 1842. We passed near *Loch Leven*, with the ruined castle in which poor Queen Mary was confined (which we passed in 1842), stopping there a moment and in view of the "*Lomonds*," past *Dollar* and *Tillicoultry*, the situation of which, in a wooded green valley at the foot of the hills, is quite beautiful, and reminded me of *Italy* and *Switzerland*, through *Sauchie*, *Alloa*, all manufacturing towns, and then close under *Wallace's Monument.* We reached the *Stirling Station*, which was dreadfully crowded, at eighteen minutes past eight (the people everywhere very enthusiastic), and after leaving it we had some good cold dinner, which reminded me much of our refreshments in the train during our charming Italian journey.

We got Scotch papers as we went along, giving harrowing details (all by telegraph) from the front, or rather from *Natal* to *Cape Town*, then by ship to *Madeira*, and thence again by telegraph here. Of nothing else could we think. Janie Ely got in at *Beattock Summit*, and went with us as far as *Carlisle*. She showed us a Dundee paper, called the "East Telegraph," which contained the fullest and most dreadful accounts. Monstrous! To think of that dear young man, the apple of his mother's eye, born and nurtured in the purple, dying thus, is too fearful, too awful ; and inexplicable and dreadful that the others should not have turned round and fought for him. It is too horrible!

---

* Sergeant footman at the time, who died in 1871.
† The Tay Bridge was destroyed in the same year (1879) in the gale of the night of December 29, when a whole train with upwards of eighty passengers was precipitated into the Tay.

HOME-COMING OF THEIR ROYAL HIGHNESSES THE DUKE AND
DUCHESS OF CONNAUGHT. SEPTEMBER, 1879.

BALMORAL CASTLE, *Friday, September* 5, 1879.

AT two I started off with Beatrice and Janie Ely (Sir Henry
Ponsonby and General Gardiner having gone on to *Ballater*)
in the landau and four, the postilions in blue, outriders in
red, Brown in full dress, and Power behind our carriage.
We arrived at four minutes to three, and waited in the carriage till we heard the train (special) was approaching, when
we got out. In two or three minutes more they were there,
and dear Arthur and Louise Margaret stepped out, and were
warmly embraced by us. I gave her a nosegay of heather.
She had also received others. The guard (Royal Scots)
were out.

When we reached the *Balmoral* bridge, we went at a slow
pace, passing under the arch composed of moss and heather,
on which was wrought, in flowers, " Welcome to Balmoral "
on one side, and " Ceud mille Failte " on the other, " A. W."
and " L. M." on the outside of each ; and there all the people stood—all our kilted people. The ladies and gentlemen,
including Lord Chelmsford and Mr. Cross, Christian Victor,
and Albert (Helena's boys), and also the Misses Pitt, were
there.

Arthur spoke a few words from the carriage, and then Dr.
Profeit said a few words ; after which, preceded by the
pipers playing, and all our kilted men and the rest following,
we went at a very slow foot's pace to the Castle.

At the gate three pretty little girls of Colonel Clarke's
(Bertie's equerry staying at Birkhall) threw nosegays into the
carriage, one being of *marguerites.* Every one who was
there followed on foot.

Only Captain Fitzgerald came with Arthur and Louise
Margaret.

When we got out, everybody having come up, Dr. Profeit
proposed Arthur's and Louischen's health, which every one
drank with cheers. Arthur thanked. Then we went in, and
Arthur, Louischen, and the two boys took tea with us in the
library.

HIS ROYAL HIGHNESS THE DUKE OF CONNAUGHT'S CAIRN.

Monday, September 8, 1879.

A FINE morning. Breakfasted with Beatrice, Arthur, and *Louischen* in the garden cottage, and at eleven we started for Arthur's Cairn, I on my pony "Jessie," Beatrice walking to the top. We were met by Arthur and Louischen, and went on to near the cairn, to the right of Campbell's path. I got off when we were near it; and here were assembled all the ladies and gentlemen, also Dr. Profeit, the keepers and servants belonging to the place with their families, and almost all our servants from the house. When we had got to the top and had our glasses filled, and were standing close to the cairn, Dr. Profeit, with a few appropriate words compliment- ary to Arthur, and with many good wishes for both, proposed their health, which was drunk with three times three. Then Arthur, with great readiness, returned thanks in a little speech. My health followed, also with loud cheering; and then Brown said they ought to drink the health of Princess Beatrice, which Cowley took up and proposed; and it was received with many cheers. Fern (who with the other dogs was there) resented the cheering, and barked very much. We all placed a stone on the cairn, on which was inscribed—

ARTHUR DUKE OF CONNAUGHT AND STRATHEARNE,
Married to Princess Louise Margaret of Prussia,
March 13, 1879.

After a few minutes we left, I walking down the whole way. We stopped at Dr. Profeit's on our way down, and here I got on my pony again.

———

VISIT TO THE GLEN GELDER SHIEL.

BALMORAL, *October* 6, 1879.

AT ten minutes past four drove with the Empress Eugénie * (who had driven up from *Abergeldie*) in the victoria to the *Glen Gelder Shiel,* or *Ruidh na Bhan Righ* (the Queen's Shiel). The evening was perfectly beautiful, warm, and clear, and bright. The Empress was pleased with the little

* The Empress was staying at Abergeldie, to which I had urged her to come for a little quiet and change of air after her terrible misfortune.

Shiel, which contains only two small rooms and a little kitchen. It stands in a very wild solitary spot looking up to *Lochnagar*, which towers up immediately above the house, though to reach *Lochnagar* itself would take a very long time. We walked on along the footpath above the *Gelder* for a mile and a half, the dogs, which had come up, following us, and the Empress talked a great deal, and most pleasantly, about former times.

When we came back to the little Shiel, after walking for an hour, we had tea. Brown had caught some excellent trout and cooked them with oatmeal, which the dear Empress liked extremely, and said would be her dinner. It was a glorious evening—the hills pink, and the sky so clear.

We got back at twenty minutes past six, and the Empress drove back to *Abergeldie* with her lady.

VICTORY OF TEL-EL-KEBIR AND HOME-COMING OF THEIR ROYAL HIGHNESSES THE DUKE AND DUCHESS OF ALBANY. SEPTEMBER, 1882.

Monday, September 11, 1882.

RECEIVED a telegram in cipher from Sir John McNeill, marked *very secret*, saying that it was " determined to attack the enemy with a very large force on Wednesday." How anxious this made us, God only knows ; and yet this long delay had also made us very anxious. No one to know, though all expected something at the time.

Tuesday, September 12.

Drove at ten minutes to five, with Beatrice, Louischen, and Harriet, to the *Glen Gelder Shiel*, where we had tea, and I sketched. The sky was so beautiful. We walked on the road back, and came home at twenty minutes past seven. How anxious we felt, I need not say ; but we tried not to give way. Only the ladies dined with us.

I prayed earnestly for my darling child, and longed for the morrow to arrive. Read Körner's beautiful " Gebet vor der Schlacht," " Vater, ich rufe Dich " (Prayer before the Battle, " Father, I call on Thee "). My beloved husband used to sing it often. My thoughts were entirely fixed on *Egypt* and the coming battle. My nerves were strained to

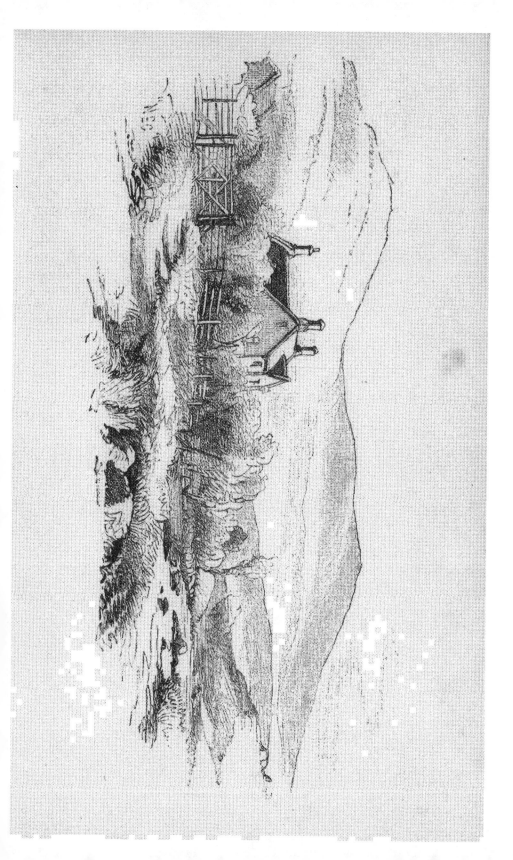

such a pitch by the intensity of my anxiety and suspense that they seemed to feel as though they were all alive.

Wednesday, September 13.

Woke very often. Raw and dull. Took my short walk, and breakfasted in the cottage. Had a telegram that the army marched out last night. What an anxious moment! We walked afterwards as far as the arch for Leopold's reception, which was a very pretty one, and placed as nearly where it had been on previous occasions, only rather nearer Middleton's lodge, and thence back to the cottage, where I sat and wrote and signed, etc.

Another telegram, also from Reuter, saying that fighting was going on, and that the enemy had been routed with heavy loss at *Tel-el-Kebir.* Much agitated.

On coming in got a telegram from Sir John McNeill, saying, " A great victory; Duke safe and well." Sent all to Louischen. The excitement very great. Felt unbounded joy and gratitude for God's great goodness and mercy.

The same news came from Lord Granville and Mr. Childers, though not yet from Sir. Garnet Wolseley. A little later, just before two, came the following most welcome and gratifying telegram from Sir Garnet Wolseley :—

ISMALIA, *September* 13, 1882.

Tel-el-Kebir.—From Wolseley to the Queen, Balmoral.

Attacked Arabi's position at five this morning. His strongly entrenched position was most bravely and gallantly stormed by the Guards and line, while cavalry and horse artillery worked round their left flank. At seven o'clock I was in complete possession of his whole camp. Many railway trucks, with quantities of supplies, fallen into our hands. Enemy completely routed, and his loss has been very heavy, also regret to say we have suffered severely. Duke of Connaught is well, and behaved admirably, leading his brigade to the attack.

Brown brought the telegram, and followed me to Beatrice's room, where Louischen was, and I showed it to her. I was myself quite upset, and embraced her warmly, saying what joy and pride and cause of thankfulness it was to know our darling safe, and so much praised! I feel quite beside myself for joy and gratitude, though grieved to think of our losses, which, however, have not proved to be so serious as first reported. We were both much overcome.

We went to luncheon after this, having sent many telegrams, and receiving many. At ten minutes past three drove with Beatrice and Lady Southampton to *Ballater.* We got out of the carriage, and the train arrived almost immediately, and Leopold and Helen stepped out ; she was dressed in gray with bonnet to match.

The guard of honor, Seaforth Highlanders (Duke of Albany's) out, and many people. Leopold and Helen got at once into the landau with us two, and we drove straight to *Balmoral.* At the bridge Louischen and Horatia * were waiting in a carriage, and followed us. Beyond the bridge, and when we had just passed under the arch, the carriage stopped, and Dr. Profeit said a few words of welcome, for which Leopold thanked. Here everybody was assembled—all our gentlemen and ladies, and those from *Birkhall* and the *Mains,* all the tenants from the three estates, all our servants, etc.

The pipes preceded, playing the " Highland Laddie," Brown and all our other kilted men walking alongside, and before and behind the carriage everybody else close following— and a goodly number they were. We got out at the door, and went just beyond the arch, all our people standing in a line headed by our Highlanders. A table with whiskey and glasses was placed up against the house, next to which stood all the ladies and gentlemen. Dr. Profeit gave Leopold's and Helen's healths, and after these had been drunk, Brown stepped forward and said, nearly as follows : " Ladies and gentlemen, let us join in a good Highland cheer for the Duke and Duchess of Albany ; may they live long and die happy ! " which pleased every one, and there were hearty cheers.

Then I asked Leopold to propose " The Victorious Army in *Egypt,*" with darling Arthur's health, which was heartily responded to, and poor Louischen was quite upset. After this Dr. Profeit proposed " The Duchess of Connaught," and at Brown's suggestion he also proposed " The little Princess." The sweet little one had witnessed the procession in Chapman's (her nurse's) arms with her other attendants, and was only a little way off when her health was drunk.

This over, we went in and had tea up stairs in my room— Louischen, Beatrice, and I. Louischen had received a very long and most interesting letter from Arthur about that dreadful march on the 25th (dated 26th, but finished later). A telegram from Sir Garnet Wolseley to Mr. Childers, with fuller accounts, arrived. The loss, thank God ! is not so heavy as we feared at first. A bonfire was to be lit by my desire on the top of *Craig Gowan* at nine, just where there

* The Hon. Horatia Stopford.

had been one in 1856 after the fall of *Sevastopol,* when dearest Albert went up to it at night with Bertie and Affie. That was on September 10, very nearly the same time twenty-six years ago !

Went to Louischen, who read me portions of Arthur's long letter. The description of his and the officers' sufferings and privations, as well as those of the poor men, made me miserable.

Only ourselves to dinner ; and at nine Beatrice, Louischen, Lady Southampton, and the gentlemen, and many of our people, walked up (with the pipes playing) to the top of *Craig Gowan*—rather venturesome in the dark ; and we three (Leopold, Helen, and I) went up to Beatrice's room, and from there we saw the bonfire lit and blazing, and could distinguish figures, and hear the cheering and pipes. They were soon back, and I went and sat with Beatrice, Louischen, and Lady Southampton, who were having a little supper in Louischen's room.

Endless telegrams ! What a day of gratitude and joy, but mingled with sorrow and anxiety for the many mourners and the wounded and dying !

CONCLUSION.

A FEW words I must add in conclusion to this volume.

The faithful attendant who is so often mentioned throughout these Leaves, is no longer with her whom he served so truly, devotedly, untiringly.

In the fulness of health and strength he was snatched away from his career of usefulness, after an illness of only three days, on the 27th of March of this year, respected and beloved by all who recognized his rare worth and kindness of heart, and truly regretted by all who knew him.

His loss to me (ill and helpless as I was at the time from an accident) is irreparable, for he deservedly possessed my entire confidence ; and to say that he is daily, nay, hourly, missed by me, whose lifelong gratitude he won by his constant care, attention, and devotion, is but a feeble expression of the truth.

> A truer, nobler, trustier heart,
> More loyal, and more loving, never beat
> Within a human breast.

BALMORAL : *November,* 1883.